D1560998

POWERSHOP 4
NEW RETAIL DESIGN

Frame Publishers
Amsterdam

HUMBER LIBRARIES NORTH CAMPUS
205 Humber College Blvd
TORONTO, ON.   M9W 5L7

CONTENTS

002

ACCESS

004

5

SORIES

005

The light touch for luxury brands

BEAN POLE
BY BETWIN SPACE DESIGN

WHERE Seoul, Korea **WHEN** March 2012
CLIENT Cheil Industries **DESIGNER** Betwin Space Design (p.491)
TOTAL FLOOR AREA 150 m² **SHOP CONSTRUCTOR** –
PHOTOS Lee Pyo-joon

For the new accessories shop of established family brand Bean Pole, Betwin Space Design opted for a light and bright interior to showcase the luxury items inside. Glass is key. Not only is the shop's sleek, angular frontage entirely glazed, but its 'nested' glass details add another dimension: the display window-within-a-window and door are framed in mirrored glass, giving a glossy, high-impact effect. This is enhanced by the store's name in illuminated letters. In the window, bags are suspended beneath silver helium-filled balloons. Inside, the same materials are used to equally dramatic effect. A hexagonal mirrored column is a strong focal point, while the long display case is topped in glass with a mirrored base that reflects the floor and thus gives the illusion of floating. The freestanding furnishings repeat the theme of layers of glass and mirror, while the wall shelves are in a neutral, light-coloured wood. These harmonise with the herringbone floor, which however is not seamless, but is placed like a rug atop the pale-grey surface beneath, which remains as a border. Chic grey is picked out again by the pegged display wall for bags, segmented in various shades and rather reminiscent of a climbing wall. The neutral palette allows product colours to pop. Meanwhile a linear black metal frame structure runs through the space, adding complexity and contrast to an otherwise light-filled interior, and matching the dark cash desk. Behind this desk, images projected onto a concertina-like folded wall add a surreal and elegantly unexpected touch.

1 In one of the windows bags are suspended beneath silver helium-filled balloons.
2 The shop's sleek, angular frontage is entirely glazed, with mirrored details.

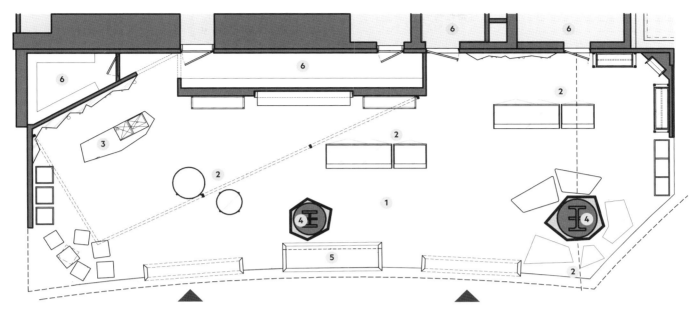

1 Retail area
2 Display unit
3 Cash desk
4 Mirrored column
5 Window display
6 Storage

5

3 A hexagonal mirrored column is a strong
focal point in the interior of the store.
4 Freestanding furnishings repeat the theme
of layers of glass and mirror.
5 Wall shelves in a neutral, light-coloured
wood harmonise with the herringbone floor.
6 Behind the sales desk, images are projected
onto a concertina-like folded wall.

6

BUCHERER
BY BLOCHER BLOCHER PARTNERS

1

WHERE Munich, Germany **WHEN** April 2013
CLIENT Bucherer **DESIGNER** Blocher Blocher Partners (p.491)
TOTAL FLOOR AREA 480 m² **SHOP CONSTRUCTOR** Korda Ladenbau
PHOTOS Nikolaus Koliusis

For Swiss horology company Bucherer's German debut, Blocher Blocher Partners was called in to create an interior fit to 'stoke the desire for luxury'. Floors of Botticini marble and walls covered in leather do just that, while the design language and lovingly executed details allude to the craftsmanship and timeless elegance of the brand. The materials palette is traditionally luxurious: high-gloss furniture, silk carpets, brass lettering, walls of dark wood and glass and a platinum-coloured metal ceiling create a rich effect, but one that doesn't oversaturate thanks to the use of cool, chic colour tones which keep the effect contemporary. Indirect lighting around the circumference imparts a floaty impression that detracts from the weight of the materials used, and an installation by artist Valeria Nascimento, with hundreds of porcelain blossoms suspended from the central space, adds to the sense of weightlessness. A staircase winds up past this floral sculpture to the first floor. In reference to the firm's founding year of 1888, the symbolic Bucherer figure of eight appears as a laser-cut pattern. Upstairs, the Bucherer customer enters the world of jewellery: here, too, there are silk carpets, while windows bedecked in greige curtains alternate with walls of gold-veined black marble, and specially designed pendant lights illuminate the consulting tables. More casual seating faces classically elegant display windows. Bucherer Diamonds has its own special section, featuring a back wall framed in brass, into which gently ribbed fabric is set. This is the fifth Bucherer store designed by Blocher Blocher Partners, following St. Moritz, Paris and Interlaken with two dependances.

1 The ground floor accommodates
  immaculately presented watch displays
  and private consulting areas.
2 Upstairs is devoted to jewellery.
3 Throughout, luxury materials create
  a sumptuous effect.

4 Marble floors and walls of leather add tactility as well as luxury.
5 Well-lit glass display cases perched on elegant long legs show off the products as though they were museum pieces.

Traditional luxury with a contemporary edge

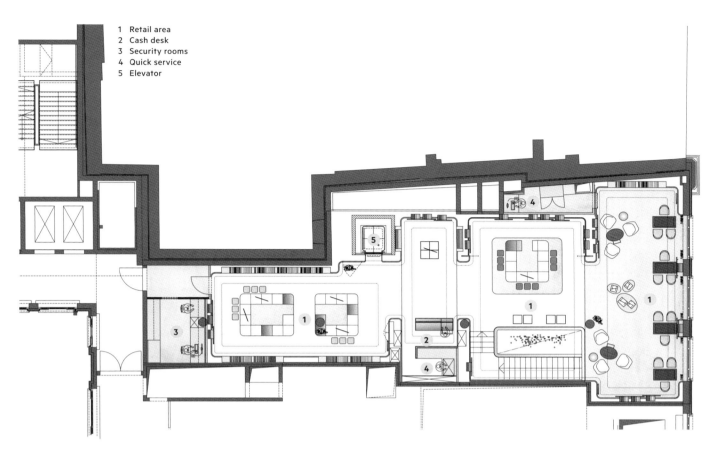

1 Retail area
2 Cash desk
3 Security rooms
4 Quick service
5 Elevator

First floor

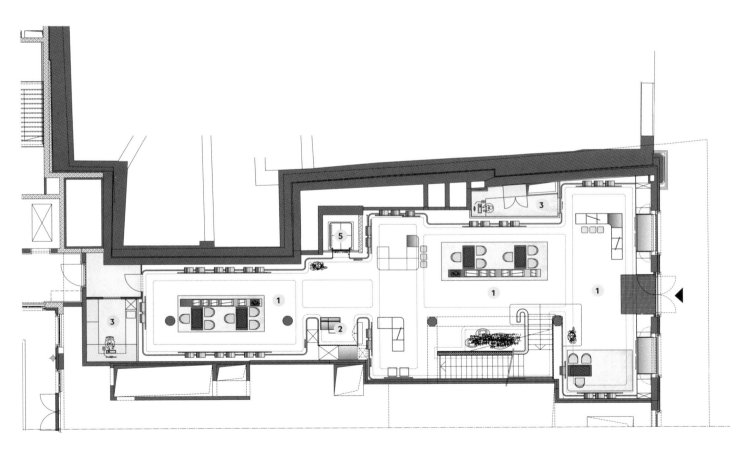

Ground floor

BURMA
BY ATELIER DU PONT

WHERE Paris, France **WHEN** May 2013
CLIENT Burma **DESIGNER** Atelier du Pont (p.491)
TOTAL FLOOR AREA 60 m² **SHOP CONSTRUCTOR** Access Agencement
PHOTOS Philippe Garcia

Designed to resemble a jewellery box, but then on a grander scale, Burma makes an eye-catching spectacle on the Rue de la Paix in Paris, thanks to a dramatic combination of black and glass. Atelier du Pont has designed an high-impact façade for the jewellery store, inspired by a portrait gallery. The jewellery in the shop window are exhibited in elliptical display cases that, held in place by a geometrical arrangement of criss-crossed wires, appear to float in mid-air. The ivory-lined cases evoke the oval frames of miniature paintings as well as settings for precious stones and cameos and the hand-held mirrors that are traditionally found on the dressing table of a boudoir. At the same time, around the display cases the glass frontage gives an intriguing view of the interior while it also reflects the street outside. The interior continues the theme, its soft tones and plush surfaces suggesting the velvety lining of the traditional trinket box. The shimmery quality is the result of the diffuse light cast by an enormous chain-mail chandelier. Atelier du Pont designed the tables with their adjustable mirrors. The glass display cases that perch on top of the glossy black cabinets contain black spheres displaying items of jewellery. A neutral colour palette emphasises the contrast of forms created by the oval mirrors and rounded chairs and the straight lines of the tables, cabinets and cases. Soft, suede-like carpeting ensures a muffled atmosphere, adding to the intimate effect.

1 Elliptical display cases, suspended by criss-crossed wires, appear to float in mid-air.
2 The ivory-lined cases reference the frames of miniature portraits, cameos used in jewellery and the handheld mirrors found in boudoirs.
3 Most of the furniture was custom-designed, giving a handcrafted, bespoke feel to the space in keeping with the products on display.

A bold, black showcase displays delicate items

CA4LA
BY LINE-INC.

WHERE Tokyo, Japan **WHEN** June 2013
CLIENT Weave Toshi **DESIGNER** Line-Inc. (p.497)
TOTAL FLOOR AREA 304 m² **SHOP CONSTRUCTOR** D.Brain
PHOTOS Kozo Takayama

For hat retailer CA4LA's largest store yet, design office Line-Inc. faced two major challenges: how to display a huge amount of headgear in the space, and how to draw shoppers to the shop in the first place – the location being set back from the main street. The second dilemma was solved by projecting a theatre-inspired illuminated roof into the street, giving the store a distinctive presence in a busy area filled with many shops. Once customers pass through the entrance, they are greeted by a 3-m-wide display showing a variety of hats and plants. The store interior was conceived as a 'a museum for hats' and appears rather like an oversized cabinet of curiosities. Classical-looking wooden shelves line the walls and coordinate with the sales desk, which shares the same style. The wooden floor continues the warm, traditional theme. The centre of the floor space is filled with a variety of freestanding shelves and display items, an antique collection of tables and chairs, all showing off a dizzying variety of hats in a suitably quirky setting. Upstairs, customers can find imported products such as the Borsalino range from Italy. At the back of the store is a professional atelier, surrounded by glass walls creating a lively atmosphere – customers can enjoy watching artisans in the process of making the hats. Next to the atelier is CA4LA's first-ever bridal section, which provides a made-to-order service.

1 A theatre-inspired illuminated roof projects into the street, giving the store a distinctive presence.
2 The dramatic treatment extends to the staircase just inside, which evokes a baronial hall.
3 The sales desk has a classical look and feel.
4 Left of the bridal area visitors can glimpse through the glass into the atelier.

5 A variety of quirky shelving and display elements allows a huge number of hats to be displayed in varied and entertaining ways.
6 An initial sketch of the entrance of the shop.

1 Retail area
2 Bridal area
3 Cash desk
4 Display 'stage'
5 Window display
6 Atelier
7 Storage
8 Office

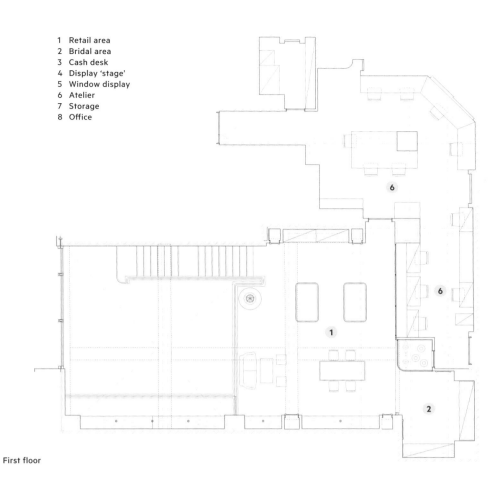

First floor

A cabinet-of-curiosities setting for classic headgear

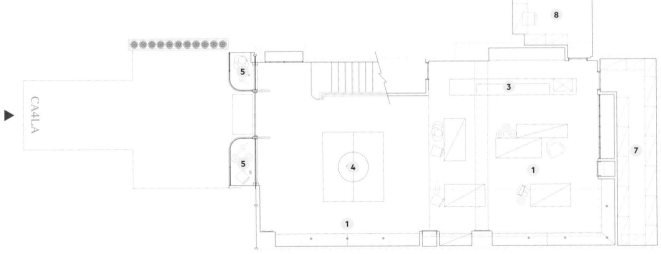

CA4LA

Ground floor

CADENZZA
BY DFROST

WHERE Innsbruck, Austria **WHEN** January 2013
CLIENT D. Swarovksi **DESIGNER** dfrost (p.493)
TOTAL FLOOR AREA 82 m² **SHOP CONSTRUCTOR** Münch + Münch
PHOTOS Bernhard Aichner

For Swarovski's first multi-brand jewellery store, Cadenzza, design agency dfrost was asked to find 'a revolutionary way' to display jewellery. A tall order perhaps, but the designers were unfazed and responded with the idea of referencing the fashion media – namely, glossy fashion magazines and online fashion blogs. Designed to resemble 'a magazine page in three dimensions,' the glass-fronted store is arranged in an open, graphic layout. Built-in and freestanding displays have backlit vertical and horizontal elements that mimic the format of magazine pages, while display tables exhibit jewellery in styled compositions reminiscent of *Vogue* or *Elle*. The 'editorial' approach mixes baubles with unrelated items such as chic table settings to create a 'lifestyle' atmosphere, presenting them in the context of style trends. And unlike in magazines, the jewellery is not unattainable but can be purchased, removed from the tableau and taken home. Displays are frequently changed to reflect seasonal trends and fashion developments, as in an online fashion blog. To make the experience interactive and engaging, the Style Hub, the area for trying on jewellery, is also the place to receive tips and advice from the store's Style Advisors. The dialogue with the brand is continued into the packaging, which comes with individual messages embossed onto it. Given the relative complexity of the curated product displays, the store benefits from an otherwise simple treatment. The façade is glass, luring shoppers inside, where an oak floor provides a neutral and unifying element and wallpaper and curtained backdrops don't threaten to upstage the jewellery.

1 The glass façade presents a mini jewellery 'catwalk' display to passing shoppers.
2 Jewellery is displayed in a variety of different ways to keep the store experience lively.
3 Displays have backlit vertical and horizontal elements that mimic the format and content of magazine spreads.
4 Display tables exhibit jewellery in styled compositions reminiscent of glossy magazines.

Jewellery store takes a leaf out of the fashion mags' book

HUMBER LIBRARIES

5 Magazine spread-like displays are presented together with real magazines.
6 A lot of thought went into creating the display concepts.

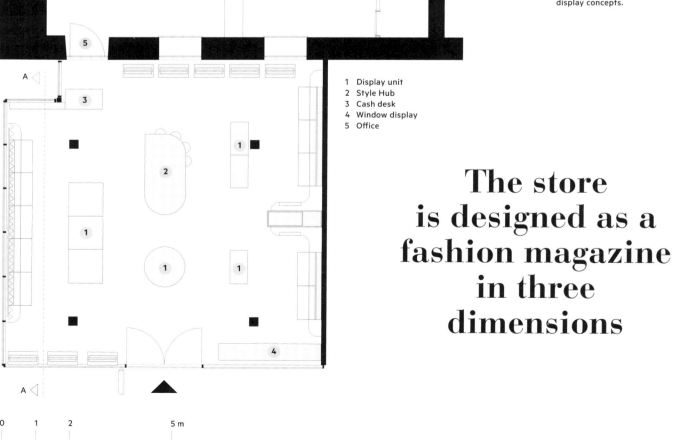

1 Display unit
2 Style Hub
3 Cash desk
4 Window display
5 Office

The store is designed as a fashion magazine in three dimensions

0   1   2   5 m

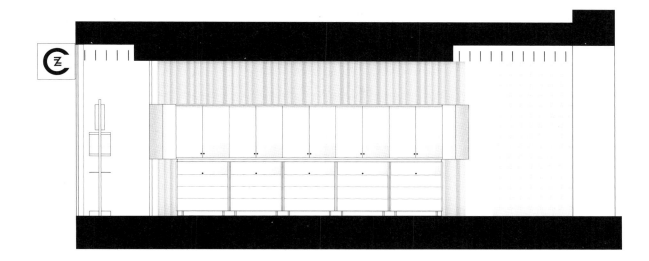

Section AA

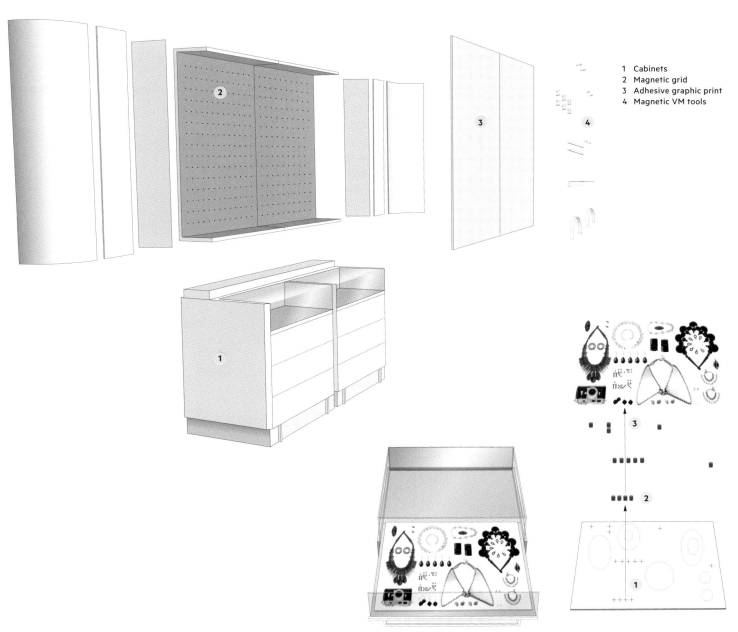

1 Cabinets
2 Magnetic grid
3 Adhesive graphic print
4 Magnetic VM tools

1 Printed/Fabric panel
2 Magnetic VM tools
3 Jewellery

6

EYE CANDY
BY CRENEAU INTERNATIONAL

WHERE Wijnegem, Belgium **WHEN** September 2011
CLIENT Bart Van Bever **DESIGNER** Creneau International (p.493)
TOTAL FLOOR AREA 135 m² **SHOP CONSTRUCTOR** Creneau International
PHOTOS Arne Jennard

'When we were asked to come up with a concept for a glasses shop, we had a clear vision of what we didn't want it to look like', says Creneau International's Andrew Theunissen, conscious of the staid reputation of the average optician. Not surprisingly, therefore, the design office's Eye Candy store in Belgium is an unusual take on an optician's space, thanks to a strong concept rigorously applied. 'The packaging became the store and the store became the packaging', says Theunissen simply. The designers came up with the idea when they visualised the process of buying a pair of glasses: 'The entire shelving system is built of boxes that serve as a display for the product. After the purchase, the box is removed from the frame, becomes the packaging and gets a carrying handle.' Another box slots in to take its place. Brand logo, displays and graphics become part of a seamless system. The packages are made of basic white cardboard, with stickers in eight different colours which add a zing to the shop space, while simultaneously dividing it into different mood zones. The delicate shop furniture in pale wood and glass detracts no attention from the colour-coded displays, allowing them to dominate the store. But one of the true beauties of the system, as the designers point out, is that every customer who makes a purchase leaves the shop and becomes a 'walking ad' for the Eye Candy.

1 The packaging serves as display and decor in the Eye Candy store.
2 Simple furnishings focus the attention on the packaging.
3 Eight different colours create different mood zones.

FREITAG STORE LAUSANNE
BY FREITAG

WHERE Lausanne, Switzerland WHEN May 2013
CLIENT Freitag DESIGNER Freitag (p.495)
TOTAL FLOOR AREA 120 m² SHOP CONSTRUCTORS Freitag and Spillmann Echsle Architects
PHOTOS Hervé Annen

Regarded as an icon of modern Swiss design, the Freitag messenger bag can be found in the design gallery of the Museum of Modern Art in New York. Made from recycled truck tarpaulins, Freitag bags have had huge success in their 20-year history, leading their inventors, the Zurich-based brothers Markus and Daniel Freitag, to open stores in far-flung places including Tokyo and New York. The most momentous opening for the brothers so far, however, was in the Francophone city of Lausanne, in French-speaking Switzerland: the 'terre romande' was, they felt, a crucial place to roll out a new store. The Lausanne retail space follows the usual Freitag formula in being all about the product – and the modular shelving system that was created to display it. The shelving system, called V30 Freitag Skid, has itself won a Swiss Design Award for what the judges termed its 'appealing functionality' and 'industrial aesthetic' – both of which sum up the brand values. Easy to stack and store, and made from recycled plastic, the angular modules can be configured in many ways – a versatility that's very much on show in the store in Lausanne, which uses few other materials, apart from wire mesh for 'walls'. The products – some 1500 bags from the famous Fundamentals range as well as all the major current items from the Reference collection – are contained in and displayed on the shelves, on two levels of an industrial space that has been rapidly and none too thoroughly washed in white – all adding to the store's quirky charm.

1   An all-white interior sets off the brightly coloured Freitag bags, which are made from recycled truck tarps.
2   The amateurishness of the interior adds to its charm.
3 & 4   The modular V30 Freitag Skid shelving system is the main element used in the store interior.

Iconic design products on iconic design shelves

FREUDENHAUS
BY AIGNER ARCHITECTURE

1

WHERE Munich, Germany WHEN May 2013
CLIENT FreudenHaus Optik DESIGNER Aigner Architecture (p.490)
TOTAL FLOOR AREA 230 m² SHOP CONSTRUCTOR –
PHOTOS Florian Pipo

For the new Munich store of FreudenHaus eye-wear, designer Marie Aigner set out to embody the brand's values of timeless style, simplicity of design and high-quality materials – but then with three distinct variations in mood, reflecting the diverse needs of different cus-tomer groups. Colour-blocking is used to great effect to create the changes in atmosphere in the rectangular two-storey space. The ground floor is the entrance level and it greets visitors with a pared-down, pristine white space spliced with a brilliant, sunshine-yellow block running the full length of the space. Glasses are displayed on the neutral, white side of the space, while the cheerful yellow area accommodates seating, storage and consultation area; the long white sales desk is also placed directly in front of it. Yellow stairs lead downstairs, where there is an abrupt transition into a space divided into two dramatically contrasting areas. A black room, dotted with circular white displays and projecting plastic-tube mini showcases, creates a feeling of high-tech drama, assisted by the shiny black floor

and raw concrete ceiling. A wind tunnel in this area puts sports glasses through their paces. The adjacent children's space is different again – light and playful, with an alcove featuring walls covered in green Lego blocks which invite small visitors to build on them. The main area is white and light, with Duplo blocks for even smaller fingers, and a scene of toy furniture arranged, upside down, on the ceiling.

1 & 2 A brilliant, sunshine-yellow block
       runs the full length of the ground-
       floor space and spills over into the
       stairs to the basement.
3   The children's area in the basement is
       partly decorated with green Lego plates,
       while a scene featuring toy furniture
       occupies the ceiling.

2

038

3

4 Adjacent to the kids' area , a dramatic black
space creates a high-tech area, complete
with wind tunnel and glass display tubes.

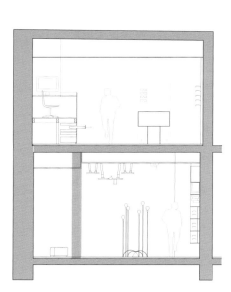

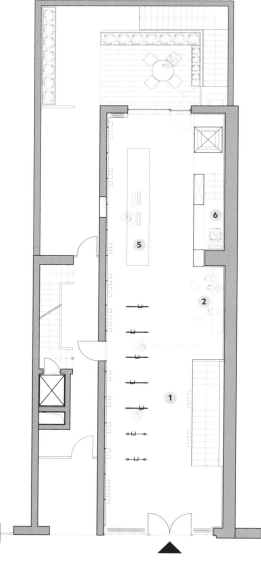

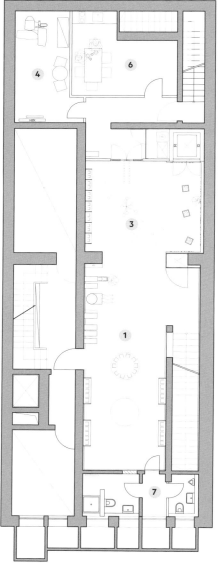

Ground floor

Basement

1 Retail area
2 Lounge
3 Children's area
4 Eye testing room
5 Cash desk
6 Office
7 Toilet

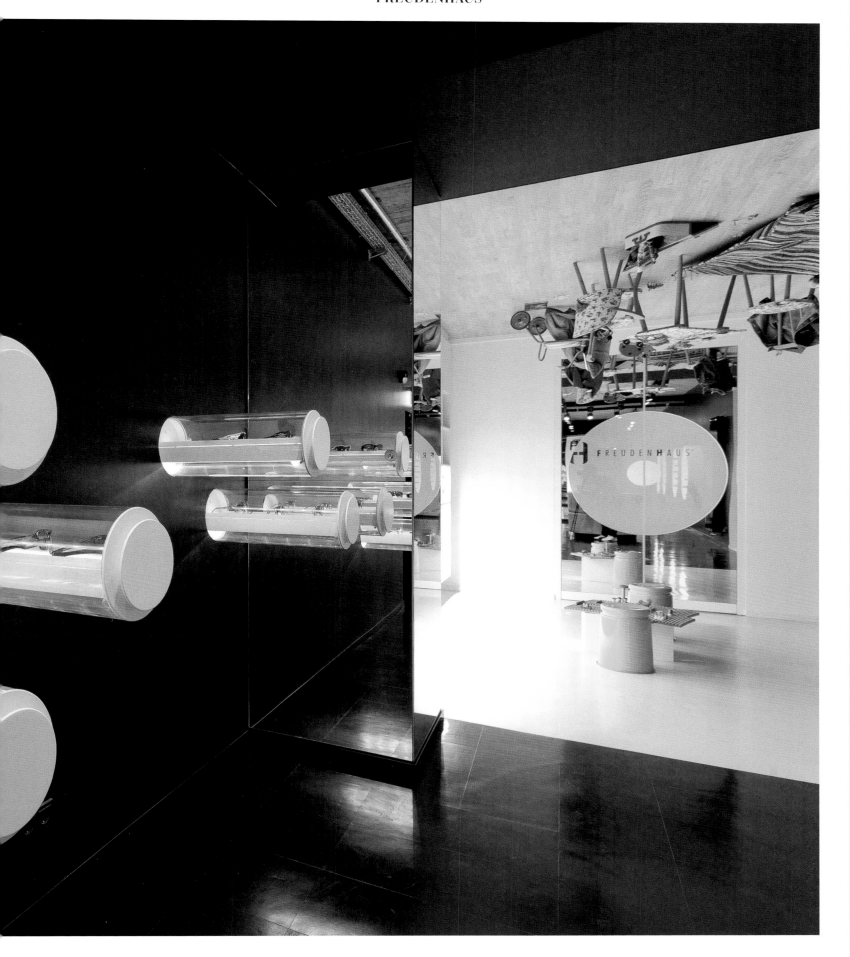

Colour-blocking signals shifts in eyewear moods

HAT CLUB
BY UP

WHERE New York, United States **WHEN** April 2013
CLIENT Hat Club **DESIGNER** UP (p.499)
TOTAL FLOOR AREA 20 m² **SHOP CONSTRUCTOR** Tristan Warner Studios
PHOTOS Julia Cawley and Harriet Andronikides

If you want to get ahead, get a hat – or so the saying goes. But at the Hat Club in SoHo, New York, realised by design studio UP, you first need to choose between no less than 420 different models, each displayed in its own Baltic birch niche. Admittedly, all the hats on show are variations on a theme – each one is a version of the classic American baseball cap. But that doesn't detract from the designers' achievement in this store, which shows maximum product in minimum space. It's all done without touching the fabric of the historic building, too. Dating back to 1898, the shop is located in the oldest freestanding building in SoHo. Stripping the space back to its bare bones revealed some beautifully aged floorboards, brickwork and beams which the designers were happy to leave exposed. They therefore devised a freestanding and adaptable retail formula for the store, which is based on the concept of a single module, repeated 420 times. The module is a rectangular plywood box which doubles as a display and storage element. Hence the rectangular shape – the closed rear of the box is for storage while the open front is ideal for display. The boxes can be stacked in a variety of configurations, so the assistants can create walls, steps and pyramids as the fancy takes them, clustering the display in the centre of the space or covering its walls – or both. The repetitive design suits the single-product concept and makes choosing the right cap an easy matter for customers.

1 The modular display means that the layout can be adjusted every week, so the shop is always changing.
2 Simple illumination draws attention to the bare brick walls and the weathered floorboards.
3 The product displays were kept simple to accenuate the original features of the 1898 interior.

A modular
approach makes
the most of a
single product

KOMPLEMENTAIR MEN
BY AEKAE

1

WHERE Zurich, Switzerland WHEN November 2012
CLIENT Komplementair 103 DESIGNER Aekae (p.490)
TOTAL FLOOR AREA 140 m² SHOP CONSTRUCTOR Gregoryclan
PHOTOS Courtesy of Aekae

For the men's branch of luxury Swiss accessories brand Komplementair (the women's store is located just next door), Aekae had to grapple with an unusually demanding location: a stone vault beneath Zurich's historic (and still operational) IM Viadukt. Reuse, appropriately enough given the original fabric, formed a large part of the project from the beginning. Recycled furniture is cleverly incorporated into the quirky freestanding shelving units that Aekae custom-designed and built for the store to showcase the range of masculine accessories on offer. These one-off pieces of display furniture in white and various woods are illuminated by strip lighting, highlighting the bags and shoes for sale but also presenting themselves almost as pieces of abstract sculpture. A unified effect is achieved thanks to the repetition of long, shallow rectangular units in the various displays – perfect for the small-sized goods they have to display. The display window echoes the rectangular format. A concrete floor and austere concrete sales desk add a modern industrial accent to the steampunk atmosphere of the original space. A freestanding concrete display wall is studded with pegs in many different styles. Reminiscent of a climbing wall, it offers a wide range of possibilities for hangable items like bags. An industrial steel staircase leads to the first floor floor, adding to the masculine palette of materials and in keeping with the area's industrial heritage.

1 Varied pegs, attached to the wall, create an interesting wall display.
2 Custom display units repeat the theme of long, shallow rectangular boxes stacked on each other.

2

An inventive recycled interior in an industrial monument

4

5

3 New structural elements in concrete
and steel are kept minimal and low-key.
4 In black, white and various woods, the
shelves incorporate vintage furniture.
5 Strip lighting highlights the products
on display.

LINEA PIU
BY KOIS ASSOCIATED ARCHITECTS

1

WHERE Mykonos, Greece **WHEN** June 2012
CLIENT Linea Piu **DESIGNER** Kois Associated Architects (p.496)
TOTAL FLOOR AREA 88 m² **SHOP CONSTRUCTOR** Korfiatis Kostas
PHOTOS Vagelis Paterakis and George Sfakianakis

According to Linea Piu's designer Stelios Kois, 'allusion to the Greek myth and tradition that saturate the Aegean' is the concept behind this luxury boutique on the island of Mykonos. Preserving the original stone building, which is typical of the island's famous 'white cube' architecture, was thus essential to the project. Within this historic shell, the new fittings and furniture were, says Kois, 'surgically fitted into place'. The selection of objects reflects various aspects of the island, and connects to its distinctive design history. The custom-made iron furniture and fittings allude to beautiful ancient finds now on display in the Mykonos Museum, and their textured surface is, says the designer, 'reminiscent of the texturing found on Alberto Giacometti sculptures'. The installation in the display room is designed to recreate the diffused mellow light that the wooden shutters introduce into typical Mykonian interiors. The polyhedral lamps reference the old Mykonos lighthouse and evoke tranquil strolls by the sea. The elegant leather stools are

intended to recall those traditional Mykonian meeting places, the square and the courtyard. 'The challenge was to orchestrate this whole synthesis in a manner that wakes up memory and brings to mind images from the life of the island', says Kois. The design is, luckily, contextual rather than scenographic, and so avoids the possible clichés of Greek island life. Brands like Chanel and Tom Ford are able to flourish in the timeless space, while the retail store is neither isolated nor detached from its location and spirit of the place.

1 Lighting was inspired by the island's old lighthouse.
2 The display room alludes to the spatial effect of the island's traditional wooden shutters.
3 Each aspect of the store alludes to the island's history, for example the iron fittings recall antique examples in Mykonos Museum.

2

A new look at
the Greek
island idyll

3

4 The simple wooden floor and brick walls
   are traditional.
5 The black-and-white theme is both
   contemporary and archaic.
6 A classic Mykonian 'white cube' house was
   the basis of the store.
7 New additions are simple and monochrome,
   so as not to overwhelm the space.

Objects refer to Mykonian history without the clichés

MALMAISON
BY DISTILLERY

WHERE Singapore, Singapore **WHEN** September 2011
CLIENT The Hour Glass **DESIGNER** Distillery (p.493)
TOTAL FLOOR AREA 815 m² **SHOP CONSTRUCTOR** Kingsmen
PHOTOS Darren Soh

Inspired by Chateau de Malmaison – the grand early 19th-century country home of Napoleon and Josephine – and located in Singapore's exclusive Knightsbridge mall, Malmaison is a rich, multi-layered retail environment. Designed by Distillery, its impeccably crafted, opulent salons present a thoughtfully curated collection of luxury objects for sale, mainly watches but also shoes, perfumes, jewellery and books. Specialist watch retailer The Hour Glass was inspired to establish this unique destination after observing how the retail environments of many luxury brands have tended to present a style of commercialised homogeneity in recent times. Distillery was engaged to craft a series of salons that would build upon the customer's engagement with Malmaison's luxury objects. These contribute to a unique retail environment which cultivates a curious state of mind and an appreciation of artisanal value. Paul Semple and Matthew Shang travelled with their client to destinations including France, Japan and India to source objects and materials. 'Our client had a unique

vision,' explains Semple. 'We drew on this to create ornate classic elements at Malmaison, but we approached the detailing and lighting in a contemporary way to bring currency to the grand vision.' Distillery designed 120 items of furniture that sit alongside antique pieces and extensive joinery in the interior. Within Malmaison, visitors discover a Parisian-style arcade, an imposing griffin, 2500 brass bees which were custom-cast in India, plaster moulding, a salon entirely lined with blue velvet, a terrarium, and Asia's first Taschen book corner. Even a private office is illuminated by a three-dimensional celestial ceiling map.

1 The store is a sequence of impeccably crafted and opulent salons.
2 Antique furnishings and ornaments join the luxury goods on display.

1   Retail area
2   Window display
3   Men's salon
4   Ladies' salon
5   Cash desk
6   Fitting room
7   Storage
8   Elevator
9   Private office
10 Staff-only area
11 Toilet

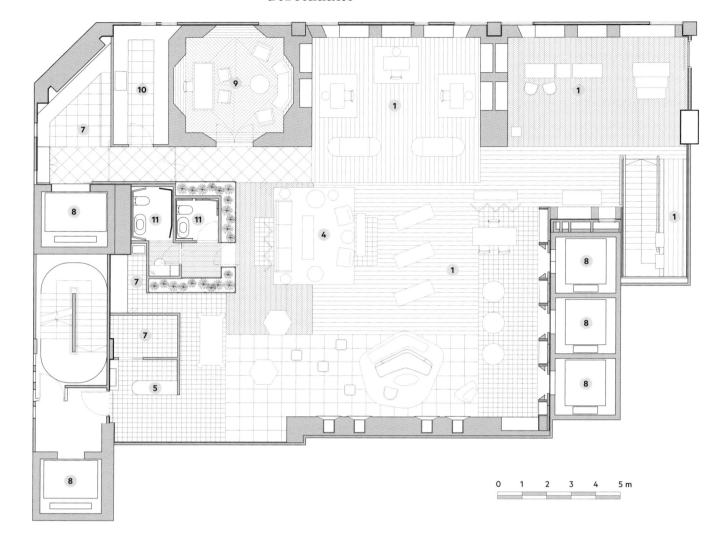

First floor

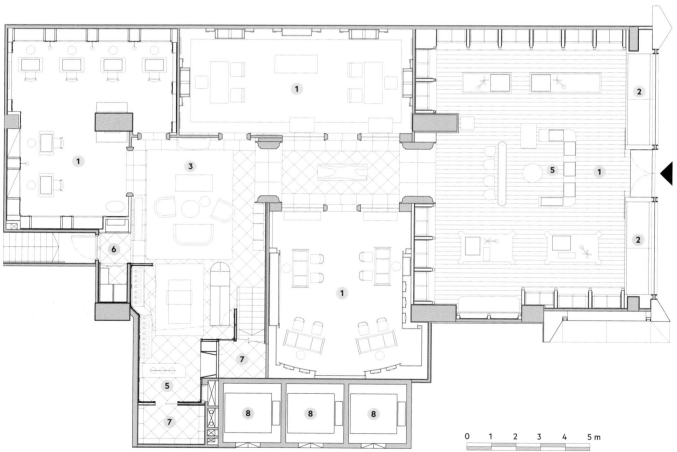

Ground floor

Classic luxury
refreshed by contemporary detailing

3 Napoleonic elements, such as an Empire
   portrait, mix with modern lighting
   and detailing.
4 Bespoke displays showcase luxurious
   merchandising.

5 & 6 A rich mix of materials, colours and objects makes this store a voyage of discovery.

7 A delightful and unexpected touch are the brass bees that adorn one of the walls.

8 The brightness of each 'star' in the celestial map was set by lighting designer Takeo Sugamata, who is also an amateur astronomer.

9 An imposing griffin features in the store, reflected in the mirror-like materials that frame it.

MYKITA
BY MYKITA

WHERE New York, United States WHEN July 2013
CLIENT Mykita DESIGNER Mykita (p.497)
TOTAL FLOOR AREA 85 m² SHOP CONSTRUCTOR Method Design
PHOTOS Courtesy of Mykita

If it ain't broke, don't fix it – or so the saying goes. And that seems to have been the motto of Berlin-based eyewear specialist Mykita for its first US outpost in New York City. The brand opted to stick to its tried-and-tested formula of a neon sign, all-white interior and hole-punched white metal walls. These are made, as in the other stores, from perforated steel angle bead that has been freed from its usual function as a heavy-duty shelving support. Individual shelf elements are instead inserted into the wall to provide each frame with its own little stage. Backlit, the functional material makes a superb presentation area, allowing the frames to really stand out against the uniform and low-key white background. As a further quirky touch, out-of-service flight attendant trolleys that may well have circled the globe for many years are given a new lease of life. Painted white, they serve as unexpected storage elements. The refurbished original grey concrete floor grounds the otherwise dematerialised white interior and completes the picture. Adding some local detail to the store, which in its basic lines resembles the brand's seven other stores worldwide, is a neon installation that brings the ceiling to life. This light installation is aligned with the old metal pipes from the building's original sprinkler system in a conscious reference to the context and the site's industrial past – a finishing touch uniting the present space with its architectural heritage, and the global brand with a particular building in New York City.

1 The storefront frames Mykita's trademark neon sign and all-white interior.
2 The perforated metal walls are backlit by LED strips which are programmed to create a nocturnal pulsating effect, while a neon ceiling installation aligns with the building's original metal sprinkler-system pipes.
3 The original concrete floor and double-height ceiling (painted white) remain, preserving the space's original character while old flight trolleys, painted white and used for storage, make interesting features.

All-white brand formula gets a local accent

PODIUM JEWELLERY
BY ART BUREAU 1/1

1

WHERE Moscow, Russia WHEN August 2011
CLIENT Podium DESIGNER Art Bureau 1/1 (p.490)
TOTAL FLOOR AREA 65 m² SHOP CONSTRUCTOR Podium
PHOTOS Frank Herfort

This is not the first Podium Jewellery store that Art Bureau 1/1 has designed for the Russian brand, but it could hardly be more different from its predecessors. Podium likes each of its stores to be unique; and its brand values – it approaches jewellery as art and often collaborates with artists – gave the designers the cue for an interior that references the psychedelic art movements of the 1960s: Pop Art and Op Art. The designers went well beyond referencing the 1960s and ended up pretty much reconstructing them, in a boutique that's a plastic fantastic environment reminiscent of period sci-fi films. The result is virtually an artwork in itself. Bright apple-green walls are the backdrop for a host of moulded white plastic displays, mirrors, and Op Art wall tiles, set off with steel bases, moulded glass tops and neon lighting. A pair of revolving plastic columns add a touch of playful drama to the space, and act as displays as well as architectural elements. The main display area is a symmetrical composition in green and white, but a more private area is concealed behind a white bead curtain. Here, there's a loungy consultation space with futuristic red ridged armchairs, adding a splash of hot colour, a cluster of shiny flying-saucer chrome lights (by Andtradition) and a pop-art rug. The only thing not redolent of the 1960s, in fact, is the iMac, which looks somewhat out of place. The rest of the interior has a seamless, time-capsule quality that makes an effective backdrop for displaying Podium's collector's-item pieces.

1 White moulded plastic display units, mirrors and columns are set off by the high-gloss apple-green walls and neon lighting.
2 The red plastic chairs and flying-saucer lights add more than a touch of Austin Powers.

A quirky take on glamour and glitz

RELOJERIA ALEMANA
BY OHLAB

WHERE Port Adriano, Mallorca, Spain WHEN August 2012
CLIENT Relojeria Alemana DESIGNER OHLAB (p.498)
TOTAL FLOOR AREA 105 m² SHOP CONSTRUCTOR Construcciones Torrens
PHOTOS Jose Hevia

OHLAB's store for jeweller Relojeria Alemana, in the Philippe Starck-designed marina of Port Adriano, is an unusual take on glamour and glitz. The designers compressed the programme – VIP area, temporary art installations, outdoor lounge, back office and signage – into five 'precious boxes', leaving the space in between the volumes as an exhibition gallery. Three of the boxes are located inside the store and two more are outdoors, extending the exhibition gallery to the terrace. Gold-coated stainless steel plates with a mirror finish cover the boxes – a touch of bling made interesting thanks to assembling the plates with a deformed set of joints, resulting in distorted surfaces and reflections. The interior space, defined only by three glazed façades, is illuminated via a matte, white, backlit textile ceiling. Every box includes an eye-level horizontal strip revealing a display: one side works as a shop window, while the other side opens to the interior of the store. On the terrace, by the sea, there are two more boxes of different sizes. One has a lounge bed with an incorporated display and the other one features the only signage of the store. The result is a collection of sculptural and abstract volumes reflecting a golden and slightly surreal environment. The project questions and reflects on the concept of luxury, proposing a game of appearances in which things are not what they seem. The simple but gold-coated boxes reflect yet distort the surrounding environment of the marina and its mega yachts, offering a new take on this playground of the rich.

1 Inside one of the boxes, the VIP lounge is covered in suede panelling and furnished with Nordic furniture.
2 The shiny but distorted surfaces reflect the surroundings in a somewhat intriguing manner.
3 The wood-lined lounge has a luxurious seating element, seeminlgy floating in the central space.

3

4   Exploded view showing the positioning of the boxes.

5 & 6   The boxes are set in a serene space with a pale stone floor and backlit tensed textile ceiling, furnished by Swan chairs upholstered in white leather, and a coffee table and lamp designed by Arne Jacobsen.

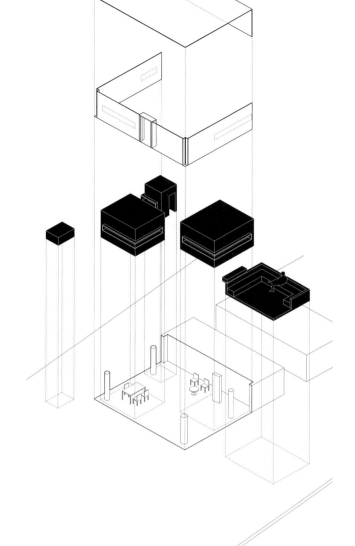

4

Every box includes an eye-level horizontal strip display

1   VIP area
2   Art installation
3   Back office
4   Seating area
5   Outdoor lounge
6   Signage box

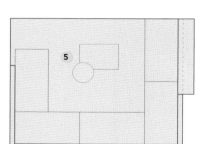

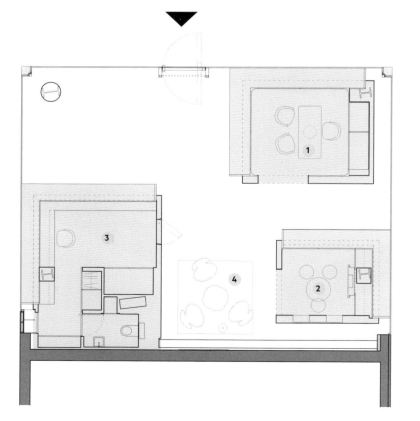

RIO
BY GLENN SESTIG ARCHITECTS

WHERE Ghent, Belgium **WHEN** May 2012
CLIENT Rio **DESIGNER** Glenn Sestig Architects (p.495)
TOTAL FLOOR AREA 53 m² **SHOP CONSTRUCTOR** Descamps
PHOTOS Jean Pierre Gabriel

Its name is Rio, the accessories store in Ghent subtly references its namesake and its owner's roots with a number of Brazilian allusions. 'In this interior, we referred to the Brazilian architecture of the late 1950s', explains the designer of the space, Glenn Sestig. 'This brutalism is legible in the use of concrete and the presence of the silver-brown travertine.' The store is designed to be a fitting backdrop to handbags and jewellery by the likes of Lanvin, Alexander McQueen, Stella McCartney, Marni, Repossi, Valentino and Saint Laurent Paris. Therefore luxury materials were a logical choice, as was the high quality of architectural detailing employed in the space. The variety of materials, features wood, concrete and natural stone. Warm-toned copper-filtered mirrors and rich walnut walls create an interesting tonal contrast with the cold materials such as concrete and marble. Concealed lighting intensifies the focus on the different textures and subtle spectrum of natural hues. Concrete beams are stacked like steps around a velvety bamboo-fibre carpet of an intense aqua blue, which adds an exotic, vibrant touch. Throughout the space, raw contrasts with refined: the offset created by luxurious silk wallpaper and American walnut identifies the concrete character of the store. The soft leather bags look desirable displayed on the hard concrete or marble shelves. The mirrors are an essential part of the concept, as they magnify the rather compact space.

1 The highly architectural space was inspired by Brazilian buildings of the 1950s.
2 The soft leather of the designer bags is accentuated by the concrete and marble display shelves.
3 An intense blue bamboo-fibre carpet adds an element of surprise.

Brazilian brutalism as a backdrop
for luxury

ZOFF
BY EMMANUELLE MOUREAUX
ARCHITECTURE + DESIGN

WHERE Iruma, Japan WHEN April 2013
CLIENT Zoff DESIGNER emmanuelle moureaux architecture + design (p.494)
TOTAL FLOOR AREA 127 m² SHOP CONSTRUCTOR Hiro Kenso
PHOTOS Nacása & Partners (Daisuke Shima)

For the Zoff eyewear shop in Mitsui Outlet Park, Iruma city (near Tokyo), French designer Emmanuelle Moureaux, a long-time resident of Japan, has reworked her signature formula of modular colour blocking. The store features a deceptively simple design composed of identical rectangular units – the colour blocks, each one measuring 80 by 16 cm – that have been stacked up to create display tables and counters, and mounted on the walls at varying heights to form shelves. Moureaux says that these slices of colour, which are versatile enough to function as furniture, fixtures and displays, are her attempt to 'capture pockets of colour that people view in their daily lives in the city'. The colours represent what she sees as an urban palette: 'the blue sky between buildings, the pockets of green in the park on the street corner, and the colourful glittering neon at night...the magenta and yellow spreading endlessly in the field of tulips, the pale blue from the crystal clear lake, and the pink petals of cherry blossoms swaying in the wind.' The

irregular arrangement of the blocks adds to the playful atmosphere of the store. 'Rationing' the colour keeps it effective and prevents it becoming overwhelming: two central display tables are composed of blocks in neutral tones and can be reconfigured as required. All the blocks, except the wall-mounted ones, are designed to be easily moved so the colour composition remains flexible and can be adjusted according to the season.

1 White walls and ceiling, a pale wood floor and neutral elements create a restrained backdrop that helps the colour blocks to pop.
2 Staggering the height of the colour blocks makes for a playful composition.
3 The stacked display units are flexible and can be reconfigured.

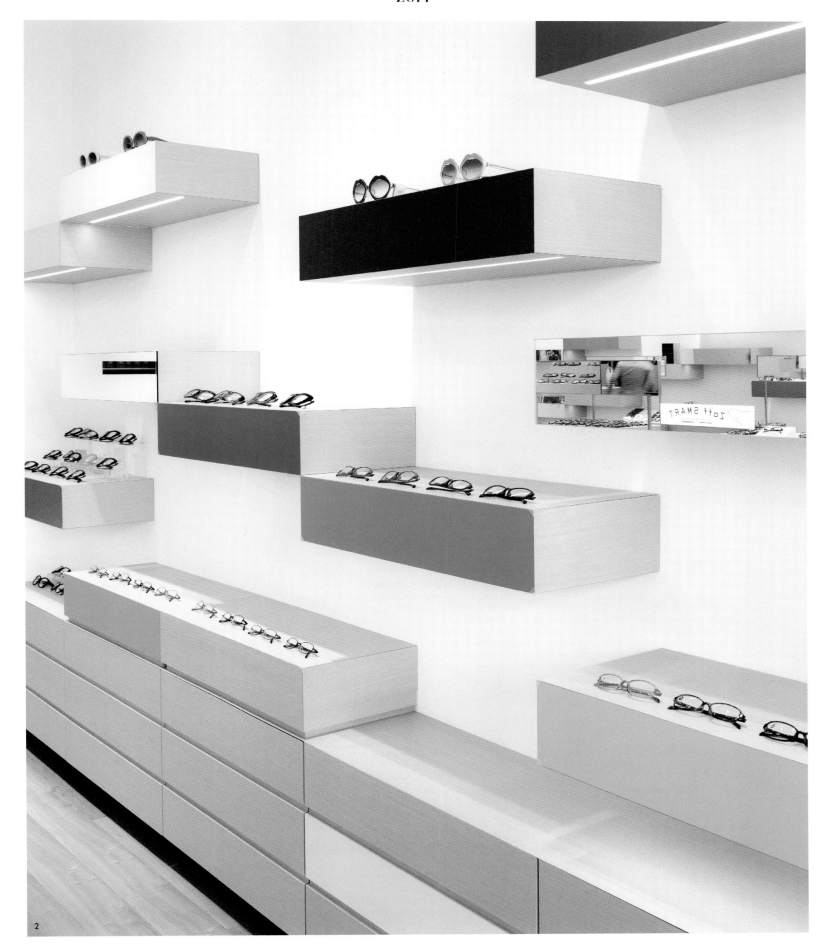

Colour blocking creates a flexible chromatic composition

ZOFF PARK HARAJUKU
BY ARCHICEPT CITY

1

WHERE Tokyo, Japan **WHEN** April 2011
CLIENT Intermestic **DESIGNER** Archicept city (p.490)
TOTAL FLOOR AREA 210 m² **SHOP CONSTRUCTOR** IDEX
PHOTOS Atsushi Nakamichi

How does an eyewear store attract attention amid all the fashionista favourites on Tokyo's cool Omotesando street? By being different of course – which for Zoff Park Harajuku designers Archicept city meant embracing transparency. 'The retail space needed to be accessible and open, making a place where everyone just wants to stop by and come in', says Archicept founder Atsushi Muroi. Therefore, there are very few visual barriers between the street and the interior. The store frontage is predominantly glass, and it showcases custom-built, illuminated glass display stands that are almost equally as transparent. 'It does not look like an eyewear retailer at first sight', says the designer. 'But more like an open-air terrace in the park. We want passers-by to naturally look into the shop and get interested in the space.' As intrigued visitors pass over the threshold into the store, the transparent elements gradually solidify into white island displays and backlit wall units. These display over 2000 frames, the complete offering of the up-and-coming Japanese

eyewear brand. Envisaging the store as a park – a public space – also inspired the custom-made pendant lights near the entrance, which are designed to resemble a fountain, a familiar parkland feature. The interior also has several strategically placed mirrors which have the effect of randomly mixing and merging different lighting 'zones' to mimic the dappled effect of daylight. The idea here is 'to give visitors a feeling of natural light in the park, not an artificial feeling', says Muroi.

1 Over 2000 frames are displayed on a
  sequence of white island and wall displays.
2 A mainly glass frontage and glass displays
  next to it give passers-by an intriguing view
  of the interior.

BODY
HEALT

080

AND
HCARE

081

ANGELICO
BY MOVEDESIGN

1

WHERE Saga, Japan **WHEN** July 2012
CLIENT Noriyuki Nakayama **DESIGNER** MOVEDESIGN (p.497)
TOTAL FLOOR AREA 50 m² **SHOP CONSTRUCTOR** Noside
PHOTOS Yousuke Harigane

Blue for a women-only hair salon? According to designer Mikio Sakamoto of MOVEDESIGN, what designates the feminity of this space is not the colour, but the concept: namely, the huge shop window fronting the space. 'I put a large element of "window display" into this space,' he says. 'Usually the salon category doesn't need this function, but here I use it to express the salon's outlook. It's like a woman saying, "I'm feminine!"' According to Sakamoto, the project is designed to look like a fashion retail space in order to suggest its gender exclusivity. From outside, a glowing blue box contains a white desk, a white sofa, three white shelves for product display and some delicate white signage – mentioning neither hair nor women. Through an opening on one side, however, the cutting space is clearly visible, again blue but with a white floor and side walls and a sequence of glass partitions. Even though blue is the world's favourite colour according to surveys, the designer confirms that opting for a single colour was a brave choice: 'I chose

blue and applied it thoroughly. It was a challenge for me to pursue only one direction, with no possibility of half measures', he says. The use of one colour effectively unifies the reception and retail area at the front with the working spaces at the back. It also lends a particularly dreamy atmosphere to the salon when viewed from street outside, suggesting the kind of temporary escape that a salon provides.

1 From the street, the salon is mostly blue.
2 The design is based on a welcoming reception space, fronted by a large window, and more functional working areas behind.
3 Inside, more white reveals itself, as does an area of natural wood which adds a contrasting warmth.

DURASAFE
BY MINISTRY OF DESIGN

1

WHERE Singapore, Singapore **WHEN** October 2012
CLIENT Durasafe **DESIGNER** Ministry of Design (p.497)
TOTAL FLOOR AREA 175 m² **SHOP CONSTRUCTOR** Exquisite Builders
PHOTOS CI&A Photography

How to attract mainstream shoppers when you're a safety equipment brand? That was the challenge facing Durasafe when it decided to open a flagship store in Singapore, and the reason that the brand turned to Ministry of Design for help. The office responded with a space that's strong on streetwise industrial chic. Like a warehouse, the store has black walls, metal staircases and cage-like balconies. But dramatic lighting, large screens and pops of colour in the wayfinding and product range make the space edgy and cool, rather than simply workmanlike. The interior is inspired by the construction and manufacturing industries, the core users of the good on show. Black floor-to-ceiling displays are based on scaffolding and take advantage of the height of the space. The signage and floor markings suggest an industrial depot, as do the watertight bulkhead doors used for the changing rooms. Yellow dotted lines on the floor denote the various different product zones. The entrance is a high point, marked by bright orange screens set back from the glazed façade. Customers pass by a big green cross as they enter the store – part of the Durasafe logo which is the only thing on display in the window. The absence of products on display avoids the workaday approach usual with safety equipment and serves to intrigue passers-by. If the promise of hard hats in a range of trendy colours, or safety boots that look more fashionable than functional, isn't enough to lure people in, the gallery-like entrance will probably do the job.

1 The enormous Durasafe logo impresses against a bright orange backdrop.
2 A scaffold-like structure is used for the staircases and shelving, creating an industrial atmosphere.
3 Bright products stand out against the dark interior.

The gallery-like entrance lures people in

Black floor-to-ceiling displays are based on scaffolding

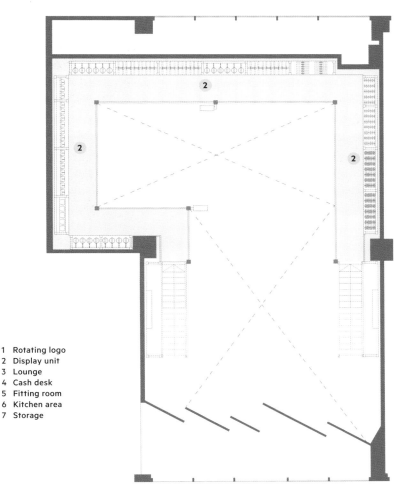

Mezzanine

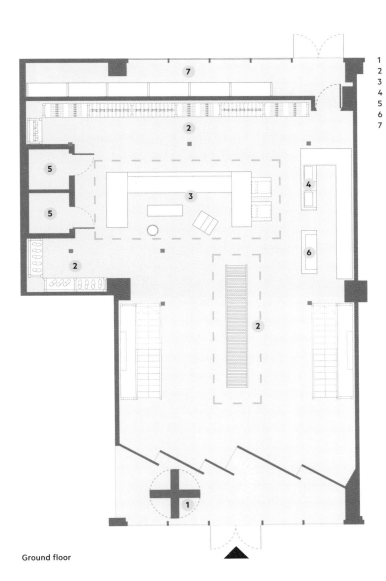

1 Rotating logo
2 Display unit
3 Lounge
4 Cash desk
5 Fitting room
6 Kitchen area
7 Storage

Ground floor

4 Signage adopts an industrial vocabulary,
   while yellow lines denote different
   product areas.
5 Watertight doors on the fitting rooms add
   to the different shopping experience.

ERNO LASZLO
BY FAK3

WHERE Hong Kong, Hong Kong WHEN November 2012
CLIENT Water Oasis Group DESIGNER FAK3 (p.495)
TOTAL FLOOR AREA 30 m² SHOP CONSTRUCTOR –
PHOTOS Trio Photo

Commissioned by legendary skincare label Erno Laszlo to design a series of experimental luxury boutiques in Hong Kong and China, local studio FAK3 opted for a fluid, sculptural and bespoke solution. Computer designed but handcrafted Corian pieces are placed on a polished black striated marble floor, and are reflected by a tinted black mirror-steel ceiling. In this gallery-like setting, the products seem to complete the design. FAK3's Johnny Wong says: 'Within the project, luxury is defined through the explorative design process and elegant articulation of fluid form. Conceptually, the Corian sculptures are like white liquid waves, with Erno Laszlo's products sitting on top to visually make them float.' The concept is striking, but simple and adaptable enough to be applied to any store space by the brand. 'The fluid forms can be uniquely defined by the context of each site, creating a different experience for each store,' says Wong's partner, Miho Hirabayashi. Meanwhile the high-contrast black and white formula with its distinctive shapes creates a strong brand identity for Erno Laszlo, which was once associated with screen icons such as Audrey Hepburn and Greta Garbo. 'Our design approach was to innovate and move away from the industry's generic retail template,' comments Hirabayashi. Nevertheless the smooth surfaces and softly curving forms are thematically appropriate, evoking the texture of well-maintained skin and the rounded angles of facial bone structure. Johnny Wong and Miho Hirabayashi, on the other hand, have dubbed the store style as 'liquid baroque'.

1 An open storefront with glass façade showcases the dramatic monochromatic interior.
2 Black-and-white striated marble flooring and dark mirror-steel ceiling throw the curved white shapes into relief.
3 The eye-catching white counter was computer designed and handcrafted in Corian.

Adventures in 'liquid baroque'

FARMÁCIA LORDELO
BY JOSÉ CARLOS CRUZ ARQUITECTO

1

WHERE Vila Real, Portugal **WHEN** October 2012
CLIENT Maria João Reis **DESIGNER** José Carlos Cruz Arquitecto (p.496)
TOTAL FLOOR AREA 522 m² **SHOP CONSTRUCTOR** –
PHOTOS FG+SG

Faced with building a pharmacy in a new area of town with no clear identity, José Carlos Cruz opted for what he calls 'an abstract and neutral character, reinforced by the absence of openings.' His solution is an intriguing, closed oval volume. Just one main entrance leads inside; otherwise the dramatic geometric structure is clad entirely in coated, perforated aluminium. Although nominally grey, the exterior is tinged with green light, thanks to the bold cross symbol that dominates the façade and acts like a billboard advertising the pharmacy. Pale by day, at night the green light of the exterior becomes a vibrant emerald, as does the sculptural cross that stands in front of the building like a thematic streetlight. 'By changing the light of the interior and of the symbol of pharmacy itself, the building gains dynamics, allowing its image to change from day to night', says Cruz. Inside, the interior is open and pristinely white, with the only colour coming from the various products displayed on the shelves. The extremely clean aesthetic speaks of hygiene and efficiency, while the curved walls give it a futuristic air. The pharmacy has two floors, with the main sales area below and a compounding laboratory, which makes medicines, above. Green and glowing, the pharmacy has carved its own territory in a nondescript corner of its hometown, making the kind of strong statement able to impose a kind of identity on a hitherto featureless area.

1 The whiter-than-white interior refers to the pharmacy's medicinal function.
2 & 3 By day the façade glows with a subtle green light, while at night the green morphs into a vibrant emerald.
4 Products add the only colour to the all-white interior.

Giving a green light to abstract geometry

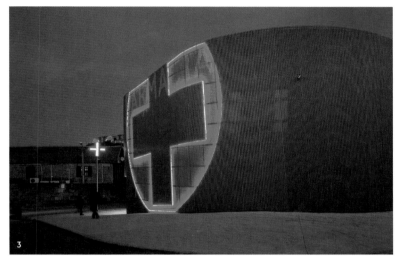

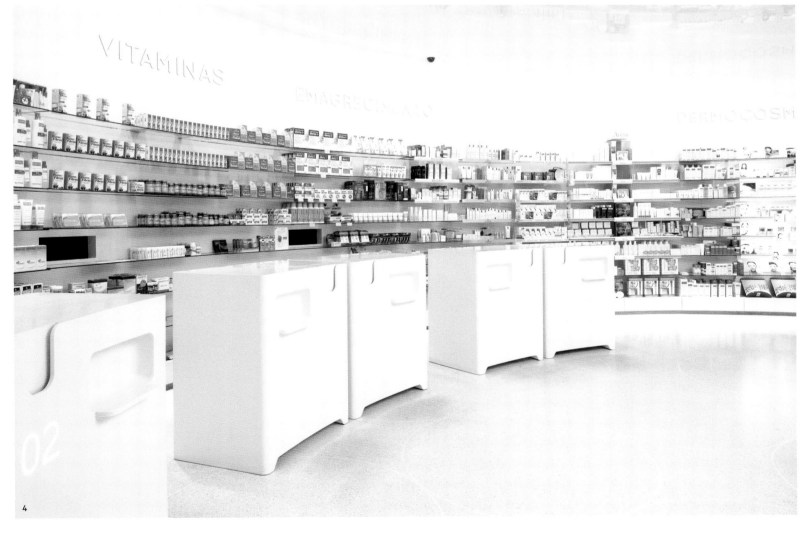

Just one main entrance leads inside

5   The architect made the interior open so
     as to be comprehensible in one glance.
6 & 7 A closed white oval contained within a
     façade of unbroken aluminium, the
     interior is abstract and neutral.

MUSSLER BEAUTY
BY DITTEL ARCHITEKTEN

1

WHERE Stuttgart, Germany **WHEN** November 2012
CLIENT Mussler **DESIGNER** Dittel Architekten (p.494)
TOTAL FLOOR AREA 240 m² **SHOP CONSTRUCTOR** Dittel Architekten
PHOTOS Martin Baitinger and Frank Bayh & Steff Rosenberger-Ochs

For a third-generation family beauty business, Dittel Architekten created a store with a distinctly domestic feel. Warm materials like wood and wallpaper combined with modern lines, while the make-up section boasts little white desks and chairs and elsewhere there are mini bathroom units, shelving units and lamps. The cosy touches encourage the customer to feel comfortable and at home, reflecting the store's mission statement: home of beauty. Despite its domestic quality, the space is well thought out, with each of the four product categories receiving its own area, which is designated by selected materials, colours and structures as well as form and function. The fragrance section is located in the central area of the perfumery. A bent powder-coated metal sheet serves as the base for the oak wood shelves presenting the flacons. It leads on to the make-up area, which contains the fixtures for the make-up brands and the cosmetics school with its little desks. The next space is dedicated to care products, and displays are tiled in white, contrasting sharply with the new product cabinets in yellow. Then the special product series of natural cosmetics is presented on a raised arrangement of single-cabinet elements. Despite the different design features of the areas, they all share an abundance of details – pieces of furniture and lamps of various kinds – that contribute to a lively atmosphere on the sales floor. A backlit visual at the cash desk and reception draws the customer's attention to the stairs leading to the beauty cabins on the floor above.

1 Display areas of different characters reflect the four different product groups: perfume, natural, make-up and care.
2 & 3 Six little white desks with chairs comprise the make-up school area.
4 Care products are displayed in a bath room-like context, with tiling and a washbasin unit.

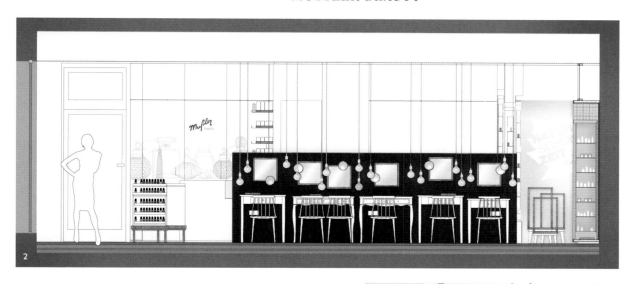

Domestic details are the key to customer comfort

BOO
STATI
AND M

098

KS,
ONARY
MUSIC

099

AOYAMA MIHONCHO
BY TONERICO

WHERE Tokyo, Japan WHEN January 2012
CLIENT Takeo DESIGNER Tonerico (p.499)
TOTAL FLOOR AREA 110 m² SHOP CONSTRUCTOR CBK
PHOTOS Satoshi Asakawa

With 1500 closed drawers and nothing on display, the serene Aoyama Mihoncho, a Tokyo paper store, is about as far away from the usual overstated retail environment as it is possible to imagine. Stretching from floor to ceiling, the rows of drawers, which conceal rather than show off the product, were intended to suggest a sample book, says Ken Kimizuka of Tonerico. His office used the drawers to unify a somewhat irregular space, creating 'one continuous surface with minimal shadows'. The modest interior was constructed using modest materials. 'The material chosen for this space was basswood, which is quite ordinary', says Kimizuka. 'In other words, it is quite common, much like Kent paper and copy papers are common for paper.' The ordinariness of the material contributes to preventing the abundance of drawers from being overwhelming, as does their precise placement. Before constructing the space, says the designer, the team did 'a detailed analysis of an actual-size mock-up design', to see how the drawers should fit together. The finished effect is greatly enhanced by the suspended fluorescent lighting, which also accentuates the long horizontal lines of the store. Lack of shadow and regular repetition lead to a certain flattening of the space: when a drawer is opened, it is a moment of some drama. 'The space is subtle and does not speak out, serving its purpose as a background space', says Kimizuka. The effect is as subtle as paper itself.

1 The modest interior was constructed using modest materials: basswood and fluorescent strip lighting.
2 Some 1500 drawers line the space.
3 & 4 When a drawer is opened, it is a moment of some drama.
5 The finished effect is enhanced by the suspended fluorescent lighting, which accentuates the long horizontal lines of the store.

How to conceal, rather than reveal, the goods

6 A rendering of the original design, which
   was intended to suggest a sample book.
7 Lack of shadow and regular repetition lead
   to a certain flattening of the space.

The effect is as subtle as paper itself

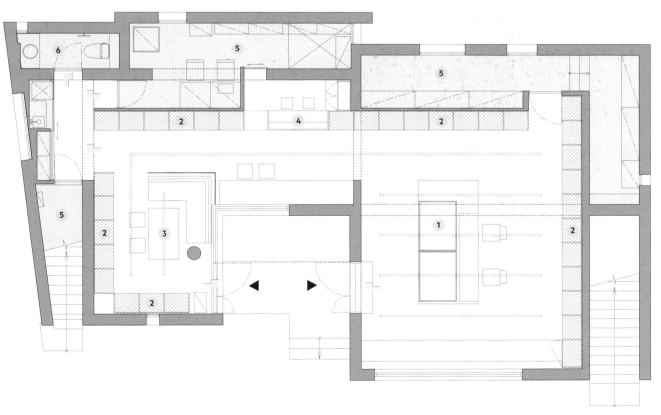

1 Display counter
2 Paper stock drawers
3 Concierge area
4 Cash desk
5 Storage
6 Toilet

BACK TO SCHOOL
BY CONFETTI

WHERE the Netherlands **WHEN** May 2012
CLIENT Bijenkorf **DESIGNER** Confetti (p.492)
TOTAL FLOOR AREA 30–70 m² **SHOP CONSTRUCTOR** Confetti
PHOTOS –

How to make the prospect of going back to school after the summer holidays an appealing, exciting idea, rather than a moment to dread? That was the challenge for design office Confetti, when commissioned to create Back to School, a seasonal shop-in-shop for all the branches of the Bijenkorf, a Dutch department store. Stocking necessities and accessories for the new school year, the branches needed a strong but general identity able to reach school kids of a wide range of ages and interests. Confetti settled on the theme: New School, New You. To express optimism and energy, the designers opted for a youthful fluorescent colour palette and a Do-It-Yourself aesthetic, with stencil-look cardboard panels fronting displays giving a fresh and surprising look. Huge, humorous thumbs-up signs, also in vivid fluoro colours, are liberally suspended from the ceiling. The thumbs-up signs are obvious references to Facebook, and 'Like' is also prominent among the stencilled statements. By channelling new media, Confetti hoped to make a universally appealing interior, one able to talk to both kids and their parents, and to the many different 'tribes' and ages of school students. While punchy and bright, the interior is also gender-neutral, so equally attractive to both boys and girls, and flexible enough to be used in the whole range of Bijenkorf locations. A colourful and playful range of products adds to the jazzy and universal effect.

1 Bright stencil-look cardboard panels front display units, giving a fresh and surprising look.
2 Huge, humorous thumbs-up signs reference Facebook, while fluoro colour and playful touches put a positive spin on the not-so-welcome idea of returning to school after the holidays.

Channelling new media for a school-age demographic

BAX-SHOP
BY DASTRO RETAILCONCEPTS

WHERE Goes, the Netherlands **WHEN** November 2012
CLIENT Bax-shop.nl **DESIGNER** Dastro Retailconcepts (p.493)
TOTAL FLOOR AREA 1600 m² **SHOP CONSTRUCTOR** Intra
PHOTOS Limit Fotografie

Dutch brothers, Jochanan en Nathanael Bax, started out on the road to success ten years ago, hiring out DJ gear. That early effort grew into a shop and a successful internet business called Bax-shop.nl. In 2012, online turnover has grown enormously, but customers were invariably disappointed by the small size (just 100 m²) of the real-life shop. It was time to think bigger – in this case, 1500 m² bigger. The brothers acquired a new 1600 m² and called in design office Dastro. These days, customers to the new store are greeted by an expansive and highly theatrical experience. On entering the space, a DJ mural announces 'Play', which is the overall theme of the shop. Visitors find themselves in a bar and lounge area, furnished in the Bax brand colours of magenta and white. Dramatic. Dramatic black portals, emblazoned with quotes about music, reference the wings of a theatre and suggest the idea of performance. These guide the customer to the 'disco', which showcases the latest in sound and light shows. Next to this, the guitar department has a totally different atmosphere, with wood-printed carpet and leather-covered walls creating a rock-and-roll environment to frame the instruments. There are rooms devoted to several instruments, but the DJ space is perhaps the high point of the interior for most visitors: bright, glossy and high-tech, it's decorated with large chandeliers and white tables. From the entresol above (housing the drum machines), there are exciting views over the shop, and visitors can try before they buy thanks to the acoustically designed rehearsal rooms and studios.

1   The store opens with a bar and lounge
    area in magenta and white, the Bax
    brand colours.
2   Black portals, each one bearing a music
    quote, are the theatrical entrances to
    the product areas.
3   Lighting, graphics and furniture emulate
    the love for making music.

A DJ and music store that's almost a nightclub

1   Lounge area
2   Guitars
3   Drums
4   Keyboards
5   Lighting
6   DJ gear
7   Rehearsal rooms
8   Cash desk
9   Storage
10 Office
11 Toilets

The 1600 m² store is a theatrical experience

4   The guitar store has leather walls
    lound wood-print floors for a touch of
    rock atmosphere.
5 & 6 Customers can try out the products in
    a range of rehearsal rooms and studios.

1

How to make a shipping container sexy

URBANEARS BOXPARK
BY 42 ARCHITECTS

2

WHERE London, United Kingdom **WHEN** November 2011
CLIENT Zound Industries **DESIGNER** 42 Architects (p.490)
TOTAL FLOOR AREA 30 m² **SHOP CONSTRUCTOR** Karmer Setbuilding
PHOTOS Courtesy of 42 Architects

Can a product that's all about our sense of hearing be presented with a strong visual impact? That was the challenge facing headphones brand Urbanears when it commissioned emerging practice 42 Architects to create its first ever store. In their approach to the compact interior – a 12m shipping container at Boxpark in Shoreditch, London – the designers built their main idea around keeping things simple, contrasting the highly colourful products against a sparse white interior. But they kept it interesting with a feature back wall created from a backlit Perspex frame, illuminated by an RGB LED light. This changes colour (according to Urbanears' seasonal palette) in response to the sounds made by customers in the shop. At night, the store becomes a colourful beacon for passers-by in the lively Shoreditch and Brick Lane area. Befitting its compact size, the shop consists of a limited palette of materials. The walls are made of precision-cut Hanex sheets, chosen for its homogenous and smooth appearance. Combined with an epoxy surfaced floor and a white ceiling that hides all services, the shop works as a deliberately non-textural backdrop for the products on display. Mirrors in the same zigzag configuration as the walls help create a feeling of space. Bespoke and quirky product fittings adds a sense of playfulness to the space; the Medis in-ear headphones are fitted in silicon moulded ears, embedded in the Hanex walls, and the Bagis headphone can be pushed into bespoke plastic plugs, which are also integrated with the walls.

1 The only colour in the all-white interior is provided by products and a Perspex LED-lit wall.
2 The products are displayed on specially molded silicone and plastic fittings.

A backlit Perspex wall changes colour
in response to shop sounds

3, 4, 5 & 6 The varied colour effects result
from customer interaction and keep
the space lively and intriguing.
7 Mirrors help to mentally extend
the compact container space.

DEPAR
STO

116

TMENT
RES

117

Boxy brilliance for a real-estate 'shopping mall'

EVEN MEGASTORE
BY JAYME LAGO MESTIERI ARCHITECTURE

2

WHERE São Paulo, Brazil **WHEN** July 2013
CLIENT Even Construtora e Incorporadora **DESIGNER** Jayme Lago Mestieri Architecture (p.496)
TOTAL FLOOR AREA 4000 m² **SHOP CONSTRUCTOR** Even Construtora e Incorporadora
PHOTOS Ary Diesendruck

For a Brazilian property developer, Jayme Lago Mestieri Architecture created an innovative retail concept – a shopping mall-style store showcasing a wide variety of real-estate projects. The designers started by hollowing out the existing building until only a shell remained. Then they applied a modular grid, splitting the space into 8-m-wide units and inserting a 'cell' into each one. Along the façade, cells are positioned in two rows, giving the building a unique character from the outside, with the white, protruding boxy forms alternating with expanses of glass. Inside the building, the boxes resemble rows of shops, and a line of palm trees growing next to the walkway alongside them adds to the illusion. While the exterior of the boxes is white, the interior walls have a darker, warmer treatment. Lighting is soft and the furniture was custom designed for the space. Each cell showcases models and graphics and has a projection area at the back. Outside the cells, the spatial treatment is lighter, with texturised white paint, glass walls and brighter, diffused lighting. The furniture – sofas and armchairs – placed around the main space is residential, creating a homely effect. The main entrance hall gives a dramatic view of all the cells. The clean plain, walls of the hall clearly place the emphasis on the cells and corridors. A ramp leads to the upper level, and lounge spaces, bars and cafés are positioned between the cells behind the glass façade. Their illumination is the basis for the external lighting and lends richness to the volume.

1 Simple design elements create impressive perspectival effects.
2 A modular arrangement of boxy 'cells' gives a sculptural profile to the exterior and interior of the building.

3 Each of the upper and lower level cubes function like a shop, selling a particular product.
4 All in all, the cells display 70 real-estate products, each one given its own, manageable area.
5 A palm tree-lined 'street' links the various enterprise units.

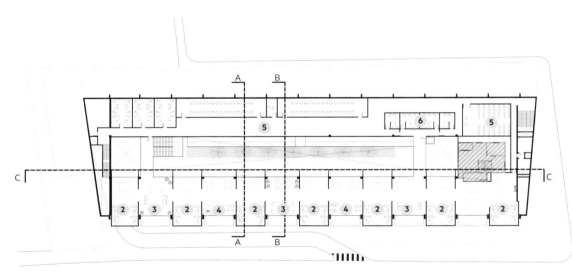

1 Institutional area
2 Enterprise units
3 Lounge area
4 Coffee corner
5 Back office
6 Toilets
7 Parking area

First floor

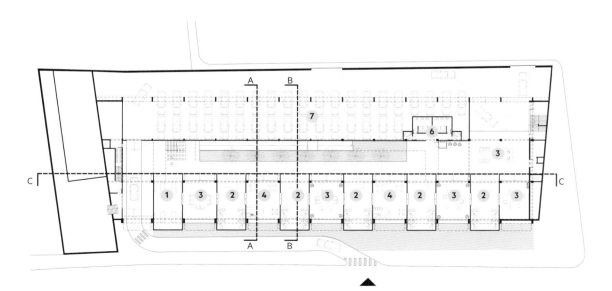

Ground floor

6 Cafés and lounge areas, reception areas and selling stations punctuate the 'mall'.
7 The row of illuminated boxes is designed to attract attention at night.

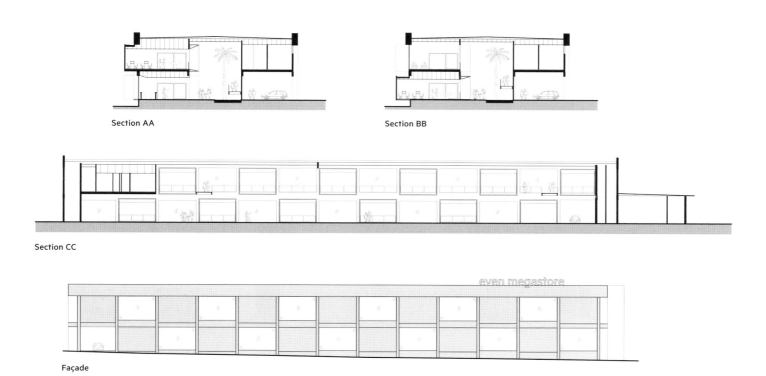

Section AA

Section BB

Section CC

Façade

Rows of 'cells' offer various real-estate products

A homage to Paris,
and the Parisian department store

GALERIES LAFAYETTE
BY PLAJER & FRANZ STUDIO

WHERE Jakarta, Indonesia WHEN June 2013
CLIENTS Galeries Lafayette and Mitra Adiperkasa DESIGNER plajer & franz studio (p.498)
TOTAL FLOOR AREA 12,000 m² SHOP CONSTRUCTOR Haras
PHOTOS diephotodesigner.de (Ken Schluchtmann)

How to convey the idea of Parisian chic in the Jakarta branch of the famous French Galeries Lafayette department store? By adding the Eiffel Tower, of course! But this solution is more interesting than it sounds: Berlin design office plajer & franz studio 'reinterpreted' the Parisian icon by placing a soaring vertical slice of it at the store's entrance – a dynamic introduction to French style and to the store's conceptual theme of 'one day in Paris'. Other aspects of the City of Light get similar thematic treatment, such as its characteristic street façades and street lights – these are encountered as sketchy, abstracted slices in various locations in the 12,000 m² store. Often, they are part of what the designers call 'indoor façades' – indoor walls made of sandblasted glass and mirror glass etched with Parisian motifs, which are used to both frame and separate the various brands within the store. The *coupole* – an emblem of the great architectural tradition of the Parisian department store – is also used as a recurring motif, reappearing as a graphic wall element or as oversized, domed ceiling lights on all four floors. The material palette, while varied to reflect the wide variety of merchandise, has a Parisian feel too, with lots of bronze and printed glass plus natural stone and wood creating a strong city feel. Neutral hues prevail, with the brand colour of red prominent at the store's entrance, where it adds a new, warm and vibrant layer to the Eiffel Tower architecture.

1 The theme of the coupole recurs as lavish ceiling lights.
2 A dramatic escalator greets visitors to the store.
3 At the entrance, a soaring installation decorated with an outline of the Eiffel Tower greets customers.

Neutral stone and wood create a strong city feel

4   Double-sided indoor walls made of
    sandblasted glass and mirror glass are
    etched with Parisian street motifs such as
    façades and street lamps.
5 & 6   Display areas are kept small-scale and
    focused, for maximum impact.
7   Natural stone, wood, glass, bronze and
    tiles give the store a 'Parisian
    streetscape' ambience.
8   Glimpses of the brand colour red is used
    selectively throughout, to add unity and
    energy to the space.

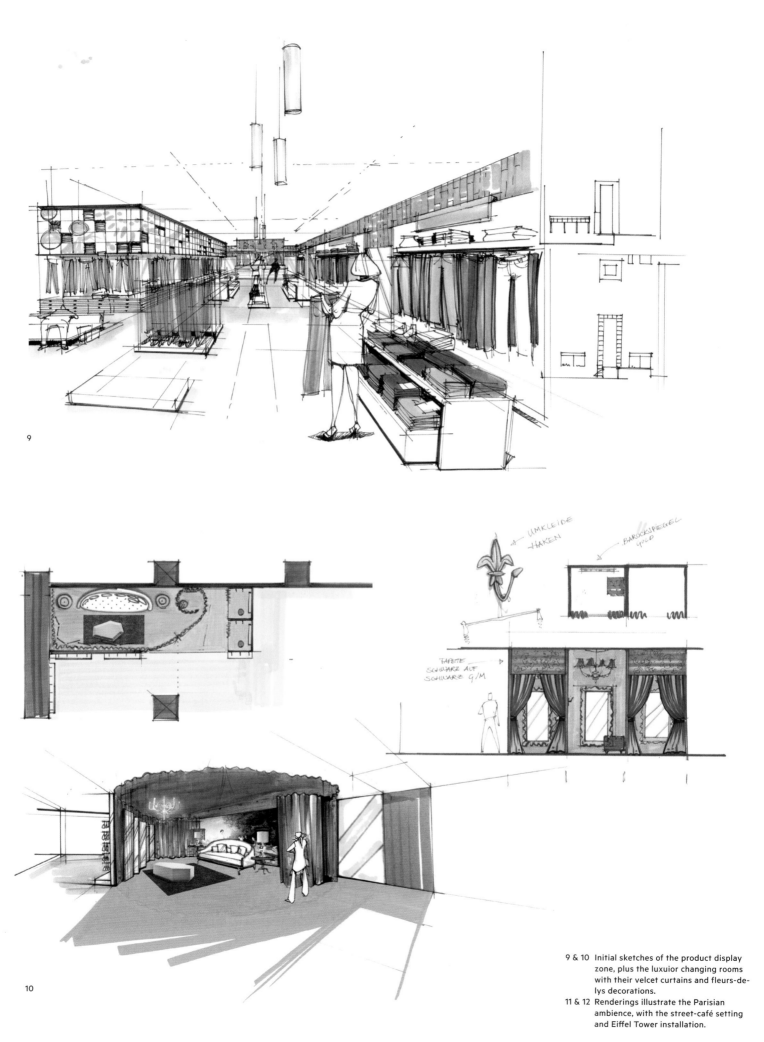

9

10

9 & 10 Initial sketches of the product display
        zone, plus the luxuior changing rooms
        with their velcet curtains and fleurs-de-
        lys decorations.
11 & 12 Renderings illustrate the Parisian
        ambience, with the street-café setting
        and Eiffel Tower installation.

Motifs include Parisian street lights and *la coupole*

LOFT
BY TONERICO

WHERE Tokyo, Japan WHEN September 2011
CLIENT The Loft DESIGNER Tonerico (p.499)
TOTAL FLOOR AREA 2500 m² SHOP CONSTRUCTOR Nomura
PHOTOS Satoshi Asakawa

A cavernous industrial space packed with shelving, storage, and must-keep items of every kind, the Yurakucho flagship space for Loft – a much-loved Japanese chainstore that sells stylish takes on everyday objects – is pretty much a pun on its name: a warehouse, an attic – a loft, in fact. For the new store, design office Tonerico decided to look back over the past 20 years of the chain's history to find inspiration for a new concept. Part of the brief was 'going back to Loft's roots'. Examining large numbers of archive photos led Tonerico's Hiroshi Yoneya and Ken Kimizuka to the idea of 'a loft within a loft', in which they could express the richness of Loft's history. 'The site was a double-layer atrium, which is a very rare in an urban street-front location', says Yoneya. It was easy to envisage the 2500 m² space as a kind of warehouse, divided into an imaginary grid and filled with 'overwhelmingly large quantities of frame racks' and no less than 3300 cardboard boxes, creating 'a totally new sense of space that did not exist before'. In this labyrinth of shelving,

graphic design and signage add a welcome unifying function. 'The selection of rugged materials, the skeleton space and the galvanised and unichrome steel frames emphasise timeless functionality, which is an underlying concept of Loft's roots', says Yoneya.

1 The concept of the interior was a 'loft within a loft'.
2 Rugged materials and galvanised and unichrome steel frames emphasise timeless functionality.

Everyday classics accented with a touch of madness

3 & 4 Rows and rows of shelves plus 330
       boxes form the store's identity.
5 & 7 In this labyrinth of shelving,
       graphic design and signage add
       a unifying function.
6   Putting together one of the 3300
       cardboard boxes that give character
       to the space.

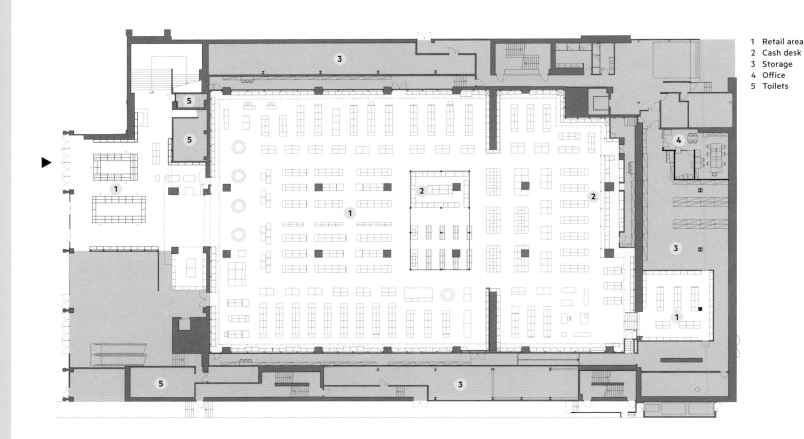

1 Retail area
2 Cash desk
3 Storage
4 Office
5 Toilets

'Overwhelmingly large' quantities of shelves and 3300 boxes create the store experience

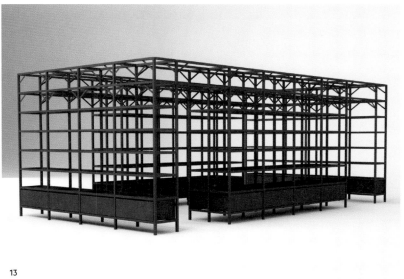

8 At this rendering the skeleton of the displays are in place and signage is added so
   customers can easily orientate themselves.
9 & 10 Putting the steel frame together
   through assembly and welding.

11 Adding a graphic backdrop of signage.
12 A rendering of the wooden shelves,
    which are painted white and black in
    the actual store.
13 The custom-made steel shelving unit.

PARIS
BY DALZIEL AND POW

WHERE Santiago, Chile WHEN December 2012
CLIENT Paris Cencosud DESIGNER Dalziel and Pow (p.493)
TOTAL FLOOR AREA 700 m² SHOP CONSTRUCTOR Cypco
PHOTOS Marcos Mendizabal

Create a modern, best-in-class department – that was the brief Dalziel and Pow received for the children's area of the new Paris store in Quilin, Santiago. The designers responded with a concept that is all about adventure, with playful architecture and furniture inspired by childhood fun – camping, treehouses, fun at the fair, skateboarding, beach holidays and hide-and-seek. The look and feel of the department is achieved through theatrical sets resembling miniature houses, rooms, and deconstructed play areas. The department is divided between fashion, toys, footwear, nursery and accessories, with each area having its own bold personality. Fashion is split by gender and age, with spaces interlinked via oversized doors and keyholes. The palette is urban and bright, with quirky, unexpected details, such as a table made of skateboards for boys and a deconstructed caravan for girls. The bespoke fixtures are inspired by outdoor adventure – rope, knots and swings. A series of patterns further helps differentiate boys' and girls'

fashion. A softer version of the pattern is used for the baby area. The toy area sits at the heart of the space and is inspired by a toy factory wonderland. Toys are displayed on a freestanding 6-m-high industrial framework, maximising the height of the space. A mezzanine wraps around the area, used as a platform for visual merchandising. Customers can stand in the middle of the space and get a 360-degree view of the toys, evoking the feeling of being a small kid in a giant toy factory.

1 The 'toy store' is the central focus and the other departments wrap around, with each area becoming more grown-up as the age range increases but maintaining a tailored 'fun and humour' thread.
2 Toys are displayed on a freestanding 6-m-high industrial framework, maximising the height of the space with the zone decorated with playful coloured geometric prints .

Childhood fun in all its quirky detail

3 & 4 Sitting within a raw concrete shell, this area is painted lighter with features including a keyhole entrance and ice-cream trolley table, appropriate for the 2–8 years age group.

5 This area exposes more of the shell, with rails constructed from steel reinforcement rods, finished in primary colours and playfully knotted like string.

6 The coloured metallic framework of the display systems also incorporated geometric patterns. Gender specific patterns define boys' and girls' areas.

7

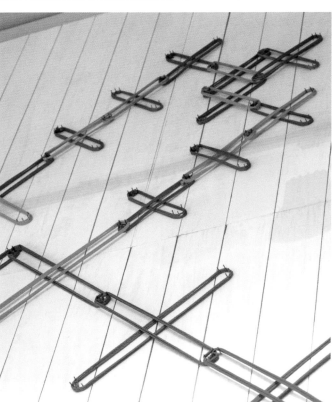

8

Each area has its own bold personality

9

1 Nursery
2 Infants
3 Junior boys
4 Teen boys
5 Junior girls
6 Teen girls
7 Nightwear
8 Fitting rooms
9 Cash desk
10 Toys
11 Shoes

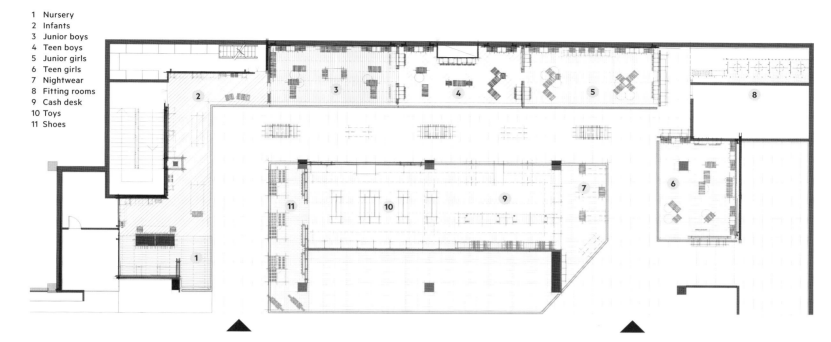

7 Each fitting room has it's own character, like movie star, rock star, etc.
8 Giant, geometric cross-stitch detailing adds another playful touch.
9 Each zone is age-appropriate; this tough, street-looking space is designed for early teens.

PODIUM MARKET
BY ART BUREAU 1/1

WHERE Moscow, Russia WHEN April 2012
CLIENT Podium DESIGNER Art Bureau 1/1 (p.490)
TOTAL FLOOR AREA 7000 m² SHOP CONSTRUCTOR Podium
PHOTOS Frank Herfort

In the former Moskva hotel, Moscow design office Art Bureau 1/1 has created a lively 7000 m² store for multi-brand retailer, Podium Market. Spread over two floors, the store had to showcase over 200 fashion brands for men and women, including American Apparel, Boy Band of Outsiders, T by Alexander Wang, Cheap Monday, and many more, covering a large range in style, target market and pricing. Art Bureau 1/1 therefore faced the challenge of unifying the large space while separating the various brands and helping a relatively varied group of shoppers to navigate among them. They responded to the demands of the store with a wide variety of angular and dramatic displays that organize the unbroken open space while showing off the merchandise and neatly dividing up the various zones. Display shelves, tables, and pedestals of different heights create an overall layered composition that evokes an interesting topographical map. Geometrical and origami-influenced forms are executed in various materials, including artificial stone, light wood, plastic and concrete. Displays are decoratively flower or star-shaped, or form bold triangles or dynamic diagonals. The changing landscape of display shapes allows shoppers to navigate easily and adds variety to the sprawling interior. The colour palette also plays an important role in unifying the space, with a neutral backdrop composed of porcelain white floor tiles and light grey raw concrete walls, with ceilings painted black. This background frames brighter accents in red, green and pink, for example the snaking metal display painted emerald that adds a touch of energy in the men's department.

1 A snaking green display sets the
   store theme.
2 At the shoe department asymmetrical
   shelves cover the wall to resemble origami.

3 Geometry and origami are themes for the varied shapes of the different displays.
4 A porcelain tiled floor and pale-grey concrete walls make a neutral backdrop.
5 Diagonal lines are used to create effect to add dynamism and direction to the store.
6 Colour accents in red, green and pink add a lively touch to the general restrained materials palette.

A changing landscape of varied display shapes

FASH

146

HION

147

16AOUT COMPLEX
BY ITO MASARU DESIGN PROJECT/SEI

1

WHERE Tokyo, Japan **WHEN** March 2012
CLIENT 16AOUT complex **DESIGNER** Ito Masaru Design Project / SEI (p.496)
TOTAL FLOOR AREA 155 m² **SHOP CONSTRUCTOR** Hearts
PHOTOS Kozo Takayama

There is no mistaking the name of this store as the first thing you notice in the interior is '16AOUT', spelled out in giant aluminium letters finished with rivets, immediately setting the space apart from other stylish shops by giving it a gallery feeling. The shiny silver letters set the tone for the high-sheen, metallic materials and colour palette used in 16AOUT complex, a store which sells not only women's fashion but also furniture and other products (allegedly, everything is for sale except the assistants). A floor of black stucco is coated with Italian resin to make it glint like water, and the walls are covered with Italian tiles which change their glittering effect throughout the day, shining gold, silver and champagne by turns. As customers browse the goods, they can admire the shifting shades of the walls. Colourwise, the store is quite neutral, but through reflective materials achieves a dreamily shimmering effect. The subtlety of the palette defines the overall approach, which is simple and streamlined. A high ceiling ensures an airy atmosphere, and fittings are kept basic and usually made of bare steel. Shelves and display cases are illuminated so that they stand out from the glittering space around them. The finishing touches are plants in huge vases, an impressive chandelier of sparkling Venetian glass and pendant lights rhythmically dotting the space. While currently a store, the idea is to also use the interior for other events, such as exhibitions.

1 The giant numerals and letters give a gallery feel to the space.
2 Colourwise the store is quite neutral, but through reflective materials achieves a shimmering effect.
3 Shelves and display cases are illuminated so they stand out from the silver-hued background.

Giant metal letters make the store shine

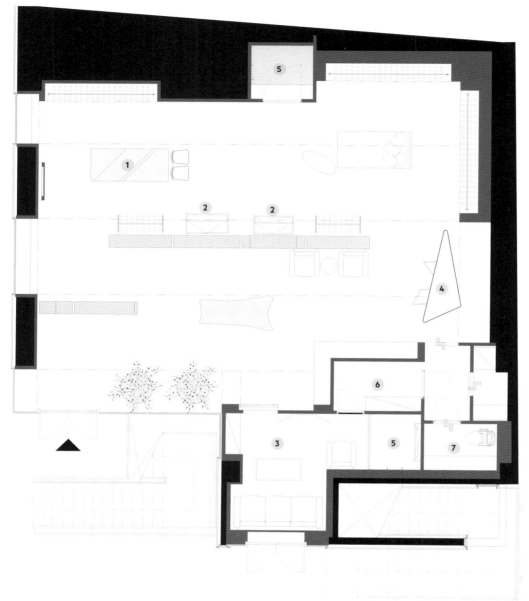

1 Display unit
2 Trunk cabinet
3 VIP room
4 Cash desk
5 Fitting room
6 Storage
7 Toilet

Silver letters set the tone for a high-sheen interior

4 Customers can view product displays
  through gaps in the giant letters.
5 The VIP lounge corner with velvet patch-
  work sofa offers a change of mood.

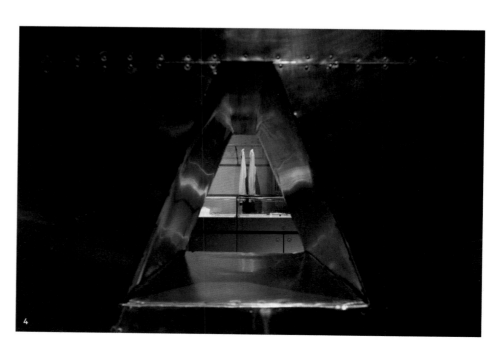

AMICIS WOMEN
BY DENIS KOŠUTIĆ

1

WHERE Vienna, Austria **WHEN** November 2012
CLIENT Vipro **DESIGNER** Denis Košutić (p.493)
TOTAL FLOOR AREA 450 m² **SHOP CONSTRUCTOR** –
PHOTOS Lea Titz

'The future vision of luxury, inspired by the fragile beauty of a butterfly', is how Denis Košutić sums up his interior for Amicis Women. Glittering, polished steel skeletons shape the basic structure of the room and at the same time serve as the foundation for all the display elements, the latter offering a strong, exciting contrast thanks to their delicate, silky surfaces. The play on transparency and semi-transparency, glitter and reflection, softness and hardness creates a dynamic effect throughout the interior. Extravagant details and materials – such as delicate lace, pleated satin silk and iridescent Murano glass – provide an element of surprise and add more luxurious depths to the composition. An experimental approach to materials sees custom-made couture lace pressed between large-format glass plates, to serve as semi-transparent room dividers. All the floating presentation boxes are coated with smooth and pleated silk and completed with gleaming metal frames and cleverly incorporated LED light strips. A one-of-a-kind carpet specially designed

for the project washes like a watercolour painting over the floor. The subtle range of colours used throughout the project is based on different nuances of nude – from light beige to soft pink to intensive apricot. The furniture, in soft pastel shades, adds to the dreamy atmosphere. 'By reaching the limits of the possibilities of design', says the designer, 'every single object has been designed meticulously down to the minutest detail so as to create a unique and unrepeatable product, a new haute couture architecture.'

1 Varied materials contrast transparency and semi-transparency, glitter and reflection, softness and hardness.
2 & 3 A pale and interesting colour palette paired with soft drapery creates a dreamy effect.
4 & 5 Polished steel skeletons are the basis for the display elements, softened by pastel furnishings.

A transparent take on luxury

AT HOME 103
BY BETWIN SPACE DESIGN

WHERE Seoul, Korea **WHEN** March 2012
CLIENT At Home 103 **DESIGNER** Betwin Space Design (p.491)
TOTAL FLOOR AREA 150 m² **SHOP CONSTRUCTOR** –
PHOTOS Lee Pyo-joon

From the outside an eye-catchingly pristine composition in white, At Home 103 conceals, rather than reveals, the fashion items inside – an intriguing approach designed to set the store apart from its neighbours on the street with their expanses of glass. Here, the only window display is to be found on the side wall of the building. Despite the contemporary appearance, the shop is a transformation of an existing building – as the interior reveals in traces of the old original fabric, in contrast to the slick new elements. The designers improved access to the building, by lowering the existing courtyard to street level – it was linked to the street by stairs originally. The ground floor of the store sells womenswear, while the first floor is for childrenswear, accessories and household item. The first floor exudes a comfortable atmosphere thanks to natural, light materials such as plywood. Fittings are kept light and flexible so that the client can transform the space according to the change of seasons. A new staircase connects the two floors, with the wall to the side of the stairs left in a stripped-back state to reveal the evidence of its history and successive renovations. Similarly, on the upper floor a concrete beam is the only trace of the former gable roof which has now been removed. Removing the roof allowed the designers to raise the ceiling, adding a roof terrace where there is also a small playhouse for children.

1 The pristine white exterior contrasts sharply with the other buildings on the street – particularly as so little of the interior is revealed.

2 Lightweight materials like plywood ensure that fittings are flexible enough to be reconfigured for different seasons.

3 Throughout the store, traces of the building's long history can clearly be seen in remnants of the original materials.

A radical renovation creates a refined and flexible space

4 The upper floor features a dramatic
  concrete beam – the only trace of the
  former gable roof which has now been
  removed, allowing for a higher ceiling.
5 The new roofterrace outside has a
  playhouse for children.
6 Unusual signage creates an intriguing effect.

BACKLASH
BY ITO MASARU DESIGN PROJECT / SEI

WHERE Tokyo, Japan WHEN October 2011
CLIENT Backlash DESIGNER Ito Masaru Design Project / SEI (p.496)
TOTAL FLOOR AREA 95 m² SHOP CONSTRUCTOR Hearts
PHOTOS Kozo Takayama

For a two-storey luxury leather clothing and goods store in Tokyo, Ito Matsaru created an interior of dramatic light-and-dark contrasts, differentiating between the main brand, Backlash, and the custom collection, Line. Each has its own, very different, floor. The lower storey of the space is given over to Backlash. Darkly theatrical, it combines aged plaster walls with a patchily black floor (the result of mixing charcoal with cement to produce an uneven tone). Fixtures include salvaged items such as a rusty metal locker and a factory workbench, and the designer compares his care in choosing these pieces with that of Isamu Katayama, the leather designer, in choosing zips and buttons for his clothes. In one corner, a heavy-toned spiral staircase leads to the contrasting, far lighter floor above, where the new and exclusive Line collection is displayed, in a totally white room which Masaru describes as like a 'laboratory or operating theatre'. A white resin floor and square white tiles keep the room clean and lean, an effect accentuated by the use of indirect white lighting and a stainless steel ceiling and fixtures and fittings. Antique sash windows were fitted here and in the space downstairs. At one end of the space is a counter for taking orders and behind it two industrial sewing machines suggesting the artisanal nature of the samples on show, plus some potted plants which, says the designer, 'emphasise the inorganic nature of the space.'

1 The lower level is dark and distressed, with aged plaster, charcoal-toned floor and salvaged fittings.
2 The exterior of the building has a dark grey mortar, which blends well with the ground floor colour palette.

3   The spiral staircase connects the dark
    ground floor with the lighter, more clinical
    space on the upper level.
4   Upstairs, a white resin floor and square
    white tiles look clean and bright.
5   Black oxide steel is seen in the framework
    of the ceiling, processed to give a rusted,
    ageing effect.

The interior has
dramatic light-and-dark contrasts

Two collections occupy very different spaces

6

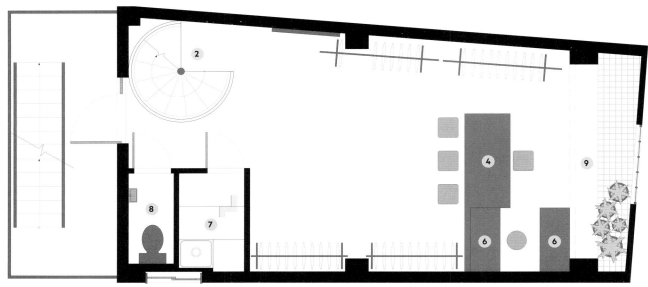

First floor

1 Display unit
2 Staircase
3 Cash desk
4 Service desk
5 Fitting room
6 Sewing mashine
7 Staff-only area
8 Toilet
9 Indoor terrace

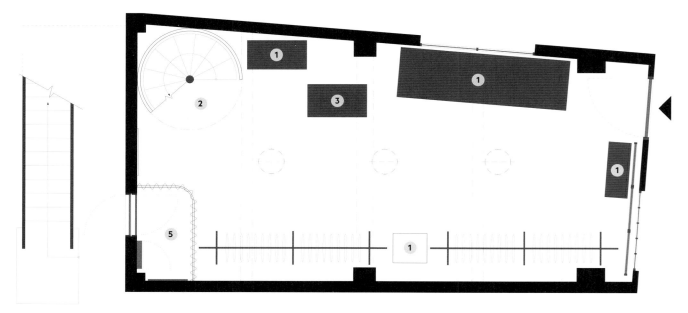

Ground floor

6 Stainless steel fittings add a clini-
cal touch.
7 & 8 Both levels have the same sash
windows, with the lower floor having
antique shutters installed to keep
out the light.
9 The initial concept sketch saw the
downstairs area designed more like
a gothic artisan's cellar.

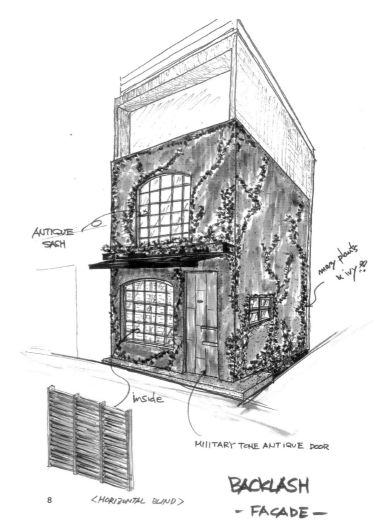

ANTIQUE SASH

many plants & ivy...

inside

MILITARY TONE ANTIQUE DOOR

8 <HORIZONTAL BLIND>

BACKLASH
— FAÇADE —

BAMBINI
BY DENIS KOŠUTIĆ

WHERE Vienna, Austria **WHEN** January 2013
CLIENT MB Fashion **DESIGNER** Denis Košutić (p.493)
TOTAL FLOOR AREA 360 m² **SHOP CONSTRUCTOR** –
PHOTOS Lea Titz

Nostalgic references to black-and-white movies influence the interior of Bambini, a children's fashion store designed by Denis Košutić with his team Marieke Kuchenbecker and Carina Habert, and explain the unusual colour choice (for a kids' store) of grey, black and white. Surreally subdued, the space avoids all the usual primary-colour clichés of environments intended for children. Instead, the store is selectively enlivened by sudden bursts of colour provided by the customised seating furniture, including bright yellow bananas and vibrant red mushrooms. Adding interest to the grey tones, a floral pattern, designed especially for the shop, flourishes across the entire space, appearing in different levels of brightness and in varying scales – a smaller size covers the wallpaper, while supersized blooms make a big splash on the floor. Classic grey wall mouldings define the merchandise presentation areas, while cage-like pillars made of copper tubing create the dramatic central displays. Thanks to their strong sculptural effect, illumination and backlighting – as well as their free positioning – these come across as mysterious objects, taking visitors by surprise. The gleaming copper contrasts boldly and unexpectedly with the matte grey and neutrally patterned background. As well as the colourful furnishings, more dreamlike objects, such as a plaster frieze of supersized mushrooms, lollipops and pears and fruit-shaped mirrors along the walls, have been added to support the fairy tale atmosphere.

1 Copper tubing forms the focal displays and changing rooms.
2 & 3 Fruit-shaped mirrors and plaster friezes on the walls add to the sweet charm of the interior.
4 The monotone palette is an unusually sophisticated choice for a kids' store.

CAPITAL ZEN
BY OPENAIR STUDIO

WHERE Bangkok, Thailand WHEN March 2012
CLIENT Central Department Store DESIGNER OpenAir Studio (p.498)
TOTAL FLOOR AREA 300 m² SHOP CONSTRUCTOR Motif Advance
PHOTOS Wison Tungthunya

Capital Zen is a multi-brand concept store that showcases cutting-edge fashion and accessories from a selection of global brands. The store is a part of the Central World complex where the designers of OpenAir Studio also styled the Just Cavalli shop (see p.202). There are five different product categories in Capital Zen: men's, women's, unisex, accessories, and furniture. The brief allowed each category its own dedicated space and called for a unique display identity for every one of them. OpenAir Studio embraced the idea of different identities by coming up with a rather fanciful concept of an urban environment – the idea being that different silhouettes in the store would suggest city features such as a church, factory, bridge, house, and crosswalk. In order to prevent visual overload, and to ensure that the emphasis is fairly and squarely on the products, the designers decided to restrict the colour palette to simple black and white. While a monotone colour scheme over a large space can run the risk of becoming dull or severe, OpenAir Studio ensured that its black-and-white interior looks sharp and fresh through the use of large-scale pattern. A bold chequerboard tiled floor is topped by glass cases (containing collections of accessories) on long black legs. A tunnel of tall black iron pillars and crossbeams adds drama to womenswear. Thick black and white stripes emphasise the length of the space, while huge white blocked shapes, reminiscent of Tetris but with all the colour removed, house irregular stacks of display shelves.

1 Bold black and white makes a dramatic fashion showcase.
2 Striped floors are the foundation for long, rectangular displays.
3 A chequerboard floor is an interesting base for the small accessory display cases.

4 Graphic black stripes paired with black
   iron architectural elements make a
   strong statement.

Big, bold statements in black and white

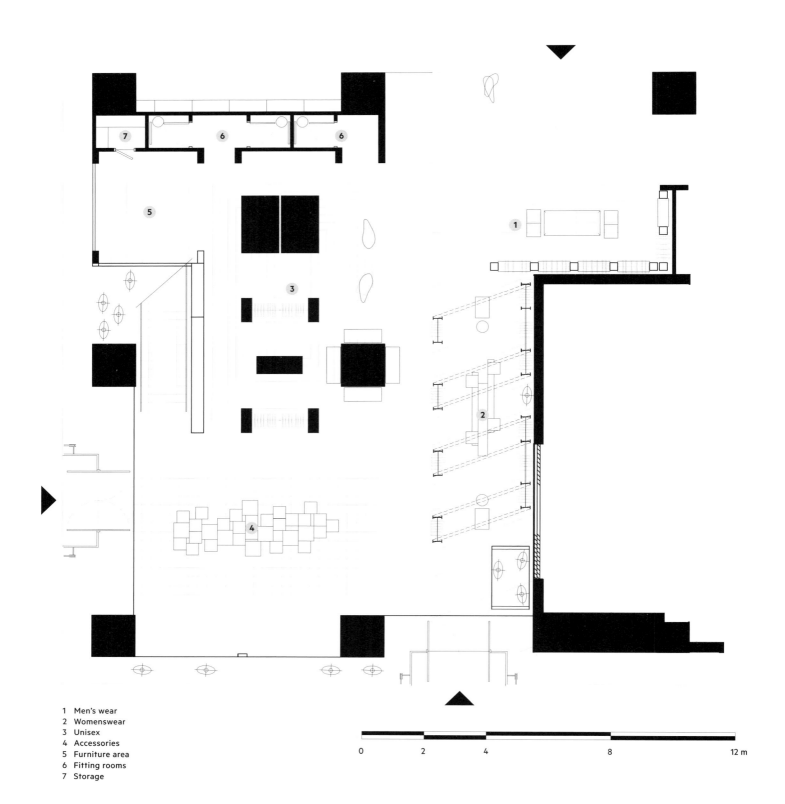

1 Men's wear
2 Womenswear
3 Unisex
4 Accessories
5 Furniture area
6 Fitting rooms
7 Storage

0   2   4   8   12 m

Large-scale patterns make monochrome look marvellous

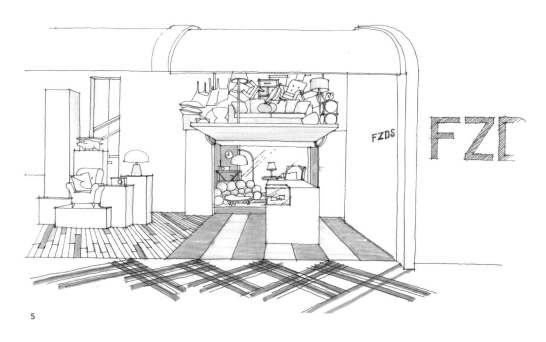

5

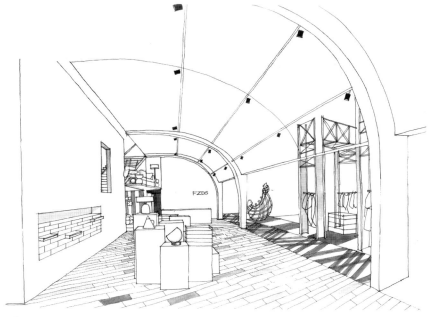

6

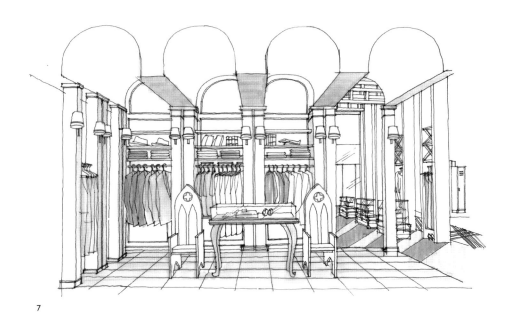

7

5, 6 & 7   Drawings of the initial interior design.

CROCODILE CONCEPT BOUTIQUE
BY UPSTAIRS_

WHERE Singapore, Singapore **WHEN** June 2012
CLIENT Singapore Crocodile **DESIGNER** UPSTAIRS_ (p.499)
TOTAL FLOOR AREA 140 m² **SHOP CONSTRUCTOR** OP3 International
PHOTOS CI&A Photography

'Being born and bred in Singapore', says Dennis Cheok, 'it is virtually impossible for me not to be familiar with Crocodile. The brand is very much ingrained into the Singaporean psyche.' So when asked to reinvent the Crocodile retail experience, Cheok, founder of design office UPSTAIRS_, focused on nostalgia, while Amsterdammer Joyce van Saane – one of Cheok's design collaborators – focused on the current label (the only one she knew). Based on this, the two quickly decided that Crocodile's key trait is its ability to adapt and survive (it was founded in 1968). Having decided that the brand's DNA was reconfigurability, UPSTAIRS_ set out to create a concept in which the key elements would be flexibility and adaptability. Taking elements from the brand's early days – louvered window shutters, mid-century timber furniture and wrought iron grilles – the designers referenced Crocodile's heritage while giving the new store a touch of pop-up contemporaneity. A dizzying array of rotating display panels add versatility to the interior: one side is a mirror wall, the other side modular, with changeable display elements in timber and leather, suitable for creating a variety of effects. At the heart of the store, The Gallery is a centrepiece serving various functions, from an exhibition space to a store-within-a-store. Here, those vintage louvres come into their own, supported by a dramatic steel frame. The all-change aesthetic convincingly reflects Crocodile's own brand development and survival, while making an intriguing space in its own right. 'We love to tell a good story', says Cheok.

1 The designers conceived the space as a transformable shell.
2 For the store's flooring, aggregate cement and black-tinted cement was used to delineate the different retail spaces.

3 The central cage-like space is a dramatic
   focal point.
4 Custom-designed merchandising racks
   in powder-coated metal were positioned
   in the walls of the central vestibule.
5 Full-height, pivoted display walls give
   the interior extreme flexibility as well
   as an unusual character.

Reconfigurable retail with a side of vintage

CTC COLOURTOCOLOUR
BY FRANK AGTERBERG / BCA

WHERE Nieuwegein, the Netherlands WHEN March 2012
CLIENT Gebroeders Coster DESIGNER Frank Agterberg / BCA (p.495)
TOTAL FLOOR AREA 140m² SHOP CONSTRUCTORS KPW International and Twin Design
PHOTOS Nick Bookelaar

sked to combine two brands (G-Star Raw and adidas Originals) in a single store without sacrificing their individual identities, designer Frank Agterberg came up the concept of two brand areas, divided by an island of colour, which he calls 'the Colour to Colour zone'. This bright yellow intersection houses the store's service, communication and fun elements, and so unites the two brands, even while each is left in full possession of its own identity on either side. Says Agterberg of the two-brand concept, 'This is the first time that two major fashion brands are combined in a single retail format. Two brands in one concept can bring out the best in each other, and from a commercial point of view it's an interesting option in cities where a monobrand store might not be profitable.' Bold simplicity enables the duo brand concept to work. The store is conceived as a basic box, with one strong colour able to hold its own against the brand identities without overpowering them. Applied floor to ceiling and coating everything in its path, the canary yellow colour creates a virtual wall between the two fashion labels. The store has its share of surprises – vintage light fittings make an unexpected addition, and the seemingly tiled islands turn out to be slatted shelves holding glossy yellow CTC gift boxes. At the latest store in Nieuwegein, the vertical composition emphasises the store's airy height, and aside from the yellow zone the décor is simple and understated: natural wood with white – a neutral background suited to both fashion brands.

1 A canary yellow zone for services divides the space between two brands.
2 The yellow is applied floor to ceiling on the central intersection and coats everything in its path.
3 The open character of the island makes both brands visible for customers from every corner of the shop.

A two-brand concept makes a bold statement

4   Each brand – adidas Originals and
    G-Star Raw – is displayed along the
    side walls, allowing for communication
    of the individual identities throughout
    the elongated store.
5 & 6   The tall yellow element emphasises
    the verticality of the space.

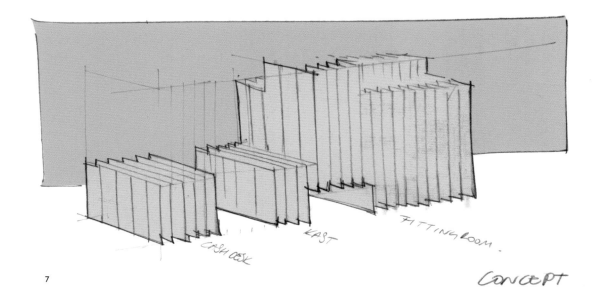

7

A shared yellow 'services' zone unites the two brands

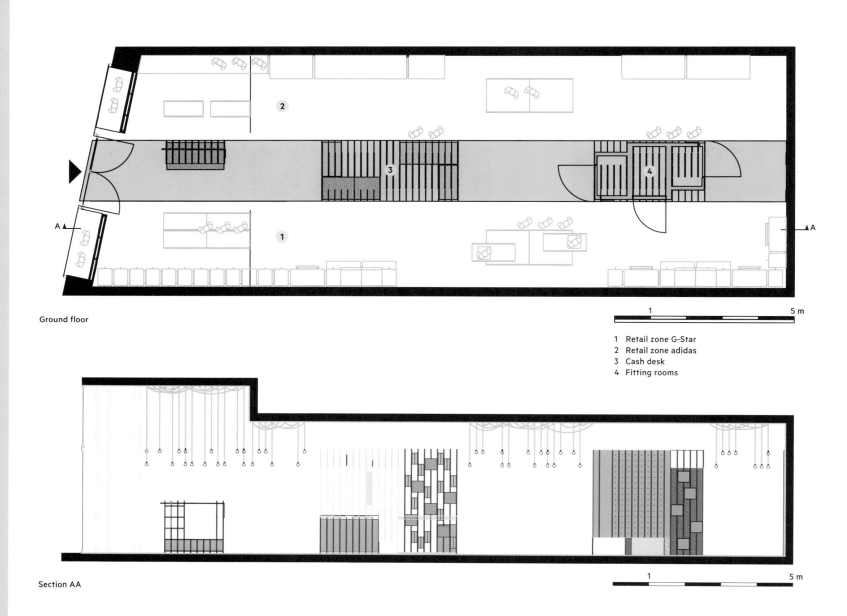

Ground floor

1   5 m

1 Retail zone G-Star
2 Retail zone adidas
3 Cash desk
4 Fitting rooms

Section AA

1   5 m

7 Sketch of the initial concept showing
    how the cash desk and fitting rooms
    would be incorporated into the
    central zone.
8 & 10 Renderings showing the role of
    suspended lights in adding an extra
    dimension to the design.
9 Detail of the finished store with
    branded packaging.

DIESEL VILLAGE
BY BRINKWORTH AND THE WILSON BROTHERS

1

WHERE London, United Kingdom **WHEN** December 2012
CLIENT Diesel **DESIGNERS** Brinkworth (p.492) and the Wilson Brothers (p.499)
TOTAL FLOOR AREA 465 m² **SHOP CONSTRUCTORS** Leckenby Associates and Portview
PHOTOS Louise Melchior

Asked by Diesel UK to collaborate on a new pop-up store with a 4-month lifespan on London's Regent Street, Brinkworth and the Wilson Brothers responded by capturing the essence of pop-up retail: a quick, simple and cost-effective installation, but with a bold concept and big on impact. Working with 465 m² spread over two floors, the designers drew inspiration from Diesel Village, the Bassano del Grappa-based Diesel headquarters, to create a series of lightweight 'house' structures that are scattered throughout the space. The houses are constructed from proprietary greenhouse kits, but are finished in a dizzying variety of different applied treatments and finishes. These play with reflectivity, transparency and solidity to create a series of diverse destinations. The effects range from a mirrored iridescent finish, smoky tints and two-way mirror, to recycled plastic sheeting and scaffold timber cladding. The mix of materials applied to the greenhouses underline the theme of the archetypal house shape, which also forms the basis of

a 2-D Village graphic icon developed by Oscar Wilson to pair with Diesel's logo in the branding of Diesel Village. Within the store, each of the houses represents a specific area of focus, highlighting different product categories, forming the changing room spaces, defining the cash wrap area and acting as the backdrop for window display. The strategic placement of each house encourages a sense of discovery, intrigue and interaction with the space. The focal point, Diesel's denim area, is nestled within the cluster of structures. A uniform grey for walls, floors and ceilings forms a neutral yet dramatic backdrop for the houses.

1, 2 & 3   The houses are constructed from proprietary greenhouse kits, but are finished in a dizzying variety of different applied treatments and finishes, from jazzy reflective glass to plain white boards.
4   Varying the scale means the house structures can display items from large to small.

184

A heritage brand finds a modern home

FILSON
BY COMO PARK STUDIO

WHERE London, United Kingdom **WHEN** April 2013
CLIENT CC Filson Company **DESIGNER** Como Park Studio (p.492)
TOTAL FLOOR AREA 70 m² **SHOP CONSTRUCTORS** Brandwacht & Meijer and Pop Store
PHOTOS Zowie Jannink

Filson is a hunting and fishing outfitter known for its special, innovative fabrics and finishes for apparel, luggage and bags. The challenge was to interpret this 116-year-old brand for a modern audience, combining its history and unparalleled functionality with a retail environment that would be both modern and respectful of its heritage. Filson's Maurizio Donadi envisioned Filson as a luxury brand where the word luxury was defined by quality and durability – in a world increasingly burdened by disposability. Filson, a brand which offers lifetime guaranties on all of its products, prides itself on the longevity of its goods – so the retail environment needed to reflect that, with materials chosen for their strength and presence. Donadi and his team at Filson envisioned a modern home nestled in the woods of the Pacific Northwest, and it was the designers' responsibility to embody all of the retail furnishings and surfaces with this feeling. Material choices and proportions were guided by the brief, with solid rough-edged oak and black-steel

fittings combining with hand-rubbed orange-red finishes to evoke the outdoors. For a contrast colour, the designers finally settled on a special green-black to work with the orange-red and provide and strong and modern contrast. Round-profile black steel was inspired by 1950s and 60s modern pieces and was used to form many of the retail fixtures. Curated furnishings were chosen to create a homey feeling and chosen for their iconic and modern properties, such as a Swiss architect's stool and the Sirocco lounge chairs from Swedish designer, Arne Norell.

1 & 2 The solid rough-edged oak and black-steel fittings combined with hand-rubbed orange-red finishes to evoke the outdoors.
3 Filson's visual merchandising team added a careful selection of decorative elements, such as vintage camping item, cut fire wood, boots, fishing lures and equipment and classic books on adventure.

4 & 5 Although seemingly casual, the store was carefully designed. To create the Pacific Northwest atmosphere, the floors and much of the walls were covered in a signature oiled oak planking that added both warmth and intimacy.

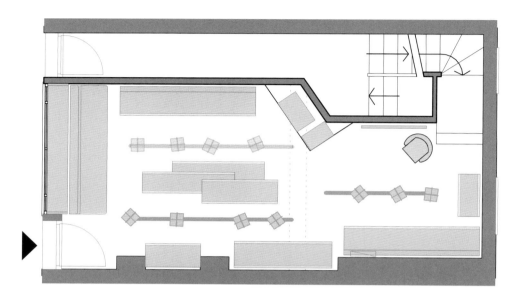

Ground floor

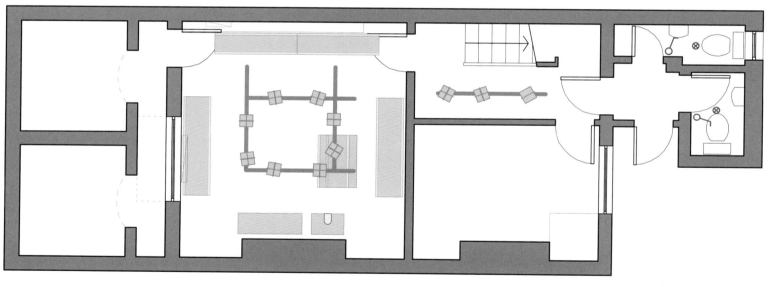

Basement

The store evokes a modern home in the woods of the Pacific Northwest

4

5

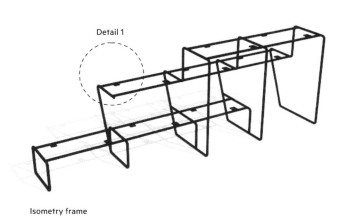

Detail 1

Isometry frame

1700

400

533+

601 18 465 18 529 18 51

181

400

141

A

267+

533+

B

C   C   D

800+

Cash machine

273

273

127

323 450

1700   797

1400

Top view

Steel frame
massive Ø 18 mm.
coated black

50

Steel plate 50 x 40,
welded to frame +
screws fication wood shelf

Wood shelf 40 mm.

Detail 1 steel connection

Side view

Front view

267

533

800

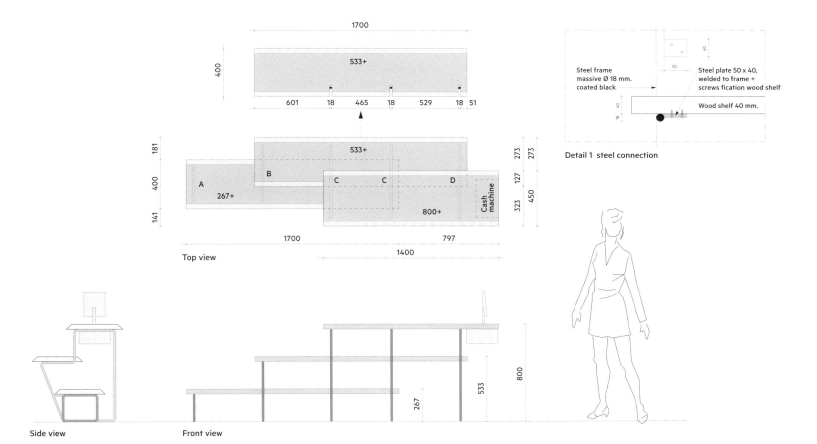

GRIGIO
BY BLOCK722ARCHITECTS+ / KATJA MARGARITOGLOU AND SOTIRIS TSERGAS

1

WHERE Thessaloniki, Greece **WHEN** May 2012
CLIENT Manto Kaikou **DESIGNER** BLOCK722architects+ /
Katja Margaritoglou and Sotiris Tsergas (p.491)
TOTAL FLOOR AREA 387 m² **SHOP CONSTRUCTOR** –
PHOTOS Achileas Menos

In shaping a new home for fashion retailer Grigio, Athens-based BLOCK722architects+ aimed at creating a multifunctional space that would offer a unique experience – so, in the city's busiest shopping street, they created a tranquil garden leading to a café, within an austere industrial shell. BLOCK722architects+ founders Katja Margaritoglou and Sotiris Tsergas took the existing ground floor of a multi-storey building and stripped it back to bare concrete which was then painted white, along with the exposed ventilation and heating pipes of the ceiling. Adding a poured concrete floor unified the space. The most dramatic intervention involved placing a 6m-high glass façade at the back of the building, which floods the space with daylight and allows the concept of the indoor garden to work convincingly. In this light-filled, rough-and-ready shell they then placed some abundant greenery and the kind of props usually associated with the outdoors – including swings, lanterns and garden furniture – blurring the division between inside and

outside. At the back of the space, just in front of the glass façade and bordering the outside patio, is a raised area which is devoted to a café (during the summer months). The café and the planted outdoor patio can be seen throughout the store, increasing the impression of ample vegetation and natural light. Display and decorative elements are created from objects used in unexpected ways. Doors become display tables, wooden frames surround hangers, and weather vanes point to the view of the café. Trompe-l'oeil prints on the walls and fitting-room curtains add further elements of surprise.

1 The store plays with the idea of indoors and outdoors – here, with a painted 'courtyard' in the interior.
2 The building was stripped back to its original concrete and brick, and painted white.
3 The café, complete with garden furniture and hanging lanterns, overlooks the patio outside.

HIT GALLERY
BY FABIO NOVEMBRE

WHERE Hong Kong, Hong Kong WHEN September 2012
CLIENT Ittierre DESIGNER Fabio Novembre (p.494)
TOTAL FLOOR AREA 100 m² SHOP CONSTRUCTOR Chen Cheong Contracting
PHOTOS Dennis Lo

For his interior for Hong Kong's HIT Gallery boutique, Fabio Novembre found inspiration in the surrealist art of Italian painter Giorgio De Chirico, from whom he has adapted the motifs of faceless figures and architecture based on the perspectival effect of rows of arches. Three walls of the store are turned into rhythmically arched colonnades, containing niches displaying clothing hanging from rails or accessories on glass shelves. In the middle of the store, there is more display space, in the surprising form of two giant blue busts facing each other. Made from wooden planes slotted together, the busts form shelves on which smaller items are displayed. A curved wall punctured by more arches separates the cash desk from the rest of the shop. While the busts and the arches are a luminous blue, the floor features a diagonal geometrical pattern in stark black and white, adding to the slightly mind-bending effect. 'The colour defining the walls – a neutral shade bordering between green and sky or cerulean blue – defies classification, so becoming the ideal backdrop for all the brands sold in the store', comments Novembre. He adds that the store design is a contemporary interpretation of Italian classicism, with its symmetry, arches and colour treatment all instantly recognisable as Italianate in origin and intended to evoke the traditional piazza. 'The HIT stores we plan to open around the globe will capture the essence and spirit of Italy in wonderful new ways', he says.

1 The walls and arched colonnades contain niches which display clothing and accessories.
2 The store has a striking symmetry, with each side displayed as a mirror-image of the other.
3 The cash desk also incorporates arches, located behind the curved wall at the back of the store.

HOCHSTETTER
BY HEIKAUS CONCEPT

WHERE Trier, Germany WHEN February 2012
CLIENT Hochstetter DESIGNER Heikaus Concept (p.495)
TOTAL FLOOR AREA 400 m² SHOP CONSTRUCTOR Heikaus Interior
PHOTOS Uwe Spoering

Hochstetter has been a force in retail in Trier for over 100 years. Naturally, then, the heritage element had to be present in Heikaus' new store concept for the retailer, but also a strong contemporary profile. As Hochstetter's retail offering is varied, combining fashion and business wear, the shop presents a variety of moods. The basement is devoted to youthful brands like Closed, Drykorn, Boss Orange and Blauer, and the interior, with its big windows and city views, is modelled on a New York loft, with dramatic black lacquered wooden flooring and a spacious arrangement of displays and furniture. Moving through the space, luxurious rugs and silk wall coverings, a lounge area, and racks made from brushed brass develop a theme of quality, upmarket lifestyles and exclusivity. A huge fountain made from stone, a glass 'dome' above it, serves as a focal point while at the same time marking a theme change to a more 'streetwise' ambience. In this area, an epoxy-resin floor with brick walls and prints of façades conjure the idea of strolling along a street full of fashion and puts the accent on urban style. Interior 'windows' link the different zones. On the first floor, the presentation of classic and business fashion is the cue for another change in tone. The highlight here is a second, particularly inviting lounge area, incorporating the plushest of sofas, a stone fireplace and a real fire, suggesting warmth and authenticity and seducing shoppers into lingering.

1 A dramatic black lacquered wood floor contributes to this store's loft aesthetic.
2 A stone fountain makes an unusual display and focal point.
3 Luxurious materials are used in the lounge and changing area.

J.I
BY LINE-INC.

WHERE Chengdu, China WHEN May 2013
CLIENT Sichuan Lessin Department Store DESIGNER Line-Inc. (p.497)
TOTAL FLOOR AREA 620 m² SHOP CONSTRUCTOR –
PHOTOS Kozo Takayama

For J.I, the first-ever shopping destination in China to stock only Japanese brands – Undercover, Plumpynuts, Frapbois and others – Line-Inc. based its design on the concept of a 'new age gallery' representing the enduring qualities of Japanese design. 'We aimed to express what is appreciated globally', explains Line-Inc.'s Takao Katsuta. 'A space that would not just follow trends, but reflect more of a universal beauty.' In the store, there are five brand shop-in-shops on the periphery of the space, plus a general area in the centre of the interior that displays nine other brands. Materials fall into the 'universal' category, with stone in two colours covering the entire floor in a pattern based on a traditional Japanese design. The five brand shops have walls also inspired by traditional patterns and made of wood and brass, creating an almost curtain-like textured effect. Each of the individual shops has a similar elegant formula, mixed with touches of its own brand personality expressed through different materials and finishes, such as parquet flooring, tiles and antique

rugs. Throughout, the store is decorated with art and vintage items that the owner has collected from all over the world, which adds interest and furthers the 'gallery' concept. On the ceiling, large, lantern-like illuminated octagons add further references to the brands' place of origin. As Katsuta says, 'The entire space condenses what is appreciated in and about Japan, and thus the store enables customers to feel the Japanese sense of beauty through its use of forms and materials.'

1 J.I's unusual curtain-like wall treatment, using wood and brass, is an adaptation of a traditional Japanese pattern.
2 The floor, made from stone in two colours, references Japan's graphic heritage.
3 The store design is based on a 'new age gallery'.

4 Luxury materials are used in surprising ways, as in this abstract wooden ceiling.
5 Each of the five brand stores adopts a different material palette. The bright ceiling light make this overall white shop-in-shop look even more white.
6 Illuminated, lantern-like octagonals add interest to the ceiling.

A new take on the traditional aesthetics of Japan

JUST CAVALLI
BY OPENAIR STUDIO

WHERE Bangkok, Thailand WHEN March 2012
CLIENT Central Department Store DESIGNER OpenAir Studio (p.498)
TOTAL FLOOR AREA 90 m² SHOP CONSTRUCTOR Motif Advance
PHOTOS Wison Tungthunya

Asked to create a shop-in-shop concept store for Just Cavalli in the Zen department store, OpenAir Studio faced the challenge of distinguishing the Italian label in the multi-brand concept store of which it would become a part – the Just Cavalli store space flows into the Galliano shop and from there into Capital Zen. The concept was a simple one – to create a multi-functional design element reflecting the brand's visual identity that could be used both as racks for merchandise display and as a partition to divide the space. For the design element, OpenAir Studio came up with a basic 60 x 60 cm module in edgy rusted metal. The finish accords well with the brand of Florentine designer Roberto Cavalli who, as well as being widely known for his detailed exotic prints, is also credited for creating the distressed, sand-blasted look for jeans which is now found as a standard in most denim collections. The rusty modules are used in varying patterns, randomly repeated to create the cage-like partitions that surround and suspend the

clothing. These modules are actually floating in the centre of the shop-in-shop space. Back-painted glass in a diagonal stripe pattern clads the surrounding walls, a semi-transparent grid that defines the space and sets it apart from the other labels that are its neighbours. The rather haphazard placement of the rusted metal grids contrasts dramatically with the glossy, linear walls, a combination that reflects the qualities of Just Cavalli, a brand that unites a certain luxury with a distinct hipster edginess.

1 A grid of rusty metal forms display areas, acts as partition elements, and totally defines the Just Cavalli space.
2 & 3 The grid is composed of 60 x 60 cm units, rather randomly constructed into structural pieces.

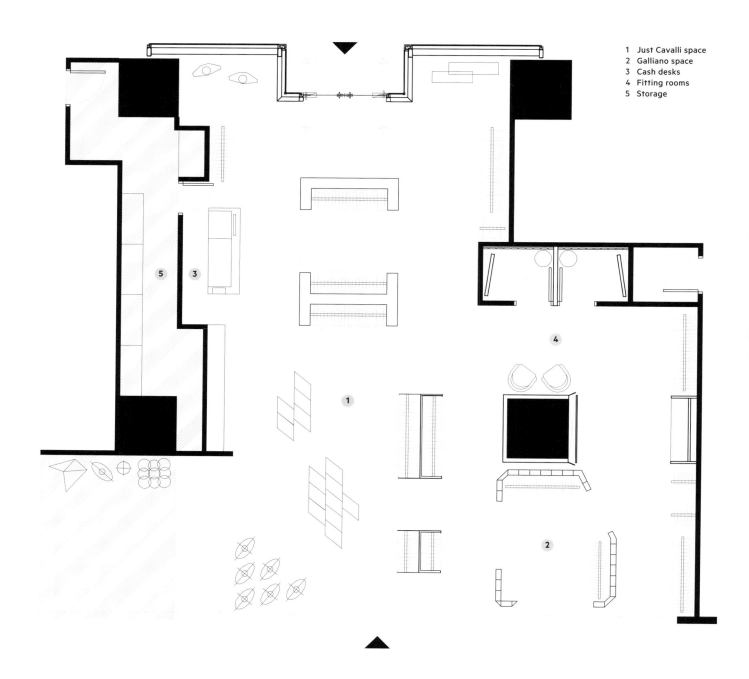

1 Just Cavalli space
2 Galliano space
3 Cash desks
4 Fitting rooms
5 Storage

A 3D-grid defines a shop within a shop

4 The rusty material has a raw, interesting texture that contrasts strongly with the luxurious garments on display.

KARL LAGERFELD
BY PLAJER & FRANZ STUDIO

WHERE Paris, France WHEN March 2013
CLIENT Karl Lagerfeld DESIGNER plajer & franz studio (p.498)
TOTAL FLOOR AREA 209 m² SHOP CONSTRUCTOR Vizona
PHOTOS Michel Figuet

The first European concept store for Karl Lagerfeld was created by plajer & franz studio under the artistic direction of the man himself and in cooperation with New York-based creative agency Laird + Partners. A fairly minimal interior with a distinct French accent, the space, in chic black and white, features strong contrasts in shapes and surfaces, blending the edgily modern and classic elements into a sleek, harmonious whole. Glass and mirror reoccur throughout the store, creating reflections and an interesting multi-dimensionality – and sometimes, even, an optical illusion. Elements of the original building are treated in a fresh and interesting way. Glass wraps an old staircase, updating it instantly. Meanwhile the neoclassical wood panelling on the first floor is restored and its pattern used as a leitmotif for the new solid surface walls by Getacore. It also appears in the form of LED-illuminated strips throughout the store. Making the space thoroughly contemporary, however, is its digital 'Karlcommunity' component: iPads allow customers to flick through the Karl Lagerfeld look books, visit and browse the website and even communicate with the designer himself via a digital guestbook. Then there are the built-in touch-screens placed in the fitting rooms to encourage consumers to capture their looks and share the pictures with friends via Twitter, Facebook or email. However, despite the digital dimension the whole, physical product offering of the brand is available here, including watches and accessories. And as a physical finishing touch, the store leverages Karl Lagerfeld's own iconic image: his ponytailed silhouette appears in several places in the space.

1 Lagerfeld's own stylized image presides over the store.
2 The black-and-white palette achieves a chic effect.

5

Classical and contemporary mixed with digital 'Karlcommunity'

3 & 4   The restored wooden panelling on the
        first level is characterised by neo-classical
        lines of french architecture.
   5   Mirrors and glass feature strongly, with
        angular modern elements adding a sharp
        contrast to the neoclassical building.

KULT
BY CORNEILLE UEDINGSLOHMANN ARCHITEKTEN

WHERE Cologne, Germany **WHEN** May 2013
CLIENT Görgens Gruppe **DESIGNER** Corneille Uedingslohmann Architekten (p.492)
TOTAL FLOOR AREA 1050 m² **SHOP CONSTRUCTOR** Starker
PHOTOS Michael Neuhaus

A fantasy-fuelled and frankly forested approach informs the new Kult multi-brand fashion store, designed by Corneille Uedingslohmann Architekten in one of Cologne's top shopping locations. Entering a woodland-themed, nature-related world of forests and fairy-tales, customers pass into a 'house' environment through which they reach the store's upper levels via the integrated escalator. The main sales area on the upper floors is divided into women's and men's areas. The women's zone is centred around the upper floor of the in-store 'house', with themes such as the multi-layered mountain-landscape walls repeated from downstairs. In one corner, there's a playful fairground scene complete with a custom-built carousel where bags and accessories are highlighted. The women's fitting rooms are located in a cosy, lodge-style setting, set around a fireplace with comfy chairs. A staircase, complete with circus light installation, leads to the men's area above, in which the highlight is undoubtedly the 12-m, illuminated 3D forest motif wall. The men's

fitting rooms too are like a woodland lodge, with their mock window, stone walls and a cosy wooden floor and ceiling. The centre of the men's zone, however, has a heavier, rough steel structure, giving a more masculine atmosphere and adding to the wide variety of instore effects achieved by the design team. Yet while the store boasts a variety of lively, differentiated zones and several changes of tempo, it also benefits from a coherent materials concept that integrates all of the space's various elements.

1 Frequent forests of antlers add to various woodland references.
2 A fairground carousel forms a playful display for women's bags and accessories.
3 Expanses of warm wood help set the tone.

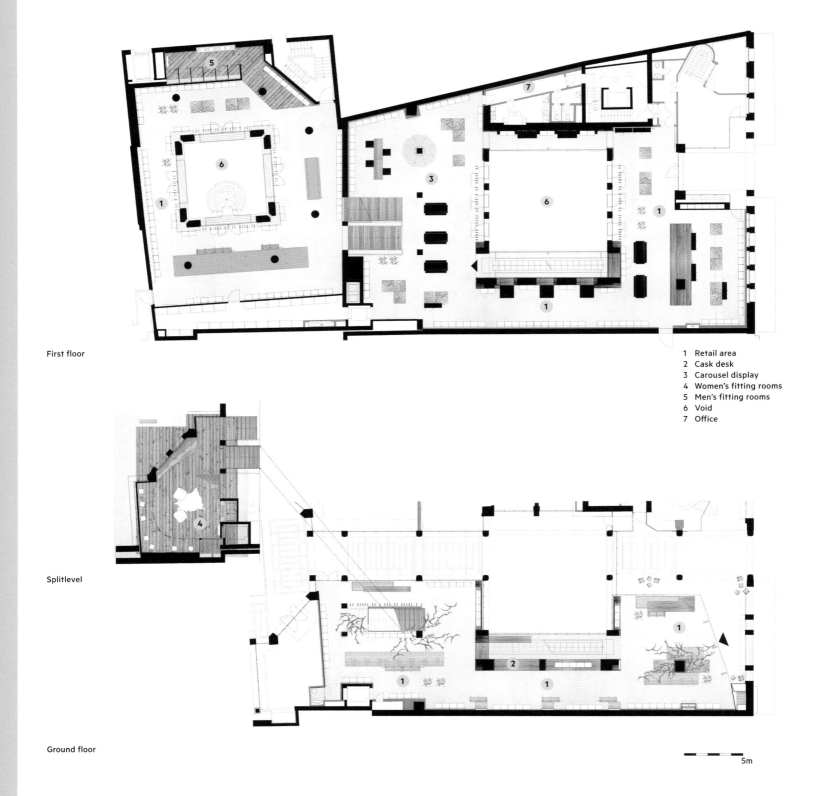

First floor

Splitlevel

Ground floor

1 Retail area
2 Cask desk
3 Carousel display
4 Women's fitting rooms
5 Men's fitting rooms
6 Void
7 Office

5m

Fantasy in the forest as an effective fashion formula

4 & 5 A staircase leading visitors to a
splitlevel deck where the women's
fitting rooms are located.
6 The men's area has a heavier, more
industrial look and feel.

A crisp white backdrop to a visual brand journey

LACOSTE
BY DESIGNLSM

WHERE London, United Kingdom **WHEN** April 2012
CLIENT Lacoste UK **DESIGNER** designLSM (p.493)
TOTAL FLOOR AREA 690 m² **SHOP CONSTRUCTOR** DG Interiors
PHOTOS James French Photography

Asked to add 'a quintessentially English twist' to French brand Lacoste's largest retail outpost, its flagship store in the heart of Knightsbridge, London, designLSM created a series of crisp white interiors organised around a stunning new focal point: a staircase in glass and steel, with lifts and a 10-m-high moving Triola wall, displaying the current Lacoste advertising imagery. These dramatic interventions solved the design team's biggest dilemma, which was how to add unity to the store, which features three floors and several awkwardly shaped spaces, while providing customers with an overview. Specific clothing collections and accessories are displayed in each room, offering a complete visual journey through the Lacoste clothing and accessory range. Within the overall white scheme, each area has its own stylistic identity and atmosphere. The Polo rooms on the ground and first floors, for example, feature pull-out shelving along a section of the perimeter walls. Polo shirts in various colours are among Lacoste's most enduring products. Here, they hang in open-fronted display units separated by clear perspex boxes, which have style guides inscribed on them. Lacoste is now 80-years old, and the store thus combines a fresh, contemporary, uncluttered feel with a distinct feeling for heritage. Both modern and historic aspects are enhanced by technology. In addition to the up-to-the-minute ad imagery displayed on the Triola wall, huge LED screens are used throughout the space to showcase archive and promotional material from the brand's long history.

1 Textured white fixtures and fittings include ridged sofas, panelled walls and patterned window blinds.
2 Open-fronted units allow for clear product displays.
3 The dynamic Triola screen rises up beside the staircase, uniting the three floors of the store.
4 A gym-like wooden floor adds a sporty touch.

215

LEVI'S
BY COMO PARK STUDIO

1

WHERE Amsterdam, the Netherlands **WHEN** December 2011
CLIENT Levi Strauss & Company **DESIGNER** Como Park Studio (p.492)
TOTAL FLOOR AREA 240 m² **SHOP CONSTRUCTOR** Brandwacht & Meijer
PHOTOS Zowie Jannink

For its new store on Amsterdam's Kalverstraat, Levi's developed a rather challenging brief for design office, Como Park Studio. Named 'Re-Store', the project was based on the idea of building a space from left-over, recycled, re-used and reclaimed materials (however, it should not look like 'junk' nor be 'designed'). It needed to perform well commercially and be colourful, friendly and fully functional as a high-street retail location. For inspiration, the designers and Levi's looked to modern art, particularly Arte Povera. They created a light and transparent framework of recycled piping that could offer great product and display flexibility. This was combined with retailing structures made from found and reused objects from areas around Amsterdam as well as from the building itself. A large portion of the structural walls was left untouched, with recycled wall panels added where necessary. The store reflects Amsterdam's history of resourceful living and conversion of bikes, homes, boats, junk and second-hand goods. Nothing was ordered or fabricated for this project. The lighting came from Levi's Bread and Butter trade fair stand earlier in the year, as did the wood on the first floor. The cash desk was made from the floorboards recycled from the first floor of the building. Shelving and changing room 'houses' were also made from reused materials, while the 'denim table' uses old doors mounted on church benches (also used for the freestanding shelves and benches). Display cabinets, hanging lamps and carts are all second hand, and the bike sculptures are created from old bikes welded together.

1 Recycled wood adds an interesting patina to the store surfaces.
2 Handmade displays were inspired by Arte Povera.
3 Old bicycles welded together make eye-catching sculptural installations for the two-storey store.
4 The big denim display table was created from recycled doors placed on old church benches.

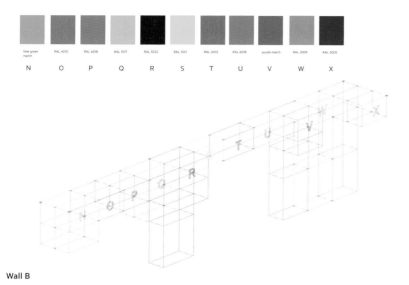

N O P Q R S T U V W X

Wall B

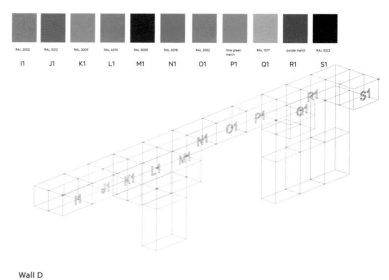

I1 J1 K1 L1 M1 N1 O1 P1 Q1 R1 S1

Wall D

A B C D E F G H I K L M

Wall A

5

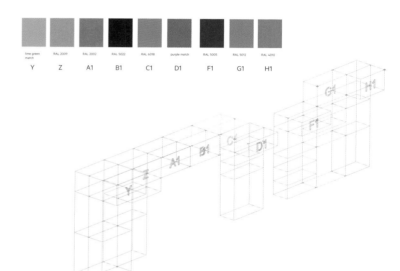

Y Z A1 B1 C1 D1 F1 G1 H1

Wall C

5 Drawings showing the colour grid used throughout the store.
6 A framework built from recycled pipes painted in various colours offers a variety of display options.

A brand interpretation of Amsterdam's recycled, second-hand aesthetic

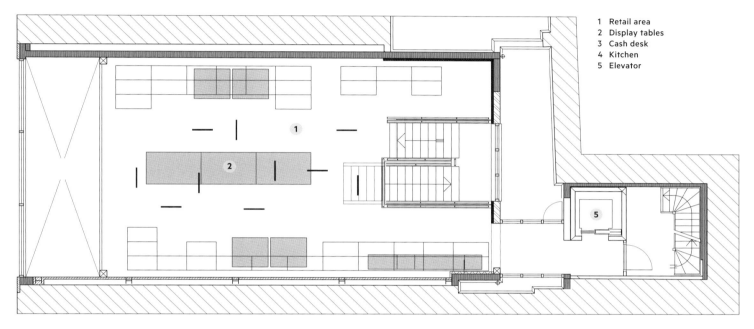

1 Retail area
2 Display tables
3 Cash desk
4 Kitchen
5 Elevator

First floor

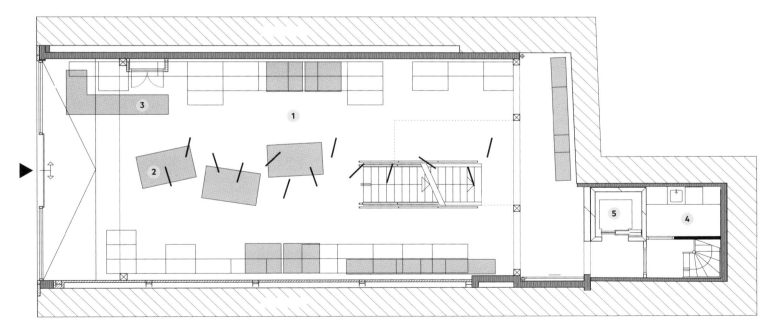

Ground floor

MAKING THINGS
BY AEKAE

WHERE Zurich, Switzerland WHEN September 2012
CLIENT Makingthings DESIGNER Aekae (p.490)
TOTAL FLOOR AREA 58 m² SHOP CONSTRUCTOR Gregoryclan
PHOTOS Courtesy of Aekae

Making Things is the name, as well as the concept, of a fashion boutique in Zurich, Switzerland. The distinctive selection of clothing, accessories and other things focuses on brands with a story of extraordinary detailing and craftsmanship. For their second venue, the owners chose a location in the former industrial district, which is quickly turning into Zurich's new hotspot. The shop is located in a temporary container structure, where construction workers used to rest between shifts, right next to Switzerland's tallest building which was recently completed. The design office Aekae studio wisely responded to the rather severe and sterile container space with a concept intended to induces warmth and cosiness – the very opposite of what might be expected from the exterior. As the shop window is not at ground level but on the first floor, they incorporated an element of surprise, so passers-by would be drawn up the stairs and into the shop. Purposefully placed mirrors on the ceiling offer a glimpse of the goods on display to the outside viewer, while augmenting the space and exposing the structure. The floor made of local timber hints at the heritage of the location, and it's reflections unleash the full charm of wood. Like abstract ribbons, the boards grow into display areas and seating of different heights, uncovering the dark floor base. A lot of onsite work was required to achieve a clean and seamless look, translating the raw-material aesthetic of a manufacturing workshop into an inviting boutique.

1 Ceiling mirrors are the solution to a first (not ground) floor window display: reflections help lure passers-by up the steps and into the store.
2 From outside, the store presents an intriguing spectacle of reflections to people on the street below.

3 Locally sourced timber is the store's most prominent material, suggesting not only warmth but also local crafts and heritage.
4 In a playful touch, floorboards are treated as ribbons that fold up to become displays and seating of various heights, exposing the black sub-floor.

Warm material and mirrors add allure to a container structure

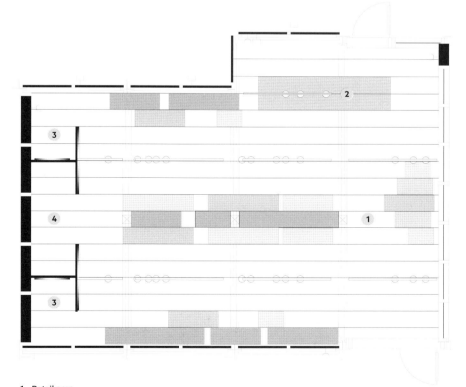

1 Retail area
2 Cash desk
3 Fitting room
4 Storage

MARC O'POLO
BY DAN PEARLMAN

WHERE Munich, Germany WHEN September 2012
CLIENT Marc O'Polo DESIGNER dan pearlman (p.493)
TOTAL FLOOR AREA 800 m² SHOP CONSTRUCTOR Knoblauch
PHOTOS Courtesy of Marc O'Polo

It's a case of going back to the brand's Swedish roots, in Munich's Marc O'Polo flagship store designed by dan pearlman. 'Nordic lifestyle' is the over-riding concept of the 800 m² store, highlighting the brand keywords: urban, modern and casual. Once past the impressive two-storey entrance, the shop mimics the atmosphere of a modernised historic apartment building, with lofty high ceilings, mouldings and floorings in herringbone parquet or black and white tiles. Empire era wallpaper combines with contemporary lighting and vintage modernist furniture. There are lots of home-like details – Scandinavian designer furniture, suitcases, photos, books and unexpected items from sports equipment to vintage shoe lasts – all bring the store to life and suggest the lifestyle of what the designers call the 'urban nomad'. Flowers, plants and fruits also find a place among the many objects and add a natural, organic element to the space, which is designed with sustainability in mind. The atrium is an especially dramatic space, with a black Nero Assoluto floor and

no less than 16,000 LED lights forming the ceiling, which modulates its intensity according to daytime brightness. Inside the changing rooms, customers are bathed in a golden light and over 300 LED lights share space with a 6-m-tall waterfall composed of Tobias Grau lamps. The clothing is displayed throughout this eclectic environment and often hangs next to artworks of various kinds, from antique prints to vintage photographs and contemporary neon signs, sending the message that the product embodies timeless quality and exemplifies good taste.

1   The store's abundant details suggest the lifestyle of an 'urban nomad'.
2   There are lots of homely details, including Scandinavian designer furniture, flowers and plants.

Nordic lifestyle is the overriding concept of the store

3 A warm herringbone floor makes the ideal base for the retail-comes-home design.
4 Every display comes complete with domestic details, like rugs, chairs and other props.
5 An eclectic take on Swedish style, with an assortment of photo frames adding to the effect.

6, 7 & 8 Renderings show the domestic
orientation of the store design.

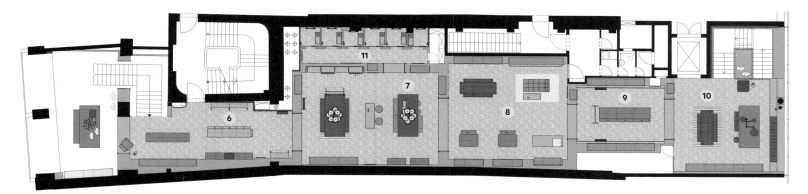

First floor

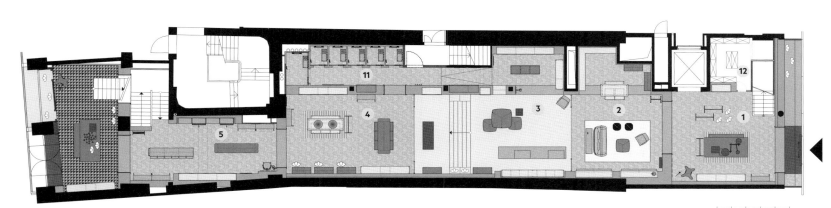

Ground floor

0 1 2 3 4 5 m

1 Foyer	7 Diner salon
2 Tea salon	8 Gallery
3 Atrium	9 Library
4 Atelier	10 Studio
5 Ladies' room	11 Fitting rooms
6 Gentlemen's room	12 Storage

The shop mimics the atmosphere of a modernised historic apartment

MAX MARA CHENGDU
BY DUCCIO GRASSI ARCHITECTS

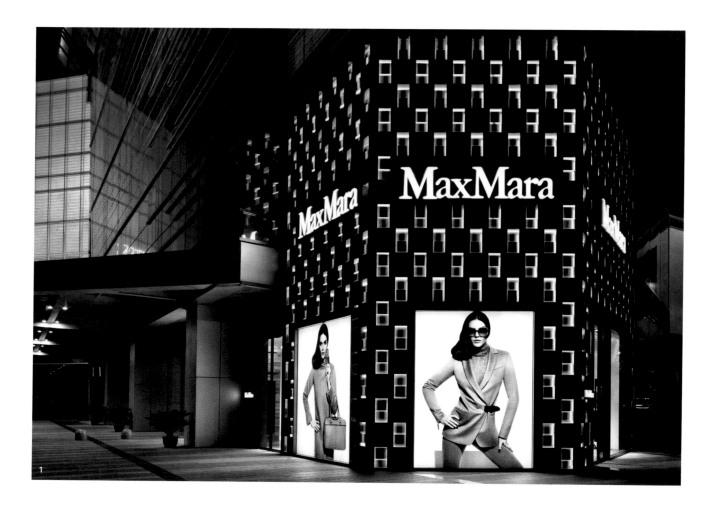

WHERE Chengdu, China WHEN July 2011
CLIENT Max Mara Fashion Group DESIGNER Duccio Grassi Architects (p.494)
TOTAL FLOOR AREA 720 m² SHOP CONSTRUCTOR Topest Construction Decoration
PHOTOS Jonathan Leijonhufvud

For luxury Italian womenswear label Max Mara, Duccio Grassi Architects shaped a serenely beautiful store in Chengdu, China. From the outside, a stunning geometrically layered, burnished-copper façade creates an unmissable spectacle, especially when illuminated at night. Inside, the interest continues in an understated way, in what the designers call the 'narration through diversified experiences.' Shoppers initially encounter a secondary entrance composed of large shop windows alternating with simple surfaces made of burnished copper that frame a semi-transparent wall, partly screening the interior, where unexpected combinations of materials reflect the natural and synthetic fabrics used in the new Max Mara collections. Wood, both recycled and ash-treated oak, plus rattan, shiny stainless steel, burnished copper plate and platinum-treated glass create textural and visual richness in the store. The staircase, with its vertical wall made from horizontal padded panels of fabric, leads to the upper level of the store, where simple volumes of different materials divide the space into several 'rooms' that unfold, progressively revealing the fitting rooms and creating well-defined areas for the collections. This level is characterized by the wooden cash desk, with its irregular shape, and the 'diamond', a box covered by glass strips made of platinum leaves that glitter like jewels. All the fitting rooms and the three VIP areas, are made from the vertical panels of padded, soft pink fabric as used on the staircase wall. The large volumes, meanwhile, are entirely covered by recycled wood, in strong contrast to the soft material of the luxurious clothing on offer.

1 At night, the stunning layered façade is beautifully illuminated.
2 Stark black frames make effective displays in the store.
3 The interesting vertical staircase wall is made from horizontal padded panels of fabric.
4 Recycled wood, glass, oak and burnished copper are used in unexpected combinations, while oval display tables contrast with the angular architectural forms.

A mix of materials
makes minimalism mesmerising

MAX MARA
HONG KONG CENTRAL
BY DUCCIO GRASSI ARCHITECTS

MaxMara

1

WHERE Hong Kong, Hong Kong **WHEN** June 2012
CLIENT Max Mara Fashion Group **DESIGNER** Duccio Grassi Architects (p.494)
TOTAL FLOOR AREA 450 m² **SHOP CONSTRUCTOR** East Joint Designs Limited
PHOTOS Virgile Simon Bertrand

For Max Mara's new Hong Kong store in one of the city's most luxurious shopping streets, Duccio Grassi Architects sought inspiration in the meeting of technology and nature. On two floors, the 450m² store boasts a 40-m glass façade, framing a second skin composed of steel, glass and moving light pulses, which surrounds the entrance and the shop windows. The irregularity of the design of this membrane allows passers-by to glimpse the interiors of the store and leaves room for the natural light to filter through. The two corner windows have as their background two high-definition LED screens, for a lively effect. Entering the store, the minimal lines of the usual Max Mara space are in evidence, but executed using an extraordinary mix of materials. Wooden volumes articulate the space, while large LED screens, showing natural images, hide behind a forest of curtains made from midollino craft sticks. The midollino sticks, themselves a natural material, lend their character to the staircase volume, which invites visitors to descend to the basement. Two huge LED screens envelope and transform the stairs into an experience, which itself leads into the warmer more intimate experience of the basement below. Here, ash-treated oak floors, walls and ceiling create a rich effect which is varied by gypsum panels that bring the natural shapes of midollino sticks to the basement. Covering the walls with these panels gives the impression of a kind of ancient fossilised forest, creating an atmospheric backdrop for the shoe collection.

1 The façade frames a second skin formed from steel, glass and moving light pulses.
2 Wrapping whole areas in ash-treated oak makes for a warm effect.
3 Midollino sticks, usually used for crafts, create richly textured walls when layered on LED screens.

4

Technology takes on nature

4 The staircase leads down into a serene space lined in ash-treated oak.
5 The form of the midollino sticks is repeated on the staircase.
6 Natural midollino sticks combine with high-tech LED screens.

MINI PACEMAN CONCEPT STORE
BY EDWARDS MOORE

1

WHERE Prahran, Australia WHEN May 2013
CLIENT Mini DESIGNER Edwards Moore (p.494)
TOTAL FLOOR AREA 116 m² SHOP CONSTRUCTOR TGC Building
PHOTOS Fraser Marsden

For the Mini Paceman concept store, Edwards Moore devised a hybrid approach for a hybrid space. Part retail store and part exhibition cum studio space, the shop was intended to host six leading international designers working across a range of disciplines, from bespoke denim to hand-made men's shoes, over a six-month period. A versatile and dynamic design was therefore critical to the success of the ever-changing concept store. Inspired by the Mini Paceman slogan, 'A new slant on things', the designers created a series of angled timber-framed pegboard surfaces. These intersect to create an interior envelope and backdrop for the display of bespoke products. The car itself makes a dramatic appearance in the window, seeming to emerge from the store in a reflective wedge designed to ensure an interactive interface between pedestrians and vehicle. This storefront wedge was finished with reflective metal laminate, contrasting with the interior angular fixtures features timber framing with pegboard surfaces. No pieces were actually fixed

to the walls, and so everything could be fabricated off-site. Plus, after the store's six-month lifespan, the components could be easily removed, restoring the site back to its original condition. An array of projecting clamp-mounted anglepoise lamps and iPads (also on clamps) were fastened intermittently throughout the store, while the muted colour scheme and pegboard surfaces ensured the space could be easily tailored to suit the differing needs of the various collaborators. Bespoke tables by Edwards Moore were also constructed from timber framing with pegboard, to add an extra display option.

1 Embedding the car in a reflective wedge is an unusual tactic, a world apart from motoring cliches.
2 The zig-zag rhythm of the store creates a dynamic impression.
3 The pegboard backdrop had to be suitable for displaying bespoke products from jeans to men's shoes.

An angular approach for versatile displays

MY BOON
BY JAKLITSCH/GARDNER ARCHITECTS

WHERE Seoul, Korea WHEN August 2012
CLIENT Shinsegae DESIGNER Jaklitsch/Gardner Architects (p.496)
TOTAL FLOOR AREA 622 m² SHOP CONSTRUCTOR Kukbo Design
PHOTOS Nacása & Partners (Nobuko Ohara)

Retail concept store My Boon is located in Cheongdam-Dong, the trendy Gangnam-Gu region of Seoul. The interior, designed by New York office Jaklitsch/Gardner Architects, was inspired by the client's motto, 'my style, my body, my soul.' Part store, part cultural destination, it is divided into three separate zones, displaying a trio of different product categories: high-end fashion, furniture and footwear; beauty products, cosmetics and vitamins; and accessories and art. The continuous element of a wooden louvred ceiling visually connects the three black-framed zones, which are punctuated by a spectacular marble juice bar and café reflecting the healthy lifestyle ethos of the store (it's also an apothecary). This bar anchors one end of the store, while the fashion area anchors the other. In between, there's a connecting zone of curated objects and accessories. It all adds up to an undulating landscape of retail, with subtle shifts in form, colour and materials defining the customer's journey through it. The palette

of materials has a raw edge, with hand-trowelled concrete finishing the walls and display elements made from recycled wood and stacked concrete planks. Polished stainless steel shelving adds to the industrial vibe, while a glowing white glass installation above the bar acts as a beacon for visitors inside and outside the store. 'It is a consumable space that seeks to reinvent retail,' says designer Stephan Jaklitsch. On the road side of the building, artist-curated LED strips add a racy touch, while on the residential side there are pantone-arrayed metal plates to add colour and screen the café.

1 Through three different product areas, the customers are taken on a retail journey.
2 Stacked concrete planks form installation-like customised display elements.
3 The marble bar is a focal point, with its glowing white lighting element above acting as a beacon for

A 'consumable' space strives to reinvent retail

5

4 Varying distances between colourful
  powder-coated steel bands create a sense
  of privacy in the café area.
5 The scheme treats each product on display
  as a work of art.

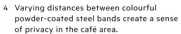
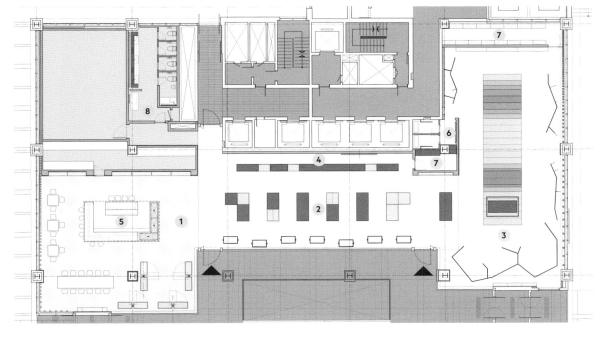

1 Café and beauty area
2 Gallery area
3 Fashion area
4 Cash desk
5 Bar
6 Fitting rooms
7 Storage
8 Toilets

N.TYLER
BY UPSTAIRS_

WHERE Singapore, Singapore WHEN November 2011
CLIENT Singapore Crocodile DESIGNER UPSTAIRS_ (p.499)
TOTAL FLOOR AREA 150 m² SHOP CONSTRUCTOR OP3 International
PHOTOS CI&A Photography

For a first flagship store for Savile Row-inspired bespoke menswear label N.Tyler, design office UPSTAIRS_ endeavoured to embody the brand's aspirations – namely, traditional English tailoring with a contemporary twist. 'Inspired by the controversial works in dissection of British artist Damien Hirst, we've created a modern-day shrine to the menswear couturier', says Dennis Cheok, founder of the design office. He calls the resulting interior, 'a curious and slightly crazed exercise in abstracting the peculiarities of the traditional English town house: the front hall, the salon, the grand atrium – all fervently curated, dissected and reconfigured as total, holistic environments.' Customers passing through the store's three quintessentially English interiors – inspired by the real-life houses of Savile Row – experience classical walls, furniture and features that are surreally sliced and spliced. Floating furnishings add to the dreamlike atmosphere, while a bespoke tailor's pedestal, positioned beneath a dramatic mirrored ceiling, emphasises the craft origins of the brand, as do doors studded with thimbles. 'This project required dramatically intricate ornamentation', says Cheok. 'We had to exercise a lot of restraint with the materials and colour palette. Surfaces were spray-painted in neutral greys and set against a raw concrete background, which we accented with brass-work details.' A key element of the project, says Cheok, was the flooring. 'For each sliver of dissected space we wanted to create a corresponding band of contrasting flooring material, laid out in geometries reinterpreted from traditional patterns.' Herringbone parquet and classical tiled surfaces accordingly found underfoot, with what seems to be half of a blue Axminster carpet positioned at the entrance.

1 The embellished front doors are studded with thimbles, announcing the bespoke garments on offer in the store.
2 The entrance carpet, table and vase appear to be 'sliced' through, indicating the abrupt end of the front hall zone.

4

Surreally sliced and spliced interiors

3 Brass, parquet, moulding, wood and
   leather create a traditional 'house on
   Savile Row' atmosphere.
4 The intermediary 'grey' zones incorporate
   floating furnishings, adding a curious
   aspect to the displays.

5 The artistic work of Damien Hirst inspired this English house setting to be 'dissected'.
6 The junctions of each zone sees classic furniture and architecture sometimes sliced in half.

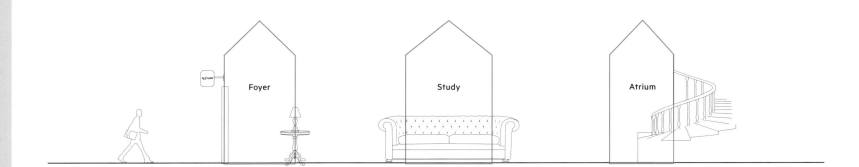

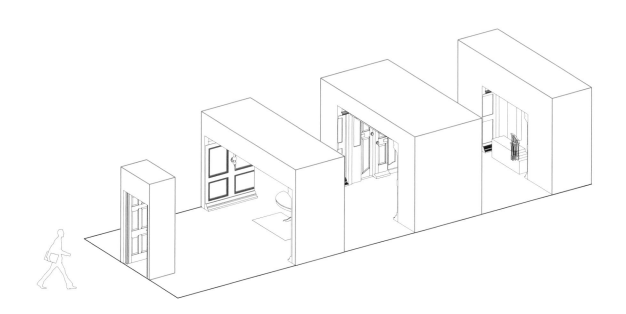

5

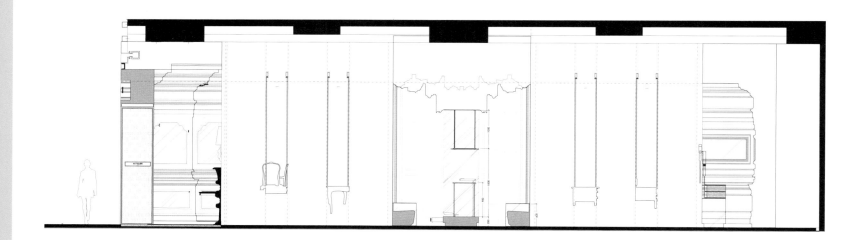

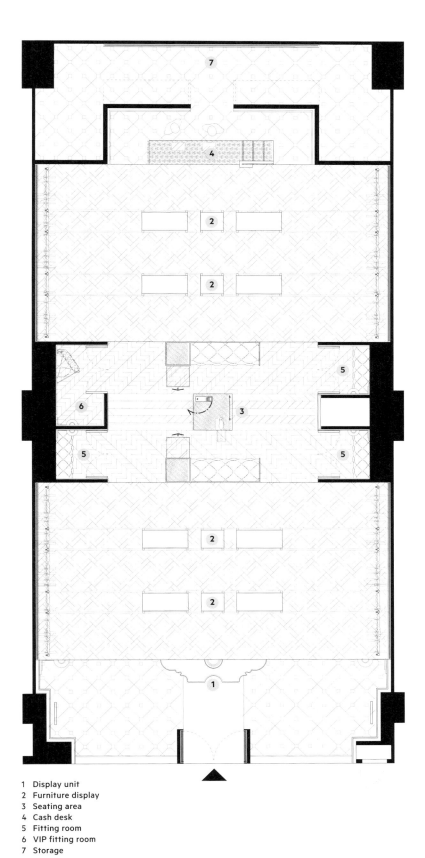

1 Display unit
2 Furniture display
3 Seating area
4 Cash desk
5 Fitting room
6 VIP fitting room
7 Storage

Abstracting the peculiarities of the English town house

NOTE ET SILENCE.
BY SPECIALNORMAL

WHERE Kobe, Japan WHEN September 2012
CLIENT Ambidex DESIGNER Specialnormal (p.498)
TOTAL FLOOR AREA 83 m² SHOP CONSTRUCTOR Itoki Market Space
PHOTOS Koichi Torimura

For an exclusive women's store called note et silence. in a Kobe shopping mall, Shin Takahashi of Specialnormal was asked to provide a simple but museum-like space with a unique twist to its design. He quickly decided that a theatrical concept, 'reinterpreting customers as actors and actresses, and the shop itself as a theatre stage' was the best possible way to fulfil to the client's desires. The theatrical setting concept naturally suggested the ideas of impermanence and flexibility. Just as a theatre changes its scenery as a play develops, so the designer wanted the store to be able to adjust its look, depending on the season and collection on display. The illusion of a theatre is assisted by the wide, diagonal frontage of the store, which is entirely glazed, putting the contents of the shop on show. To create unity in the space, only one colour was used: white. This simple backdrop helps to throw the collections into relief, and focuses customer attention on the clothing. Flexibility is added in the shape of a mobile box unit, measuring 2.5 m in width,

and mobile wall units, which are suspended from the ceiling – without ever touching the ground. The 'set' elements can be moved around in the store to create a variety of effects, and the floating effect guarantees a playful sense of drama. The feet of customers are visible behind them, rather like actors moving behind a curtain. Arched openings frame views and suggest doorways, while the square openings, which reference windows, contain two sets of display shelves.

1 Display units that appear to levitate give the retail space a dreamlike quality.
2 A wide, diagonal glazed façade puts the store on show like a stage.

A theatrical setting seems to float on air

3 The movable box and wall elements can be used to reconfigure the shop.
4, 5, 6 & 7 The mobile units slide on runners placed on the ceiling, so rearranging them is easy and results in entirely different atmospheres.

OLYMP & HADES
BY CORNEILLE UEDINGSLOHMANN ARCHITEKTEN

WHERE Leipzig, Germany **WHEN** November 2012
CLIENT Görgens Gruppe **DESIGNER** Corneille Uedingslohmann Architekten (p.492)
TOTAL FLOOR AREA 680 m² **SHOP CONSTRUCTOR** Starker
PHOTOS Michael Neuhaus

For the Olymp & Hades store in Leipzig's Paunsdorf Center, the designers at Corneille Uedings-lohmann Architekten did a bit of thinking inside the box. Customers are not only greeted by a dramatic entrance resembling a rectangular black steel box, but the whole store frontage is treated as a composition of boxes – this time in oak, fronted by glass – that create a transparent border zone between the shop and its mall setting. They also act as frames, creating multiple shop-window display areas. Entering the store, the rectilinear theme continues. Shoppers are guided by a dramatic 35-m-long rectangle, a wooden pedestal display element which runs through the centre of the store and contrasts with the grey, seamless PU floor. Above this display element is a corresponding white ceiling strip, adding lightness to the space and emphasizing the linear dynamic. Various zones are defined along this horizontal axis by smaller, rectangular black display unites that punctuate the space. A range of wall treatments, in black, white and mosaic, correspond to the zonal organisation. The monochrome treatment of the interior sets off the clothing which, abundantly displayed throughout the store, adds welcome splashes of colour to the space. In the fitting room area at the rear of the store, the rigid rectangular shapes give way to more dynamic and energetic forms, with star-shaped white ceiling elements set in sharp relief against a black background. Magenta curtains and curving banquettes complete the softer, lusher effect for a touch of customer comfort.

1 Oak boxes act as a transparent border zone between the shop and the mall outside, while also creating multiple shop-window display areas.
2 Black rectangular display elements help create smaller zoned areas, which are complemented by different wall treatments.
3 In the fitting room area, curves and colour make an appearance in the interior.

A 21ˢᵗ-century translation of 'Japanese-ness'

ONITSUKA TIGER
BY LINE-INC.

WHERE Tokyo, Japan WHEN April 2012
CLIENT Asics Corporation DESIGNER Line-Inc. (p.497)
TOTAL FLOOR AREA 268 m² SHOP CONSTRUCTOR Sogo Design
PHOTOS Kozo Takayama

'As a Japan-born brand, we felt it was important to find the best way to show the concept of "made in Japan"', says Line-Inc.'s Takao Katsuta of the Onitsuka Tiger flagship store that the office designed in Omotesando. Instead of literal – and probably clichéd– references to the idea of Japan, the designers decided to transform the essence of Japanese-ness into a more contemporary expression, creating a store that would seem fresh and unexpected not only to foreigners, but also to Japanese people themselves. Situated in a back street, the flagship obviously needed an eye-catching façade to draw the attention of passers-by. For the exterior walls, the designers created a custom black mortar containing a sumi ink, which is traditionally used in Japanese calligraphy. Pressing cedar boards onto the sooty mortar gave an interesting woody texture. Inside, the black sumi mortar is also used for some of the interior walls, notably as a dramatic backdrop for the sales desk, creating a sense of unity in the two-storey building. On the ground floor, a western-styled

herringbone floor was installed, but using the Japanese material bamboo, to suggest a synthesis of Japanese and western cultures. In order to heighten the beauty of the bamboo, each piece was tinted in a range of colours including green, and then randomly placed. Upstairs, the striking wooden louvered ceiling is based on the design of the patterned soles of Onitsuka Tiger shoes. It contrasts with the clean, sporty-looking white acrylic floor.

1 The ground floor features a bamboo herringbone floor, part of an east-meets-west design which pairs Western furnishings with Japanese materials and aesthetics.
2 & 4 The striking louvred wooden ceiling upstairs is based on the patterned soles of Onitsuka Tiger shoes.
3 As the façade has a large glass surface, louvre the ceiling of the first floor can be easily seen from a distance.

259

PODIUM SPORT
BY ART BUREAU 1/1

1

WHERE Moscow, Russia **WHEN** August 2012
CLIENT Podium **DESIGNER** Art Bureau 1/1 (p. 490)
TOTAL FLOOR AREA 450 m² **SHOP CONSTRUCTOR** Podium
PHOTOS Frank Herfort

A multi-brand sports clothing store located in a luxury shopping centre, Podium Sport stokes active clothing and products with a fashionable edge. In order to give the 450m² Podium Sport store a distinctive and appropriate look, designer office Art Bureau 1/1 referenced the colours, forms and materials associated with sports, creating an appropriately high-interest, high-energy interior. The shop was loosely based on a fitness club, with plenty of custom touches: unique displays are paired with an original, specially designed wallpaper. Starting with the giant frame constructions acting as window displays fronting the store's glass façade, many pieces have stepped corners which give a pixelated, vintage computer game look. Shelving and hanging units resemble locker-room fittings, with the circular mirrors above them again suggesting dressing rooms. Most of the display furniture suggests sports equipment, including mobile metal racks that suggest hurdles and gymnasts' bars. Mats and punchbags add to the range of athletic props. The colour palette is sporty too, with grey floors and ceiling animated by energetic yellow running stripes and walls highlighted in vibrant red and blue or multi-coloured stripes. The wallpaper design, especially created for this store, adds a further dynamic touch. Based on a three-dimensional pixelated pattern, it contributes an eye-catching optical illusion in rich shades of magenta. The tile-like pixels of the pattern are mirrored by real tiles, which cover the surface of a raised podium feature, resembling a catwalk, in the store. Brightly coloured merchandise and mannequins in active poses complete the picture.

1 Displays are based on locker-room furniture and gym equipment.
2 An original custom wallpaper, based on a pixelated pattern, adds a lively optical effect.
3 Blocks and stripes of bright colour make for a high-energy space.

4 Large frames with pixelated corners make effective window displays fronting the glass façade.
5 Sporty props, including ramps, mats and punchbags, add to the atmosphere.
6 A rendering of the custom wallpaper.
7 Shelves with rounded edges display the shoe collection.
8 Bright colours result in a buzzy effect.

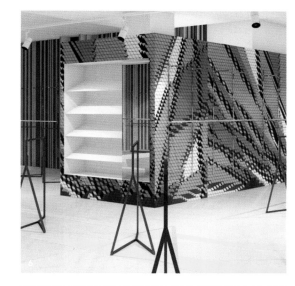

Athletic themes create an adrenalin rush

PUMA
BY PLAJER & FRANZ STUDIO

2

WHERE Osaka, Japan WHEN December 2012
CLIENT Puma DESIGNER plajer & franz studio (p.498)
TOTAL FLOOR AREA 580 m² SHOP CONSTRUCTORS Max Brilliant and Nomura
PHOTOS diephotodesigner.de (Ken Schluchtmann)

To conjure a truly Puma-themed store that packs a global branding punch yet makes plenty of local references, plajer & franz studio teamed up with Ales Kernjak, Puma's head of store concepts and the director of the project. As well as a retail destination, the new Puma flagship was designed to be a social hub – a cultural meeting point and space for events and happenings of various kinds, including sports tournaments. The lower two floors (totalling 580 m²) of the three-storey building are therefore devoted to shopping, while the upper levels feature the events spaces, including an open rooftop, surrounded simply by the light façade construction, dedicated to sport and culture. The boldest statement in the store is the impressive cone-shaped staircase which, backed by a sweeping wall of trainers, emphasises Puma's heritage as a footwear brand. On the ground floor, Japanese design is referenced by the use of simple forms and materials like concrete and wood, and seating concepts influenced by origami. These elements combine to present the black label and sports-lifestyle products showcased here in rather a high-fashion atmosphere. Upstairs, the performance store space is more traditionally 'sporty.' Wrapping almost the entire exterior space – apart from the ground-floor, lantern-like expanse of glass – is a red metal mesh façade that is partly transparent. This rises above the building, forming the 'walls' of the rooftop sports and performance area. The white Puma logo makes a strong signal outside, while inside too white ceramic and graphic pumas make regular appearances in the space.

1   The red-and-white colour scheme reflects Puma's brand but also has a strong Japanese identity.
2   The Puma trademark pops up in various forms in the store.
3   The simple forms and concrete and wood of the ground floor convey a Japanese aesthetic.

4 Industrial materials contribute to
  the technical atmosphere.
5 Upstairs, a more sporty space projects
  a more functional profile.
6 Bold graphic details add interest
  and movement.

A global brand gets strong local references

4

5

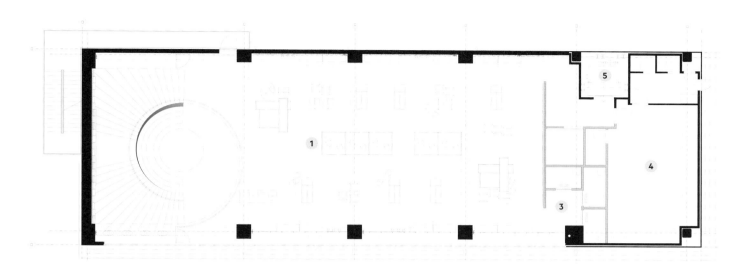

1 Retail area
2 Cash desk
3 Fitting rooms
4 Storage
5 Elevator

First floor

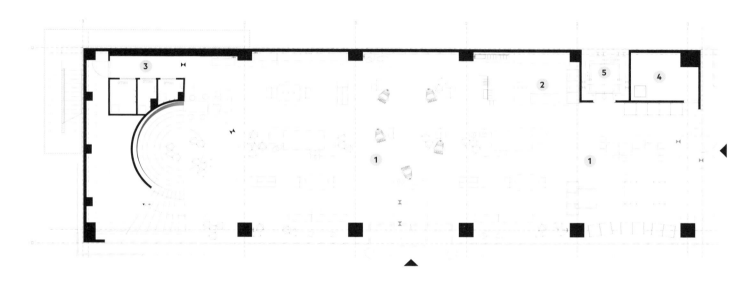

Ground floor   0 1 2 3 4 5 m

White curtains go with the flow

SOHO
BY HEIKAUS CONCEPT

WHERE Trier, Germany **WHEN** July 2011
CLIENT Soho **DESIGNER** Heikaus Concept (p.495)
TOTAL FLOOR AREA 200 m² **SHOP CONSTRUCTOR** Heikaus Interior
PHOTOS Uwe Spoering

Proving that pale can be interesting, Heikaus constructs a deceptively simple interior for a luxury womenswear store. A simple white curtain sweeps over the walls of Soho, suggesting the softness and femininity of the women's fashion on offer there. The drapery makes a subtle backdrop for the store's exclusive garments, which hang from simple brass rails. Simplicity is also the key to the white free-standing display elements which alternate with golden glass cubes throughout the space. An interesting contrast is provided by the cast iron columns which suggest past eras, as do the panelled wall panels used at the rear of the store. The iron pillars give a graphic perspectival effect, since they begin with the façade and then dot their way through the space. Indirect lighting provides a bright daylight effect, in keeping with the natural skylights at the back of the space, that greatly enhances the softness of the materials and colours of the interior and the fashion on show. A lounge area harmoniously mixes different styles of furniture, while the changing room creates an indulgent atmosphere: shag-pile carpet and mirrored walls are enclosed by more flowing white curtains to form an elegant and private atmosphere for customers to try out new looks. Products are further enhanced by some custom lighting using recessed and power-rail mounted spotlights from the Stella II and Neal series of Heikaus' own Professional Retail Light lamp collection.

1 A pale but interesting interior is partly based on simple modular shelving.
2 White curtains cover much of the wall space, while garments are displayed on simple brass rails.
3 Simple free-standing display elements create a sense of movement through the store, even when seen from outside.

SOV DOUBLE STANDARD CLOTHING
BY PROPELLER DESIGN

1

WHERE Tokyo, Japan WHEN March 2013
CLIENT Film DESIGNER Propeller Design (p.498)
TOTAL FLOOR AREA 173 m² SHOP CONSTRUCTOR Brio
PHOTOS Nacása & Partners

Japanese fashion brand Double Standard Clothing, by Masahisa Takino, has many different faces, in the form of various sub-brands. There's DSC, a mid-priced range; Sov, a more exclusive collection; D/him, a menswear brand; DSC accessories and the newest line, Wedding, a collection of dresses, made-to-measure suits and wedding rings. The challenge for Propeller Design was to incorporate all of these into a single store in Tokyo's ritzy Marunouchi district, located within one of the biggest office and shopping complexes near to the city's central station. The store had to be 'full of antitheses', according to Propeller's Yoshihiro Kawasaki, who aimed at creating 'an environment both modern and classic, cool and emotional, casual and feminine.' Curved glass walls flank the entrances, and a herringbone wood floor and geometric, textured wood-tile walls create a traditional, almost heritage feel. They contrast strongly with the black ceiling, which makes a striking contemporary statement and ties in well with the black frames that articulate the entrances and windows and the black fittings. Square geometric display blocks and black vertical posts inscribing rounded shapes define the space's different areas without breaking up. For the lighting in the shop Propeller Design decided to work with lighting designers Shift+N2. A dramatic chandelier, strip lighting around the periphery and talk, skinny mirrors add light and sparkling reflections to the interior. The subdued tones are a great setting for Double Standard's trademark red mannequins, and the bright red is echoed by several display units in the store. Rows of simple metal racks meanwhile display the collections in an uncluttered way.

1 Classic meets quirky, thanks to traditional details like the herringbone floor and eccentric touches like the red mannequins.
2 Vertical black posts create separate circular areas without breaking up the space.

Classic and contemporary contrasts define diffusion brands

3   Strips of light create movement in the space.
4   Blocky black displays add an angular look.

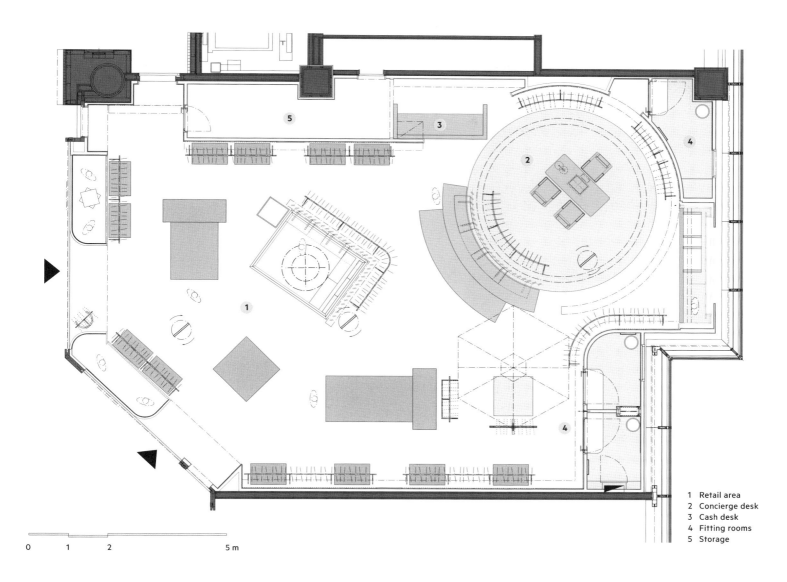

1 Retail area
2 Concierge desk
3 Cash desk
4 Fitting rooms
5 Storage

0   1   2   5 m

Gold gilds every surface in a cylindrical store

STELLA CADENTE
BY ATELIER DU PONT

2

WHERE Paris, France WHEN March 2012
CLIENT Stella Cadente DESIGNER Atelier du Pont (p.491)
TOTAL FLOOR AREA 50 m² SHOP CONSTRUCTOR Farc
PHOTOS Sergio Grazia

Seen from the street, the Stella Cadente boutique forces passers-by to do a double-take as they navigate the rather staid Boulevard Beaumarchais in Paris. For what they see is not the average city fashion boutique, but a glittering tunnel of gold. The shop's glass frontage is surrounded by a border of mirror glass containing a golden inner layer inscribing a circle. Inside, the interior sticks to this rounded profile, the cylindrical shape a novel and dramatic departure from the usual retail conventions. Gold leaf covers just about every surface, including the mannequins. Products are displayed in the rectangular golden recesses and niches that puncture the curved walls of the space. Spotlights on the ceiling and strip lighting in the recesses make the most of the gleaming golden surface by bathing it in light. Simple, uncluttered window displays – at the most using a suspended golden mannequin or two – and one simple, long, rectangular and of course golden display table in the centre of the space maximise the effect by avoiding clutter. The sparse nature of the design achieves an effect that is monumental and at the same time quite cave-like. The impression is of a primeval space coated in the richest of materials. This is Atelier du Pont's second store design for Stella Cadente. The first, in Dubai, has been described as 'midway between an ice palace and a crystal maze', but was not realised. The second follows the theme of a single material, but substitutes glass for gold.

1 Displaying products in well-lit, gold-covered niches gives them an aura of preciousness.
2 From the street, passers-by see the glittering tunnel in its entirety thanks to the glass frontage.
3 The golden background makes product colours pop.

STILLS
BY DOEPEL STRIJKERS

WHERE Amsterdam, the Netherlands **WHEN** September 2011
CLIENT VeldhovenGroup, Stills atelier **DESIGNER** Doepel Strijkers (p.494)
TOTAL FLOOR AREA 188 m² **SHOP CONSTRUCTORS** Heijmerink Wagemakers and Krant Interieurbouw
PHOTOS Wouter vandenBrink

An intricate wooden lattice infiltrates every corner of the Stills flagship store, designed by Doepel Strijkers. The grey-painted grid unites the two storeys of the space and makes loose furniture superfluous, by acting as both a hanging and flat display, as well as a stage for mannequins. While the grid is fixed, its modular organisation allows for the products to be positioned very flexibly. 'This makes the design a clever response to rapid retail interiors and enables connection to current themes like future resistance and durability,' says the design office's Eline Strijkers. The design does a lot with a few materials. It also reflects the values of the Stills label, whose clothes are based on research into the intrinsic qualities of materials, resulting in new processes, effects and combinations. The store interior was visualised as a close-up of a textile's structure. Starting off with a grid structure that filled the entire space, during the design process the designers removed parts of the grid, to create recesses, sight lines, product visibility and movement through the space, using rules based on units of 30 cm. The measured uniformity of scale ensures a harmonious effect. Dressing rooms, lighting and all possible display options are integrated into the latticed volume, so clothing, shoes, bags, books and mannequins form the variation within the continuous structure. Clothes hang from the grid, or are folded flat on clear glass shelves placed here and there. Dressed mannequins appear to have scaled the structure in order to perch atop it.

1 The light grey wooden lattice acts as
   a hanging and flat display element, and
   as a stage for mannequins.
2 The grid is counterbalanced by voids in
   modular variations based on a 30 cm unit.
3 In the all-grey structure, products provide
   the only colour and variation.

A light grey wooden lattice fulfils every store function

SUPREME
BY BRINKWORTH AND
THE WILSON BROTHERS

WHERE London, United Kingdom WHEN September 2011
CLIENT Supreme DESIGNERS Brinkworth (p.492) and the Wilson Brothers (p.499)
TOTAL FLOOR AREA 150 m² SHOP CONSTRUCTOR Syntec
PHOTOS Louise Melchior

According to Brinkworth's Director Murray Aitken, the concept of the London Supreme store is 'almost anti-design, it's about creating a perfectly functioning space, with minimal decoration'. But although this space has a certain rawness, it is not lacking in sophistication. Brinkworth, together with the Wilson Brothers, was asked to design the New York skate brand's first and only European store. The designers opted to make the basement the main trading area of the two-storey space, while the stockroom and back-of-house facilities are on the ground floor. Cutting back a substantial area of the ground floor to create a double height-void added an open, airy feel to the basement. A galvanised steel staircase leads customers downstairs, where painted breezeblock walls and furniture in industrial materials contrast with the luxurious herringbone parquet flooring laid throughout the store. Above the staircase hovers one of two bird-like sculptures by skateboarder and artist Mark Gonzales. Adding to the gallery like atmosphere

is the bespoke display furniture made by the designers, which includes clothing rails made from galvanised steel, referencing skate-able street furniture. Upstairs, in the space reserved for the cash desk and skate equipment, Supreme's graphic skateboard decks are displayed on the walls, together with skate photography by Ari Marcopoulious. High contrast is a major feature of the project. As Oscar Wilson says, 'The rich parquet floor introduces a touch of warmth to the space that is then flipped again by the sheer "Skate Pop" of the two huge Mark Gonzales birds.'

1 Seen from outside, breezeblock walls evoke an industrial ambience.
2 Bird-like sculptures by skateboarder and artist Mark Gonzales create a 'skate-pop' ambience.
3 The rich parquet flooring unifies the store and adds warm.
4 Bespoke display furniture references skate-able streetscapes.

Skate-pop with a side of industrial meets luxury

TADASHI SHOJI
BY OPENAIR STUDIO

1

WHERE Bangkok, Thailand WHEN April 2012
CLIENT Central Department Store DESIGNER OpenAir Studio (p.498)
TOTAL FLOOR AREA 40 m² SHOP CONSTRUCTORS Motif Advance and Time Enterprise
PHOTOS Wison Tungthunya

Japanese-American fashion designer Tadashi Shoji is known for the figure-flattering qualities of his clothing – the result of a little clever material trickery using pleats, ruching and other sleights of hand with fabric. For this shop-within-a-shop, OpenAir Studio imitated Shoji's own trademark techniques by flattering a rather small and hidden space, tucked away in the corner of a multi-brand area devoted to high-end fashion brands, with some crafty dress-up tactics. It was important, giving the setting, to make the space visually striking from a distance. OpenAir Studio therefore hit upon the idea of featuring shiny, light-reflecting materials to create texture and interest. Accordingly, the walls of the space are lined by folded stainless-steel modules that are stacked and rotated in an alternating pattern, creating an asymmetrically angled surface that dances with glittering reflections, beckoning shoppers from afar. A lilac border along the top of the walls adds very visible yet subtle signposting to the Tadashi Shoji collection. The shining backdrop to the space makes a

perfect stage for the very feminine, detailed garments that are Shoji's speciality. The intricately textured and crafted wall is an effective counterpoint for the intricately pleated and ruched dresses on display, and the jewel-like effect gives a feeling of luxury and exclusivity. The rest of the space is kept rather simple but dramatic. Clothes are displayed on mirrored platforms on rails made from bent brass tubing. The fitting room is another mirrored space, this time using upholstered panels to create a soft effect.

1 Garments look dramatic atop mirrored platforms on rails made from bent brass tubing against shimmering stainless-steel walls.
2 The fitting room features mirrors and upholstered panels for a soft effect.
3 Folded stainless-steel modules that are stacked and rotated in an alternating pattern create a glittering, angled surface.
4 The intricate effect mimics the complex detailing of the clothes.

Fantastically facetted walls maximise a small space

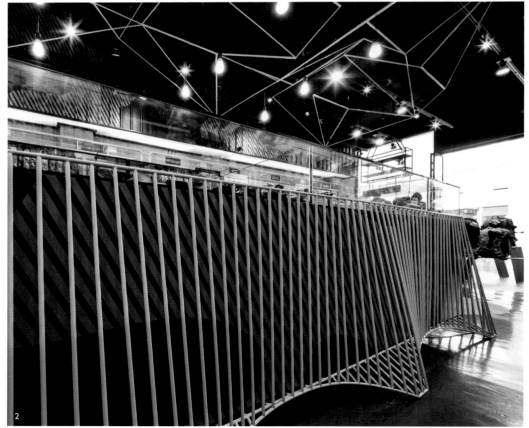

Taking a cue from Batman's cave

TANK STORE
BY SUPERMACHINE STUDIO

WHERE Bangkok, Thailand **OPENING** December 2012
CLIENT Tank Store **DESIGNER** Supermachine Studio (p.499)
TOTAL FLOOR AREA 120 m² **SHOP CONSTRUCTOR** –
PHOTOS Wison Tungthunya

'Customers should feel as though they've walked into Batman's cave', says Supermachine Studio's Pitupong Chaowakul of the retail space his office designed for Tank Store, an outdoor activity brand selling technical products from torches to outdoor gear. Chaowakul wanted the interior to embody the idea of choosing equipment for an exciting, action-hero type adventure. Simple outdoor items, grouped in the store according to category, are thus elevated to the status of essential kit for exploration and survival. To create a cave-like effect in the interior, the designer opted for a dark palette: a mix of black and grey background shades achieves what Pitupong Chaowakul calls a 'heavy-duty' effect, enlivened with some dramatic detailing in khaki – a colour with appropriately outdoorsy and military overtones. The dark, no-frills background focuses customer interest on the functional, practical nature of the equipment on sale. Hundreds of 8mm steel rods were used to craft the store's focal point, its central display, which adopts a wave-like, rippling profile. In khaki, like the shelves, counter, graphics, and what the designer calls 'the triangulated cloud chandelier' which adds interest to the upper area of the space, the display forms a dramatic base on which the smaller items are showcased. Set off beautifully against the dark background of the store, these sculptural khaki steel installations can be seen through the shop's glass frontage, offering passers-by an intriguing preview of what's inside and adding a layer of complexity to a relatively simple retail format.

1 The dark colours used as background focus customer interest on the functional items on show.
2 Hundreds of 8mm steel rods were used to craft the store's focal point, its central display, with its wave-like, rippling profile.
3 Khaki, with its military overtones, is used for the graphics, shelves, displays and installations.

TIGER OF SWEDEN
STORE CONCEPT
BY KONCEPT STOCKHOLM

1

WHERE London, United Kingdom **WHEN** October 2013
CLIENT Tiger of Sweden **DESIGNER** Koncept Stockholm (p.496)
TOTAL FLOOR AREA 260 m² **SHOP CONSTRUCTOR** KS Projekt
PHOTOS Ed Reeves

Tiger of Sweden has always been of a *different cut*, ever since the founders, Marcus Schwartzman and Hjalmar Nordström, ventured into tailored suits out of a small atelier on the west-coast of Sweden in the early 1900's. Now is the time for the next step; together with the architects Koncept Stockholm, the vision of *The New Lux* is applied to all Tiger interiors world-wide, starting off with a new flagship store in London. 'We've worked with Koncept for ten years. They know exactly how to dress our core values. Nice-looking interior design is one thing, but to create an environment functional and beautiful, while fully incorporating the brand, this, Koncept Stockholm does very well', says Jonas Nyström, Retail Director at Tiger of Sweden. Over the next few years, 50-something stores will transform. 'The strength of Koncept Stockholm's work is creating a concept that works wherever we are in the world and whatever the size of the shop,' Nyström explains. No matter if you're stepping into the flagship store on Piccadilly Circus or visiting Täby Centrum

outside Stockholm, you will immediately recognise the casual elegance of Tiger of Sweden. Mirror glass meets rough textures and creates depth and space within the retail area. The clothes are accessible, presented gallery-style along walls or on an L-shaped podium. A play on graphics, harmonizing blacks, greys, and whites frame the custom-made, sculptural furnishings. The many innovative design features of *The New Lux* all adhere to the core values of Tiger of Sweden; individualism, high fashion, urban feel, and Scandinavian tailoring.

1 The shop front of the Tiger of Sweden
   St James store.
2 An architectural clean-cut store concept
   with graphical use of black, white and grey.
3 The floor plan is strict in form and furniture
   is sculptural with a monolithic feel.

A play on graphics, harmonizing blacks, greys, and whites frame the custom-made, sculptural furnishings

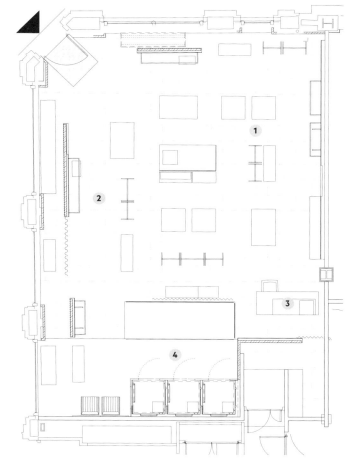

Ground floor

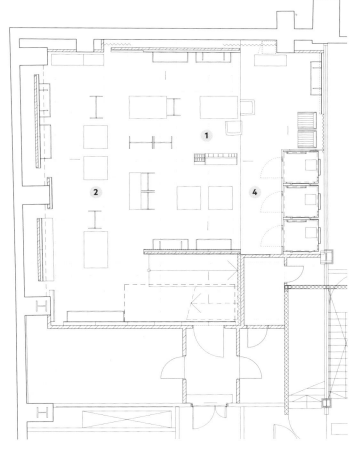

Basement

4 The clothes are accessible, presented gallery-style.
5 Street like flooring creates a dynamic between high precision materials and rougher textures.
6 Sleek pieces of furniture in tactile materials like satin maple and brushed aluminium with tailored velvet panels are positioned on thick premium wool carpets.

1 Men's area
2 Women's area
3 Cash desk
4 Fitting rooms

UM
BY AS DESIGN SERVICE

1

WHERE Shenzhen, China **WHEN** July 2011
CLIENT World First Holdings **DESIGNER** AS Design Service (p.491)
TOTAL FLOOR AREA 126 m² **SHOP CONSTRUCTORS** Creative Furniture and Project Department
PHOTOS Sing Studio (Sum Sing)

For a men's underwear store for World First Holdings in Shenzhen, China, AS Design Service decided to focus on the idealised masculine traits of capability, self-confidence, steadiness, dignity and virility: an image of maleness at its most regal. To explore this concept, they chose a colour palette of deep charcoal grey, with accents of high-energy yellow – the traditional colour of royalty in China. Rich, dark materials including suede wallpaper, travertine, black stainless steel and black glass suggest steadiness and virility, with attention-grabbing yellow mannequins implying strength and royalty. The letter 'M' for men, male and masculine appears hugely magnified in the store in graphic black and white, creating a bold and dramatic impression. A yellow grid construction is filled with boxed products. When the sales assistant picks up the box at the front, subsequent boxes are automatically pushed to the front thanks to the mechanics of the system. The small screens demonstrate the latest fashion shows from top brands, exhibiting the season's most stylish products for customers and contributing liveliness to the store. The storefront is entirely glass, and the window display features a replica of a streamlined futuristic vehicle that appeared in a sci-fi movie, operated by one of the yellow mannequins. A combination of abstract and modern, it suggests the masculine love of control, dynamism, gadgets and speed. The designers add that it's also 'hilarious to imagine that it is a huge banana, in order to associate it with that most important part of men…'

1 The letter 'M' for men, male and masculine appears hugely magnified in the store in graphic black and white.
2 The futuristic yellow vehicle in the window is a replica from a film.

Celebrating the masculine love of control, dynamism, gadgets and speed

3 Yellow, used for mannequins and displays
in the store, suggests royalty through
traditional Chinese colour association and
contrasts strongly with the dark materials
otherwise used.
4 A yellow grid filled with boxed products
is automated so as to instantly move new
products to the front as boxes are sold.

UM COLLEZIONI
BY AS DESIGN SERVICE

1

WHERE Macau, Macau WHEN November 2012
CLIENT World First Holdings DESIGNER AS Design Service (p.491)
TOTAL FLOOR AREA 126 m² SHOP CONSTRUCTORS Creative Furniture and Project Department
PHOTOS Sing Studio (Sum Sing)

For the UM Collezioni women's multi-brand fashion store, AS Design Service devised the concept of fashion as a sea, using the motif of waves which inspired the unique shape of the shop's focal point: the island display unit. The choice of the sea as a metaphor is intended to suggest UM Collezioni's search for the best luxury brands in the ocean of clothing labels, which it then brings back to the store in a suitcase – another motif which recurs in the interior. Customers go with the flow in the fluid circulation of the shop, finding some suitcases opened and some closed, the latter increasing their feeling of curiosity. The wave-shaped island display unit creates a relaxed atmosphere, and makes an interesting platform for the product offering. The designers have lovingly detailed the various suitcases, exploring the motif through various luxury materials including glossy PU, leather and mirror glass. Sets of suitcase shelves are set in a metal framework finished in solid wooden veneer, for a lightweight look. The suitcases usefully distinguish between the different brands, without favouring one over another. The walls are finished in a glossy PU coating in a chic grey, with horizontal channels recalling the wave theme while serving the practical function of supporting the smaller wooden shelves. Recessed spot lighting makes the most of all the luxurious surfaces and clothing on offer. All in all, the store evokes a holiday feeling – a heady mix of sea, stylish suitcases and premium fashion.

1 The walls and sales desk are finished in PU in chic grey.
2 The store focal point is the wave-shaped island display unit, finished in solid wood veneer.

Riding the wave of fashion on a suitcase

3 Wave-like displays and suitcases
 used as shelves create a holiday
 feeling in the store.
4 & 5 The suitcases, sometimes open and
 sometimes closed, which are used
 to display.

UMIX
BY AS DESIGN SERVICE

2

WHERE Macau, Macau **WHEN** November 2012
CLIENT World First Holdings **DESIGNER** AS Design Service (p.491)
TOTAL FLOOR AREA 142 m² **SHOP CONSTRUCTORS** Creative Furniture and Project Department
PHOTOS Sing Studio (Sum Sing)

UMix is a multi-brand store housing the collections of top men and women's underwear and home-wear labels. Asked to come up with a core design concept for UMix's retail spaces, AS Design Service focused on the unisex angle, developing the idea of the differences between the sexes coexisting with a philosophy of mutual tolerance. Difference is expressed in the store by the use of polygonal display units of different sizes and angles that contrast with, yet complement, each other. For the wall displays, the designers used a concealed metal A-A system to create adjustability and variability for different display combinations. The walls are finished in parallel ribbing, which is made from middle-density fibreboard, its surface sprayed with matte white PU coating. The grooves in the walls hide a large number of hardware components, each able to accommodate a range of accessories, including shelves and hanging racks. The walls are therefore flexible and the displays can easily be changed, making the visual effects of the overall space

more eye-catching. The marine blue display stands add a touch of colour to relieve the uniform whiteness. They are constructed similarly to the wall displays, with their grooves concealing hardware components that can also mount a range of accessories according to different needs. In addition to meeting the practical needs of an underwear store, the designers have succeeded in creating a playful space – a lavishly layered, almost Op Art interior that intrigues the eye and presents the product range in a different light.

1 The interior is a composition of white parallel lines and marine blue polygons.
2 The grooves create an Op Art effect.

3 For the wall displays, the designers used a concealed metal A-A system to create adjustability and variability for different display combinations.
4 The grooves of the floor displays also conceal hardware components that can mount a range of accessories according to different needs.
5 Marine blue polygons add contrast to the space.

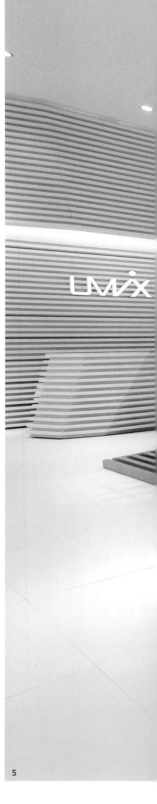

Marine blue display stands relieve the uniform whiteness

Urban extremes define a masculine lifestyle space

WORMLAND
BY BLOCHER BLOCHER PARTNERS

WHERE Oberhausen, Germany WHEN September 2012
CLIENT Theo Wormland DESIGNER Blocher Blocher Partners (p.491)
TOTAL FLOOR AREA 2020 m² SHOP CONSTRUCTORS Korda Ladenbau and Schlegel
PHOTOS Nikolaus Koliusis

Urban, industrial, rough around the edges – that's men's lifestyle concept store Wormland, which combines fashion with music, art, fragrances and reading material. The designers made the most of the extremely high ceilings of the space by fashioning a three-tonne steel framework for the store. Measuring 17 metres wide and 11 metres high, this honeycomb construction connects all three floors along the escalators. The webbed surface is reminiscent of the outer shell of the Oberhausen Gasometer, a local industrial monument. On the ground floor, the structure forms an urban stage for men's fashion. Materials reflect the urban and industrial theme. Solid oak flooring, anthracite stone, exposed concrete, rough plaster and steel dominate the interior design. Visible mechanics emphasise the industrial ambiance, as do the metal surfaces of the clothing racks. In contrast to the two-toned, grey and brown theme, the 33 dressing rooms stand out thanks to their bright colours reflected in oversized mirrors. Giant photographs, backlit by

LEDs, provide more brightness. Each floor has its own highlights that form variations on the basic design theme. On the ground floor, suspended steel elements and large concrete cubes and polygons function as display surfaces, completing the rough look. An eye-catcher on the first floor is the raw steel structure framed by a cube of exposed concrete. Clothing is suspended from this structure over a floor of cognac-coloured oak. Walls of stacked, cube-like cabinets are yet another attention grabber. The second floor, which also features a spacious coffee lounge, is divided up with freestanding walls that constantly afford new perspectives.

1 The ground-floor ceiling bears a large-format motif of the New York City skyline.
2 *Wollen, haben, sein* (wanting, having, being) are three key words adorning the cashier stations at Wormland stores.

Exposed concrete, rough plaster, oak and anthracite stone add to the urban and industrial theme

3 A library-like book section adds some graphic brightness.
4 Concrete cubes and polygons make tough displays.

YOUTOPIA
BY DAN PEARLMAN

WHERE Ravensburg, Germany **WHEN** March 2013
CLIENT Youtopia **DESIGNER** dan pearlman (p.493)
TOTAL FLOOR AREA 1000 m² **SHOP CONSTRUCTOR** Gerhard Koening
PHOTOS Guido Leifhelm

It's a place for 'Youtopian' dreams – Youtopia being a fantasy-directed concept store aimed at younger fashion fans. Four storeys and 1000 m² of space play tribute to fashion innovation and fun. 'Curious, brave, friendly' announces a monkey sign outside the store, and those seem to be the values that the designers at dan pearlman have tried to embody. Apes – among the most playful of animals – are a theme throughout the store, stencilled graffiti-like onto walls or appearing as masks on mannequins. Wire mesh and metal grid walls create a cage-like aesthetic which combines with recycled materials to further the industrial vibe. Stools are made from reclaimed car tyres and salvaged pieces of furniture dot the space. As the names given to each floor suggest – from Sparkling Jungle to Brave New Brainiac – each one aims to create a different atmosphere. Many items in the space reference the fantasy of the clientele. There's a circus horse in one corner, while the changing rooms look like little beach huts made from reused wood in chevron patterns. Then in the Monkey Lounge there's a Fliewatüüt – a fantasy all-in-one vehicle that featured in the famous German kids' TV series, *Robbi, Tobbi und das Fliewatüüt* – a perfect allusion for the customer demographic. There's an instore photo booth too, named Photopia (what else?). Also in keeping with the interests of the target group was a Facebook campaign tying in with the shop's opening, a map of monkey sightings and a monkey-themed launch party.

1   Retro elements, such as the fairground unicorn, bring fun and drama to the store.
2   Suspended frames animate a dark interior space.
3   A changing room has a mural of butterflies and humming birds.

Childhood nostalgia and fantasy appeal abound

4 Monkey graphics and ape references
   are found throughout the store.
5 Recycled wooden planks painted in
   contrasting colours add to the fun feel
   of the store.
6 The Monkey Lounge in one corner of the
   store doubles up as a stage for events.

FOOD

BEVE

316

AND
RAGE

317

An artisanal approach for a unique food concept

BILDER & DE CLERCQ
BY ...,STAAT CREATIVE AGENCY

WHERE Amsterdam, the Netherlands WHEN February 2013
CLIENTS Rogier Leopold and Diederik van Gelder DESIGNER ...,staat creative agency (p.490)
TOTAL FLOOR AREA 200 m² SHOP CONSTRUCTOR Den Dekker Project Management
PHOTOS Ewout Huibers

Amsterdam's Bilder & De Clercq is a food retailer with a difference. In the store, customers find everything they need to create 14 different dishes, each one packaged as the ingredients for two portions and step-by-step instructions for making it. The shop also stocks everything else they might need for their meal, including fine wines, fresh bread, desserts, kitchen equipment and a variety of organic products such as jam and olive oil. ...,staat creative agency created the whole concept for the brand, right down to the denim aprons (made by students of The Amsterdam Jeans School). Rather than traditional supermarket aisles, the store is equipped with bespoke display furniture. Simple grey shelves line the walls, while the display islands are composed of stacked, white 3D frames that create an airy and light effect. Each display island shows off two dishes, and visitors can browse among them as though visiting a market with various stalls. An inviting counter opposite the entrance integrates a coffee bar, cash registers and the kitchen.

The grey palette is combined with warm wooden tones and a touch of copper green, giving a fresh look. The artisanal ambience is boosted by the hand-crafted tiles, copper fittings, custom-made furniture in wood and steel, concrete floor and a sprinkling of vintage furniture. Product presentation has a casual touch and packaging is simple – more small-scale delicatessen than big supermarket. It all adds up to a light, contemporary, industrial aesthetic combined with the traditional but updated feel of a quality grocer's shop.

1 Display islands are composed of stacked, white 3D frames that create an airy and light effect.
2 A welcoming tiled counter opposite the entrance unites a coffee bar, cash registers and the kitchen.

Product presentation has a casual touch

3 & 4   Simple grey shelves line the walls,
        harmonizing with the concrete floor.
5, 6 & 7 ...,staat created the entire brand
        identity for Bilder & De Clercq.
8 & 9   The denim aprons are made by
        students of The Amsterdam
        Jeans School.

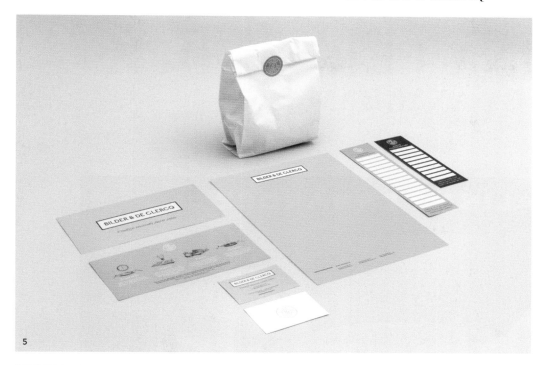

5

8

6

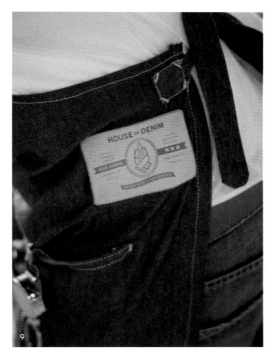

9

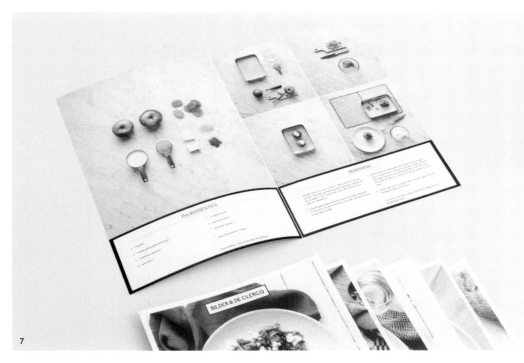

7

CATALINA FERNÃNDEZ
BY ANAGRAMA

1

WHERE San Pedro Garza García, Mexico WHEN March 2012
CLIENT Catalina Fernãndez DESIGNER Anagrama (p.490)
TOTAL FLOOR AREA 80 m² SHOP CONSTRUCTOR –
PHOTOS Caroga Fotografo

For a boutique pastry shop in San Pedro Garza García, Mexico, design office Anagrama created a deceptively simple interior to accompany a rather chic, sophisticated house style. It's an effective combination that evokes both the Catalina Fernandez brand's upwardly mobile aspirations, as well as its authentic origins as a home-based bakery (founded by Catalina herself in 1988). Having grown into a fully-fledged pastry shop, the brand owner wished to upgrade her bakery and identify it with a more sophisticated sphere. Anagrama therefore developed an elegant brand identity, with a sans serif typeface chosen for its neutral and timeless associations. The various boxes and bags were decorated with delicate details in golden foil which, like Catalina's pastries, took many hours of attention to detail. The store's interior, however, evokes the brand's reliable and down-to-earth origins, with a look that suggests both a kitchen and a warehouse: white containers of sugar, flour, and yeast are placed liberally all over the store. A vertical display structure with shelves above the refrigerators takes advantage of the space's high ceilings. The walls, of enamelled white brick, look impeccable, as well as old fashioned; their shiny surface suggests a sugar coating. A simple concrete floor and contrasting gold coloured rear wall keeps the materials and colour palette restrained and simple. Modern furniture by the likes of Eames creates an interesting contrast with the aged, artisanal bricks, again adding to the aura of timelessness around the brand. A suspended circular lighting fixture helps to pull the whole thing together.

1 A chic and elegant house style is combined with a more rustic, yet still stylish, interior.
2 White enamelled bricks look sugary and smooth, while white storage containers emphasise the honest ingredients of the pastries.

Sugar-coated brickwork for a chic but homely bakery

CHOBANI SOHO
BY A L M PROJECT

WHERE New York, United States **WHEN** July 2012
CLIENT Chobani café **DESIGNER** a l m project (p.490)
TOTAL FLOOR AREA 65 m² **SHOP CONSTRUCTOR** –
PHOTOS Patricia Parinejad

An honest, artisanal approach to the interior of Chobani, a yogurt bar in Manhattan, reflects the healthy simplicity of the products on offer. A l m project used natural materials to transform the landmark SoHo building into a restful but vibrant modern space: Corten steel, diamond plate and hardwood planks, put together with minimalist precision, frame the transparent glass envelope that reveals the goodies within. Outside ledges act as benches, encouraging customers to linger and extending the presence of the store into the street. The interior palette continues the themes of the façade, by combining reclaimed local redwood, rusted steel and concrete, with accents of copper lighting, wire glass and Corian. Three zones define the small space: the public area revolves around the 'harvest table', an earthy centrepiece showcasing produce from local farms and the range of Chobani pre-packaged yogurt. Then there's the serving unit, dubbed 'the pantry', which holds the various Mediterranan ingredients used in the yogurt creations prepared to order. Finally, the 'yogurt master bar' is a preparation area, where Chobani's yogurt masters work their magic under the eyes of both customers and passers-by. 'Drawing inspiration directly from the yogurt and its rural origins, the design reinterprets the barn in a contemporary way, creating an austere environment, meticulously detailed and flooded with natural light', says a l m's Andrea Lenardin Madden. According to the designer, the mix of old, new, natural and cultural references suggests 'timeless rituals and a lifestyle that offers a change in pace.'

1   A seamless glass box detailed in Corten steel and wood, Chobani's transparent frontage tempts passers-by with the sight of delicious treats.
2   Natural materials and Mediterranean colours evoke a more traditional way of life.
3   Fresh produce and warm detailing adds old-world charm to the space.

Mediterranean lifestyle infused into a bustling SoHo intersection

DIAGEO CONCEPT STORE
BY FOURFOURSIXSIX

1

WHERE Bangkok, Thailand WHEN October 2012
CLIENT Diageo DESIGNER Fourfoursixsix (p.495)
TOTAL FLOOR AREA 150 m² SHOP CONSTRUCTOR Sense Sign
PHOTOS Owen Raggett

An unusually curvaceous store concept was Fourfoursixsix's winning entry in an invited competition to produce a retail design for drinks brand Diageo. The brief had asked for an innovative design solution to enhance the customer purchasing experience and create a benchmark retail concept within the sector. The brand also wanted a high product density in the small space. Inspired by luxury retail window displays that highlight key products in order to drive brand value and desirability, the designers created a plan that showcases the bottled offerings in sweeping, white curved forms. The design is based on six intersecting circles. The arching shapes differentiate between product types and provide smaller, intimate spaces within the store. Each product group is clearly labelled in black type, while shelves separate the offering within that range, which are also graphically labelled. The result is an elegant gallery-like space, dominated by a ribbon of displays which creates a dynamic line through the space, attracting attention and allowing customers to easily navigate and view the products, which seem to unfold in a natural way. Meanwhile, the flowing forms subtly echo the sinuous shapes of the bottles they contain, and suggest the liquid contents inside them. Lighting also sticks to the curved lines of the display. A dark wood floor accentuates the rounded white lines. For the client, the design was also an effective way of increasing product density in a relatively small space, ensuring that revenue per m² predictions were easily met.

1 The store's walls are a continuous curving ribbon of white display units.
2 The four-sided island form in the centre of the space is also based on arcs.

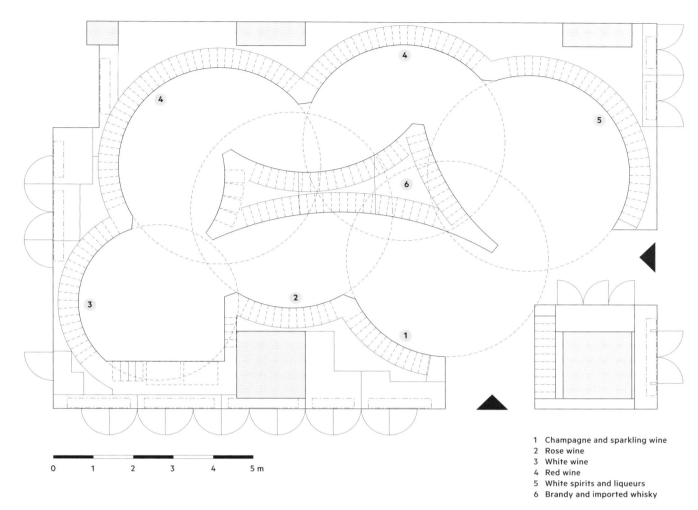

0   1   2   3   4   5 m

1 Champagne and sparkling wine
2 Rose wine
3 White wine
4 Red wine
5 White spirits and liqueurs
6 Brandy and imported whisky

Elliptical elegance frames homely preserves

LA CHAMBRE AUX CONFITURES
BY NOËL DOMINGUEZ ARCHITECTE

WHERE Paris, France WHEN April 2012
CLIENT La Chambre aux Confitures DESIGNER Noël Dominguez Architecte (p.497)
TOTAL FLOOR AREA 30 m² SHOP CONSTRUCTOR Titom
PHOTOS Fred Toulet

A stylish boutique devoted to jam, and only jam? It might sound unlikely, but in the trendy Le Marais district of Paris, Noël Dominguez has created a simple but chic second store for La Chambre aux Confitures, an upmarket purveyor of preserves, and pulled off the feat with aplomb. Starting off with an awkwardly shaped and badly oriented room, the designer decided to restructure it into a finer, and easier to handle, form: the ellipse. The new elliptical profile is elegant and gives instant coherence to the space, helpfully evoking the rounded shape of a jam jar. It also provides eye-pleasing flowing lines for the shelves and cabinets in birch plywood that cover the walls. Here the jams are lovingly presented in their small glass jars, carefully sorted according to colour and demonstrating a jewel-like brightness thanks to some judicious lighting. The display elements are conceived as a cabinet de curiosités, framing the homely products as though they were exotic rarities. In one corner of the store, a copper-fronted screen conceals the stairs and kitchen.

The screen can fold out to allow the store staff to give jam-making demonstrations. The warm copper finish adds to the honey tones of the store, while alluding to the copper pans traditionally used to prepare preserves. Fluted coated-glass lampshades pick up the same hues. As a finishing touch, a minimal but eloquent window display presents several jars of the jam under a bell jar, looking like precious specimens.

1 In the old-fashioned window, an elegant product display is positioned beneath fluted glass lampshades.
2 Giving the interior an oval shape resolved its awkward angles.
3 Birch plywood shelves display the jams as though they are rare collectables.

Cake boxes inspire a simple space for teatime treats

LES BÉBÉS CUPCAKERY
BY JC ARCHITECTURE

2

WHERE Tapei, Taiwan WHEN August 2012
CLIENT Les Bébés Cupcakery DESIGNER JC Architecture (p.496)
TOTAL FLOOR AREA 56 m² SHOP CONSTRUCTOR –
PHOTOS Kevin Wu

A glass house-shaped façade fronts Les Bébés Cupcakery, but into this transparent expanse the designers have inserted a dark, opaque door and a deep-framed window. These details add to the store's mystique, and give the simple act of walking inside a heightened drama. The window-within-a-window showcases the product against a backdrop of more products. Design office JC Architecture wanted to embody the 'purity, elegance and simplicity' of the store's cupcake products, while also creating an interior that would not overshadow the baked goods for sale. The client was also keen to have a different look, one without the French patisserie associations used by other cake shops. For these reasons, a rather minimalist direction was pursued, with none of the sugary colours or cute decorations that are often seen selling similar products. The inspiration, in fact, was not the cupcake itself, but its foldable packaging. The interior was visualised as a series of flat spaces that fold up to form a 3D box to contain the product. The floor, wall and ceiling use the same colour tone to reinforce the idea of a folding box made from one material, while the cutaway details on the walls, used for shelving display and bar counters, extend the concept. The colour palette of grey and yellow is based on the brand colours of Les Bébés Cupcakery, but grey predominates in order to provide a neutral background that helps the products to pop. Yellow, being a stronger colour, is used much more sparingly as an accent.

1   A minimalist interior is an antidote to the
    usual sugary solutions for cake shops.
2   The house-shaped façade of Les Bébés
    Cupcakery is glass – but with a mysterious
    opaque door and deep-framed
    display window.

Folding the box

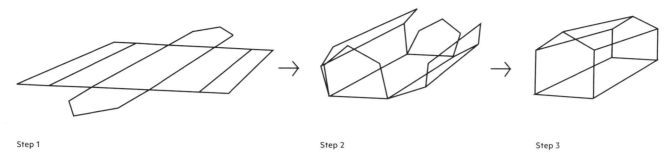

Step 1   Step 2   Step 3

Cut the function we need

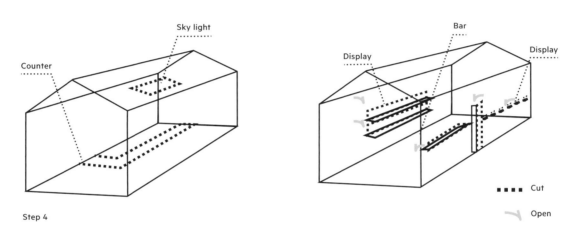

Step 4

4

3 The extraordinary shopfront will attract passers-by, especially at night.
4 A sketch of how the cupcake packing box became the starting point for the interior design.
5 The shelving on the wall shows different samples of the packaging boxes of the shop.

LOBLAWS
BY LANDINI ASSOCIATES

WHERE Toronto, Canada **WHEN** November 2011
CLIENT Loblaws **DESIGNER** Landini Associates (p.496)
TOTAL FLOOR AREA 7900 m² **SHOP CONSTRUCTOR** Icon
PHOTOS Trevor Mein

The brief of Loblaws was to create 'the world's best food store' and so Landini Associates set out to redefine the whole supermarket genre. Firstly, the space – an iconic old ice hockey stadium – was designed as a social hub. Social spaces, including a cookery school and numerous places to eat, were added to the shopping areas to create community appeal (there are few public facilities in the area). Welcoming warmth is expressed by a palette rich in orange and red (the brand colours), and by a giant artwork – a huge blue maple leaf, made from the old stadium chairs and referring to the supermarket's location in Maple Leaf Gardens – that greets visitors at the entrance. A key decision for the designers was to avoid the usual supermarket solution of harsh fluorescent lighting, instead opting for a system that lights the produce and signage, while creating alternating areas of shadow and brightness that humanise the space. Stripping back the walls to their original concrete surfaces suggests authenticity and a sense of history, while wood fixtures

and bright linoleum floors soften the industrial effect. Stainless steel and glossy black and white tiles add to the rich textural mix. Signage is a key element of the project, and the designers used a number of approaches, from utilitarian stencils to wall-covering expanses of colour to moulded concrete to nostalgic fonts evoking the 1950s. Throughout the store, there is much attention to food as theatre, with a giant 6-m-high wall of cheese, extensive glass-topped display counters and market-like expanses of colourful fruit and vegetables.

1 The warm palette is rich in orange and red, the brand colours.
2 & 3 The numerous places to eat in-store adds an interactive aspect and a certain social appeal within the

4 Lighting the products and signage, while allowing some areas to be darker, avoids the bleak atmosphere created by fluorescent light.
5 Huge, colourful graphic signage adds drama but also makes wayfinding simple.
6 The theatrical display of cheese is additionally indentified with large lettering.
7 The blue installation made of chairs – recalling the building's previous incarnation as a stadium – is an eye-catching aspect that greets visitors at the entrance.

Shadows and brightness humanise the space

MERKUR HOHER MARKT
BY BEHF ARCHITECTS

WHERE Vienna, Austria **WHEN** June 2012
CLIENT Merkur Warenhandels AG **DESIGNER** BEHF Architects (p.491)
TOTAL FLOOR AREA 3000 m² **SHOP CONSTRUCTOR** –
PHOTOS Bruno Klomfar

In contrast to most Merkur supermarkets in Austria, the company's subsidiary at Hoher Markt offers food only in the form of fairly exclusive products. Another unusual factor is the location, in one of Vienna's oldest and most historically important areas. For these reasons, BEHF Architects opted for a restrained and sophisticated approach, with the supermarket's new façade integrating itself beautifully into the environment without any of the usual brash supermarket signage or signals. The verdigris copper of the leaf-patterned sunshades BEHF added to the windows subtly evokes the green of Merkur's brand identity, and creates interesting patterns both inside and outside the shop. Inside, the food and drink offering is spread generously over three levels. Attractive products and presentation are intended to encourage the customer to browse the various zones. There are also spaces to linger over a coffee or lunch, before heading home with the shopping: the first floor houses a Dallmayr Café with its specialist tea and coffee assortment, while the second floor has the Kim Kocht restaurant and an extensive wine selection. The levels can be accessed via a staircase and three panoramic elevators, giving a broad overview. The interior uses materials traditional to the area – copper, brass, hand-painted tiles and wood. Floors, walls, ceiling and furniture are primarily in shades of grey, which are selectively complemented by brass, polished steel, matte stone and wood. The subtle qualities of the environment effectively highlight the value of the products and goods on offer.

1   A predominantly grey interior is warmed by touches of wood and bronze, as well as by the colourful food products on sale.
2 & 3   The verdigris copper sunshades on the outside of the building also create eye-catching effects inside the shop.
4   Visitors are tempted in the café and restaurant.

Proof that a supermarket can be chic

MISTRAL
BY STUDIO ARTHUR CASAS

WHERE São Paulo, Brazil WHEN September 2012
CLIENT Mistral DESIGNER Studio Arthur Casas (p.499)
TOTAL FLOOR AREA 126 m² SHOP CONSTRUCTOR Souza Lima
PHOTOS Fernando Guerra

Despite selling mainly via the internet, wine distributor Mistral wanted a real-world showcase – and then in a space of just over 100 m². Studio Arthur Casas rose to the challenge with a curved design that makes the most of the compact interior and manages to fit in all the various functions – sales space, cellar, storage, interactive gallery, reading room and wine-tasting area – that the client desired. The curve of the store creates a path along which these spaces gradually appear, while also conveying the sensuous nature of the product itself. The upper part of the curved pathway is lined by wooden laths, adding organic texture to the interior, while below is a glass area, mirrored above and backlit below, where bottles are suspended to great effect. An interactive table showcases a monthly selection of wines, with sensors underneath each bottle allowing relevant information to be projected onto the table screen, so visitors can learn about the wine's place of origin or watch interviews with the producers. At the back of the store, the wooden laths form a bookshelf, and a Lina Bo Bardi chair invites customers to read next to a double-height wall decorated with more bottles. A tasting space was created in the entresol above, with two tables that can be joined together if needed. Separated from the main corridor by a glass door, a double-height cellar has its own air conditioning system for storing rare wines. Throughout, the bottles are presented in surprising ways, becoming a sort of texture for the store as a whole.

1 A curved 'pathway' invites visitors to explore the store.
2 Bottles emerge surreally from backlit expanses of glass, tempting customers to reach out and touch them.
3 & 4 The vertical design makes the most of the double-height space.

2

Bottles form a textural backdrop for a wine store

OLD AMSTERDAM CHEESE STORE
BY STUDIOMFD

WHERE Amsterdam, the Netherlands **WHEN** April 2013
CLIENT Old Amsterdam **DESIGNER** studiomfd (p.499)
TOTAL FLOOR AREA 95 m² **SHOP CONSTRUCTOR** Jan van Eijken Bouwmaterialen
PHOTOS Johannes van Assem

You can't get more Dutch than cheese. And among Dutch cheeses, Old Amsterdam is a premium brand. So it was logical for Old Amsterdam to open its first (pop-up) flagship store in the Dutch capital – in Amsterdam, in the heart of the city on Dam Square, which is frequented not only by Amsterdammers, of course, but by throngs of tourists for whom cheese makes an ideal souvenir. Studiomfd was asked to design an interior for the temporary store to reflect the current rebranding of Old Amsterdam. The new direction of the brand is all about authenticity, and the honest experience of the cheese, as a quality and traditional product. The store therefore has an appropriately aged and honest appearance. The distressed wooden floor, with its saw-blade texture, stairs and wall covered in classic white marble and the countertop of Belgian granite all testify to traditional standards of quality and to natural, genuine materials. Tourists can savour images of Amsterdam in a vintage poster-style mural showing the landmarks of the city.

The city, in its most traditional aspect, is thus closely associated with the cheese brand. Halfway through the shop, the floor changes into a black and white tiled pattern and the materials become lighter. The lighter furnishings offer a framework for other cheeses, displayed on refrigerated tabletops. And because the store is a pop-up, the interior was built in modular elements so that the entire retail 'set' can be moved easily to a new location.

1 & 2 Natural materials, including a distressed wooden floor, marble wall and granite counter, create an authentic impression in a store selling traditional cheese products.

3 Behind the cash desk, display shelves are topped with mini Amsterdam canal houses.
4 Piles of wrapped cheeses create a market-stall effect.
5 Halfway through the space, a tiled floor introduces a lighter mood for a range of other products.

Going Dutch with a traditional touch

Section AA

Tourists can savour images of Amsterdam

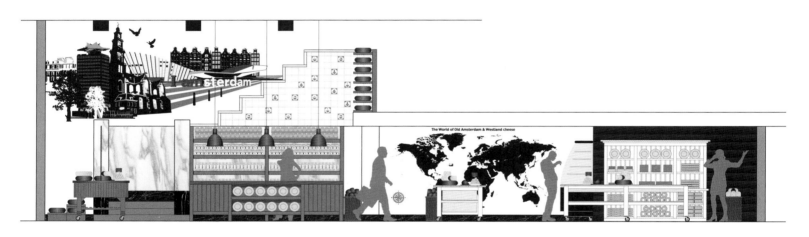

Section BB

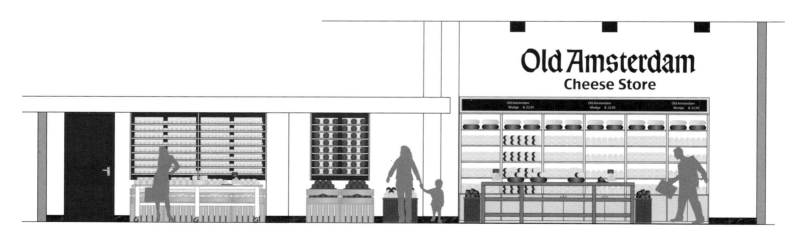

Section CC

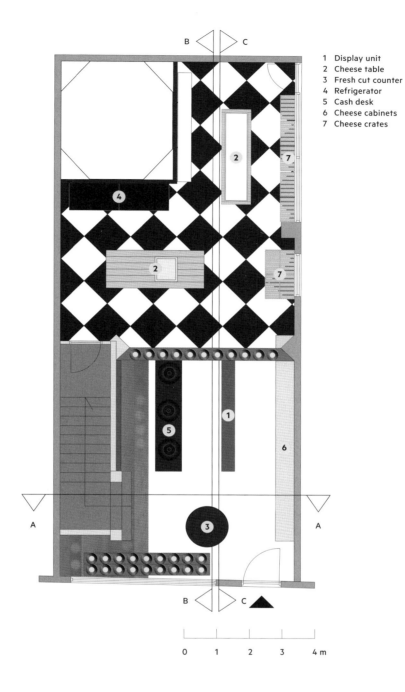

1 Display unit
2 Cheese table
3 Fresh cut counter
4 Refrigerator
5 Cash desk
6 Cheese cabinets
7 Cheese crates

0 1 2 3 4 m

6 A vintage poster-style mural in black and
white depicts the landmarks of the city.

PATCHI TAKHASSUSSI
BY LAUTREFABRIQUE ARCHITECTS

2

WHERE Riyadh, Kingdom of Saudi Arabia **WHEN** July 2012
CLIENT Patchi Saudi Allied **DESIGNER** Lautrefabrique Architects (p.497)
TOTAL FLOOR AREA 707 m² **SHOP CONSTRUCTORS** Dal Al Arabia and Unidecor
PHOTOS Luc Boegly

For its longtime client, the Middle Eastern luxury chocolate company Patchi, design studio Lautrefabrique remodelled a neo-classical villa into an impressive confectionery showcase. A graphic new façade, a huge screen of white aluminium composite panels studded with luminous monograms, was designed to catch motorists' eyes from afar, maximizing the roadside location. Two display windows below this flag-like element hint at the goodies inside. The interior, with its double-height ceilings, feels luxuriously cool and spacious. White floors create a dematerialised, floaty effect, while sumptuous materials, including ebony, Corian, black and white painted glass and mirror add a feeling of precious exclusivity to the numerous displays. Oak features prominently among the materials, being used for a long sculptural display element with delicately ridged edges which sweeps sinuously through the ground floor, and for a blossoming fan-like canopy on the first floor, which shelters a more intimate lounge-like area.

On the walls, transparent shelves lined with jewel like pieces of crystal and glass alternate with ebony displays profusely covered with bowls and trays of tempting chocolate delicacies. Combinations of black and white and dark and light add graphic definition to the space. The rich woods in a variety of shades suggest the range of chocolates on offer. A panoramic elevator transports visitors to the pastel-tinted, more intimate space of the first floor, which is dedicated to baby and wedding gifts. Behind the scenes is the 118 m² area given over to workshops and services, as well as an attic warehouse.

1 The first task concerned the external appearance of the premises. Removing the aspect of the neo-classical villa in favour of an eye-catching façade.
2 Various woods, including ebony, make appropriate displays for chocolates.
3 A sinuously ribbed sculptural element in oak sweeps through the ground floor.

An opulent setting for chocolate luxuries

4 A fan-like oak canopy shelters a more intimate lounge-like area on the first floor.

5 White floors and stairs dematerialise the space and give a floaty effect.

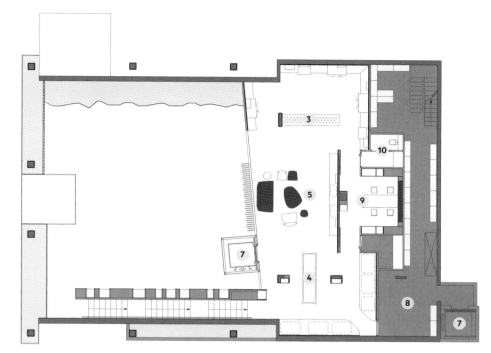

1 Retail area
2 Display units
3 Baby gift area
4 Wedding gift area
5 Lounge
6 Cash desk
7 Elevator
8 Back of the house
9 Office
10 Toilet

Mezzanine

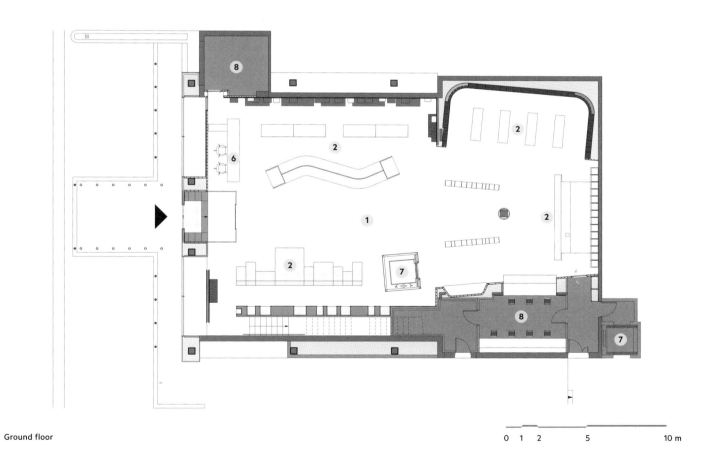

Ground floor

0 1 2   5   10 m

SPRINKLES ICE CREAM
BY A L M PROJECT

WHERE Beverly Hills, United States **WHEN** May 2012
CLIENT Sprinkles Ice Cream **DESIGNER** a l m project (p.490)
TOTAL FLOOR AREA 106 m² **SHOP CONSTRUCTOR** –
PHOTOS Trevor Dixon

All-American associations – namely, the traditional soda shop – inspired a new venture for well-known US cupcake brand Sprinkles. For Sprinkles Ice Cream, a l m project evoked customers' childhood memories while updating the nostalgic soda-shop image with clean minimal lines. The austere white façade sets the tone: it consists of metal shields with a laser-cut perforation that suggests pastry doilies and lace tablecloths. An illuminated cone logo and a pin-mounted red script announcing 'ice cream' signal the store and its contents. Inside, light filtered by the façade creates beautiful patterns. Expressing the creamy quality of ice cream, the interior is defined by the smooth, sculpted shapes of the main material, white Corian, which is used for both the round counter centrepiece and the walls. Accentuated by the pattern of the penny tile base and floor, and red perforated metal sliders mounted service-side of the display cases, the built-in cabinetry fully integrates both equipment and product. Above the centrepiece, a light rotunda

features a red text – Thomas Jefferson's original ice cream recipe, evoking further heritage associations. 'We chose white to honor the organic dairy used as the main ingredient of Sprinkles Ice Cream, and the white Corian that is simultaneously soft and very, very crisp', says designer Andrea Lenardin Madden. 'I think smooth was really the main quality that I was looking for.' The pops of red in the interior echo the colour of Sprinkles' trademark red-velvet waffle cones, which she also used for the logo of the store. The designers won a Los Angeles Design Award and best of year merit in *Interior Design* magazine for their work on the store.

1 The façade consists of metal shields with a laser-cut perforation that suggests pastry doilies and lace tablecloths.
2 & 3 Red accents enliven the all-white store – a reference to Sprinkles' unique red-velvet cones.
4 A round centrepiece and counter is topped by a light rotunda featuring the original American ice cream recipe by Thomas Jefferson.

2

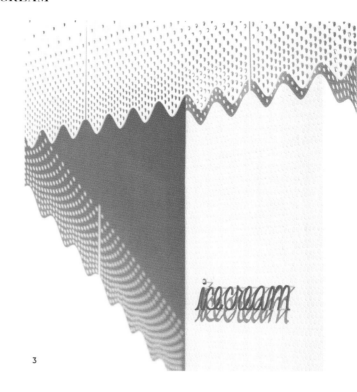

3

A contemporary take on the all-American soda shop

4

SWEET ALCHEMY
BY KOIS ASSOCIATED ARCHITECTS

3

WHERE Athens, Greece **WHEN** January 2012
CLIENT Stelios Parliaros **DESIGNER** Kois Associated Architects (p.496)
TOTAL FLOOR AREA 96 m² **SHOP CONSTRUCTOR** Korfiatis Kostas
PHOTOS George Sfakianakis

When Stelios Parliaros, who is considered to be the best pastry chef in Greece, asked Kois Associated Architects to design his new store, he specified that the space should be as far as possible from the usual cake and sweet shop interpretations. The designers responded with a light-filled store based on the concept of alchemy – 'a notion associated with darkness mystery and mysticism', according to the designer Stelios Kois. Wrapping the shop in a transparent, punctured bronze façade was the first step in creating the illusion of a 'chamber of treasures and forbidden fruits'. The floor-to-ceiling bronze grid, which is repeated throughout the store, contains jars and containers in which sweet treats appear beautifully illuminated as though they were the precious ingredients for magical potions. Still more confections appear to advantage in open display counters, each one with its own set of shiny scales for weighing the tempting products on show. Natural materials like wood, copper, bronze and iron were chosen throughout the interior for their authenticity and alchemical associations. The various displays, meanwhile, cleverly mimic the 'enigmatic devices, rare distillations, crystals and potions' of the alchemist's trade, giving an impression of richness, colour and abundance. The bronze shelves also ensure a high degree of transparency. 'Light and shadow change throughout the day giving the space a unique atmosphere every moment', says Kois. 'Serenity is followed by tension and drama.'

1 A floor-to-ceiling bronze grid forms a transparent façade.
2 Natural materials like wood, copper, bronze and iron suggest authenticity.
3 Glass jars and containers suggest an alchemist's store.

Sweet treats transformed by the magic of light

4 Bronze grid shelving displays products
   and diffuses light.
5 Daylight effects are an important part
   of the store experience.
6 Open displays create a feeling of variety
   and abundance.
7 Candy colours are set off by a warm,
   neutral background.

Reinventing the teahouse as a take-away concept

T2B
BY LANDINI ASSOCIATES

WHERE Sydney, Australia **WHEN** July 2013
CLIENT T2 tea **DESIGNER** Landini Associates (p.496)
TOTAL FLOOR AREA 55 m² **SHOP CONSTRUCTOR** Faculty Shopfitting
PHOTOS Sharrin Rees

A wholly new take on the teahouse, T2B is a fresh and fragrant retail concept devoted to the time-honoured brew. Selling an adventurous range of teas to take away, or to enjoy on the premises, T2B is the second brand of T2, and the first in a planned series of take-out points. The store also sells a small range of food items, plus 200 kinds of packaged tea. Landini Associates created the interior, which rethinks teahouse conventions for a new generation. A large cast concrete bar showcases the making of tea in a theatrical manner and reflects the experimental approach – the store allows customers to design and blend their own brews. In order to create more drama, an angled mirrored ceiling was installed over the bar, and the signage is made of extruded concrete letters surrounded by a huge splash of expressionist paint. Other features include the tea library at the rear of the store, made from black oxidised steel shelving and canisters. This dark palette allows T2's trademark orange packaging to stand out under the intense lighting, in glowing shades as rich and warm

as the beverage itself. Creating an additional zone in the space, a small steel 'dry bar' ledge acts both as a place to stop, drink and chat and a rail to protect customers from the level changes at the site's threshold. Finally, two small back of house areas are hidden behind a vertical projection screen, displaying film of seas and forests and a massive secret pivoting door of tea.

1 A massive cast concrete bar makes a theatrical focal point in the store.
2 An angled mirrored ceiling over the bar creates more drama, while the black shelves on the side walls frame T2's glowing orange packaging, which evokes the colour of tea.

WEIN & WAHRHEIT
BY IPPOLITO FLEITZ GROUP

WHERE Sulzbach, Germany **WHEN** November 2011
CLIENT Weinkellerei Höchst **DESIGNER** Ippolito Fleitz Group (p.495)
TOTAL FLOOR AREA 80 m² **SHOP CONSTRUCTOR** Planausbau
PHOTOS Zooey Braun

Charged with displaying over 600 different wines and spirits, delicatessen items and gifts within a space of just 80 m², Ippolito Fleitz completely encased this wine store's two long walls in shelving units. Made from white lacquered and brushed oak, these curve sensuously to meet the rear wall. Their 501 separate compartments are strictly organised for an elegantly homogenous look which is broken only by square shelving elements in a fresh green. At the centre of the store, a checkout counter, an elevated table for wine tasting and a packaging station are grouped together, with three additional presentation units between them and the wall. Their cubic geometry emphasises the material interplay of white laminate and bleached oak. The central units stand on an oblong-shaped epoxy resin-coated concrete floor. Outside this zone, the floor is made from contrasting rough oak boards. The ceiling echoes this pattern, with a shimmering canopy of 150 hand-blown glass vessels in four different shades occupying the centre section.

LED lighting illuminates two-thirds of the glasses. They are framed by a mirrored border which seems to increase the height of the space and multiplies the already large selection of wines. Glass and oak are the dominant materials in the space, both chosen to reference the world of wine – wine bottles and wine glasses, oak casks and cork oak. Their use results in a sensual ambience designed to tempt shoppers to indulge. A new corporate identity was also developed to reflect the store design.

1 White lacquered and brushed oak shelves present the wines as though they are books in a library.
2 The canopy of glasses is an attention-grabber.

365

3 The warm, glowing canopy of glasses
offsets the very rational bottle display.
4 Good organization means that 600-plus
products can be displayed effectively in
a compact space.

The 501 separate compartments are strictly organised

4

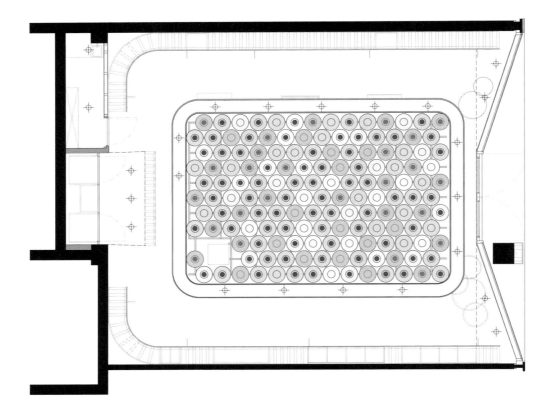

5

◄ C

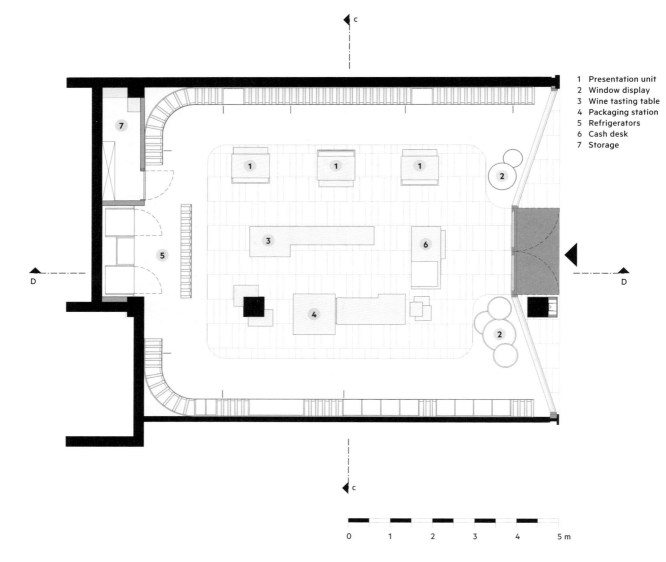

1 Presentation unit
2 Window display
3 Wine tasting table
4 Packaging station
5 Refrigerators
6 Cash desk
7 Storage

D ► ---- D ►

◄ C

0   1   2   3   4   5 m

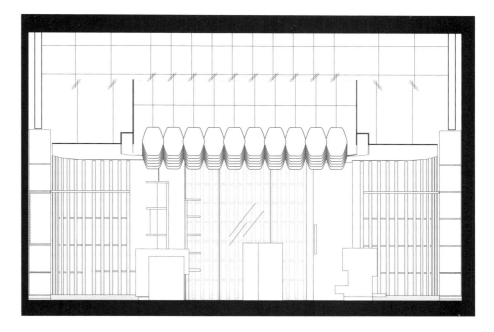

Section CC

Compartment chic and a real glass ceiling

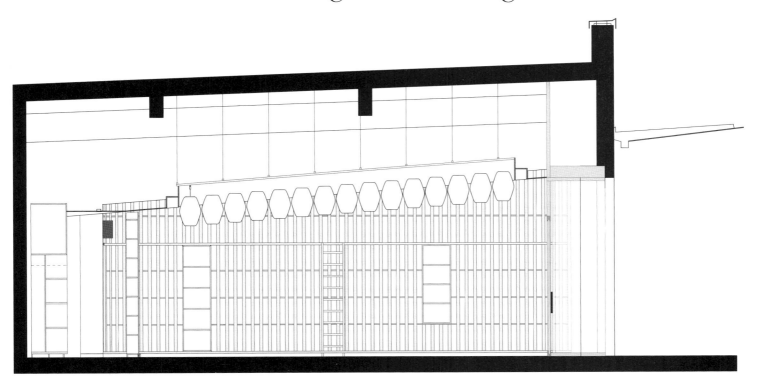

Section DD

5 A plan showing the colour scheme for the installation of glasses.
6 Hanging the 150 glass vessels to the ceiling.

FURN
AND
PROD

370

TURE
HOME
UCTS

371

AS GOOD AS NEW
BY i29 INTERIOR ARCHITECTS

WHERE Amsterdam, the Netherlands **WHEN** October 2012
CLIENT As Good As New **DESIGNER** i29 interior architects (p.495)
TOTAL FLOOR AREA 30 m² **SHOP CONSTRUCTOR** –
PHOTOS Ewout Huibers

Is grey the new black? Well it is at i29 interior architects' pop-up store As Good as New. Following on from the designers' super-successful Gummo office project, which gathered together lots of discarded pieces of furniture and sprayed them all grey, the i29 team decided to create a range of similar pieces for sale to the public. The resulting grey furnishings were then displayed as in installation-cum-store, As Good As New, in Amsterdam's arty SPRMRKT. To create the collection required a lot of furniture hunting. All the used and abused finds were sourced locally via Marktplaats (the Dutch answer to eBay) and vintage markets. Everything was then spray-painted with polyurea hotspray to conform with the matte-finish, battleship-grey colour theme. From old Chesterfield sofas to ancient Mac computers and unlovely ornaments, every piece was given the same treatment. Together, they form a surreal 'living room'. 'Selecting these items, was an adventure in itself,' says i29 interior architects' co-founder Jaspar Jansen. 'We selected quite outspoken and weird items. The collection of second-hand furniture in one finish becomes a powerful sculptural image, it has an alienating effect.' Adds his partner Jeroen Dellensen: 'The funny thing is that especially the "off" pieces, the pieces that are normally rejected in modern interiors, become the most interesting. But the message of this work is mostly about giving attention to re-used furniture. We are giving these items a second life. And in the case of the more vulgar pieces we've even up-cycled them aesthetically.' And probably inspired many people to try it at home, too.

1 Battleship grey paint unites an odd collection of second-hand furniture and gives it a sculptural presence.
2 The designers sourced the items locally via auction sites and vintage markets, hoping to raise awareness of the potential of recycled furniture.

BACCARAT
BY RAFAEL DE CÁRDENAS / ARCHITECTURE AT LARGE

WHERE New York, United States **WHEN** June 2013
CLIENT Baccarat **DESIGNER** Rafael de Cárdenas / Architecture at Large (p.498)
TOTAL FLOOR AREA 445 m² **SHOP CONSTRUCTOR** JRM Construction Management
PHOTOS Floto + Warner

On the eve of its 250-year anniversary, French crystal manufacturer Baccarat commissioned Rafael de Cárdenas' office, Architecture at Large, to create a high-visibility outpost for the brand in Manhattan. The designer set out to underscore the brand's high-end heritage while underlining Baccarat's modern aspirations as a contemporary international lifestyle brand. Combining classical and contemporary styles achieved the objective of attracting a younger, broader audience, without alienating the brand's traditional following. Baccarat's traditional items mingle in the shop with its edgier, newer offerings. The storefront, fittingly enough, is a double-height etched glass façade that, while sporting a modern geometrical pattern, suggests traditional artisanship. Inside the store, a brushed Nordic black granite floor is combined with geometric strips of Macassar ebony and mirror-lined walls – luxury materials used in a fresh but still elegant way. Both the entrance area and jewellery bar feature video panels which connect customers with Baccarat's 250-year history. A shimmering collection of chandeliers lights up the entrance space, showcasing the brand's crystal expertise and creating stunning lighting effects in the store. An 'icon wall' composed of interlocking Nordic black granite niches displays the larger products. As customers move on through the store, they encounter a variety of equally luxurious spaces. The 'lounge' room, with its diamond-patterned hardwood floor and tufted grey suede walls, frames Baccarat's decorative and novelty pieces. In the 'dining room', a display of stemware and barware sparkles beneath a trio of ornate chandeliers, while the 'lighting room' with its dark, yet reflective, silver–black plaster walls bring the bright and refractive crystals to the foreground.

1 The façade of etched glass bears a contemporary geometric motif.
2 At the store's entrance, a cluster of brushed Nordic black granite and Macassar ebony pedestals make opulent display.

3 In these coloured section-elevations you can see the store is divided into four zones.
4 Display shelving in polished stainless steel and glass was custom designed by Architecture at Large, while all treatments include Macassar ebony, tufted Maharam 'suede' walls, and custom Venetian plaster.

5 White-gold leaf displays punctuate the space and highlight the brand's signature and seasonal objects.
6 In the entryway, a grand double height space strung with crystal chandeliers is enveloped by faceted Macassar Ebony interspersed with reflective mirror strips.

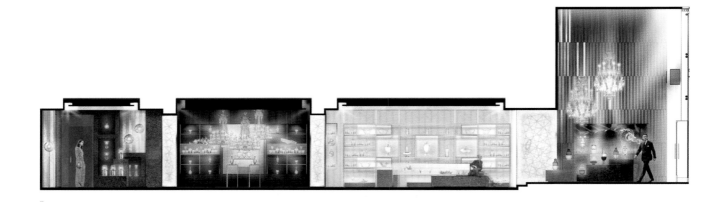

3

1 Jewellery area
2 Tableware area
3 Lighting area
4 Lounge
5 Storage
6 Toilet

A light approach to luxury

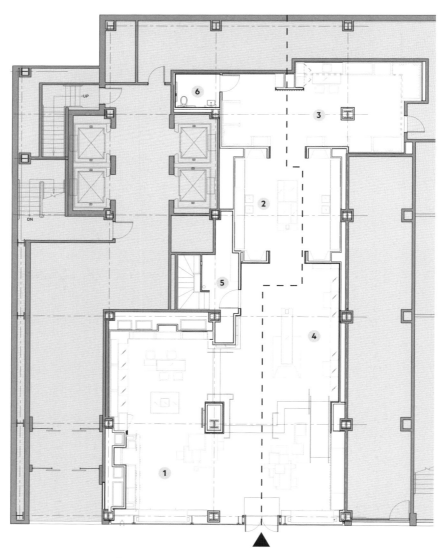

BORK
BY IPPOLITO FLEITZ GROUP

2

WHERE Moscow, Russia **WHEN** August 2011
CLIENT Bork **DESIGNER** Ippolito Fleitz Group (p.495)
TOTAL FLOOR AREA 215 m² **SHOP CONSTRUCTOR** Ganter Interior
PHOTOS Zooey Braun

For Bork, which produces high-end domestic appliances for the Russian market, Ippolito Fleitz came up with a boutique concept borrowed from the fashion industry. Spacious presentation areas are used to underscore the quality and individuality of the products. Meanwhile, the sales element is pushed discreetly into the background as other elements – such as a testing counter, home accessories in floor-to-ceiling shelves and incised patterns in the wooden panelling – come to the fore, creating a cosy, home-like feel, thereby portraying Bork appliances as the natural companions of an upmarket lifestyle. The interior of the flagship store uses a range of natural materials. Stone flooring, anthracite display units and a brushed-metal sales counter combine with walnut wall panels with a geometrical pattern carved along their tops, adding a warm, domestic touch. All the fittings and units are strictly geometrical. Product display accentuates each item's form by placing the appliances against bright, white backgrounds framed by dark wood. In the centre of the space, further products are presented on anthracite pedestals. An LED band lights these from beneath, so they appear to float. An additional focal point is the light cube on the ceiling, which is encased within metal panels. A dynamic colour gradient printed on the glass inside it is Bork's corporate colour. The intense orange hue defines the emotional centre of the space and functions as a strong visual sign, visible from the outside. The colour is also reflected in illuminated light cubes, which provide a complementary contrast to the display units.

1 An orange light cube presides over the space adding colour and drawing the different elements together.
2 A brushed metal cash desk adds to the range of natural materials

3 Displaying products against brightly
lit white backgrounds framed in wood
accentuates their form.

1 Retail area
2 Display units
3 Window displays
4 Cash desk
5 Back of the house
6 Storage

The boutique concept is borrowed from the fashion industry

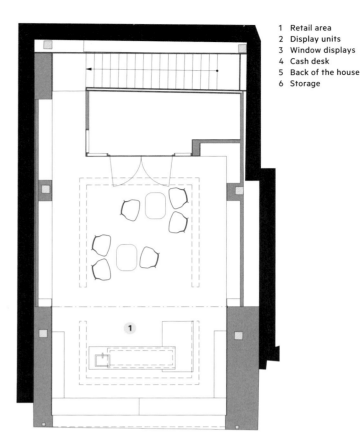

First floor

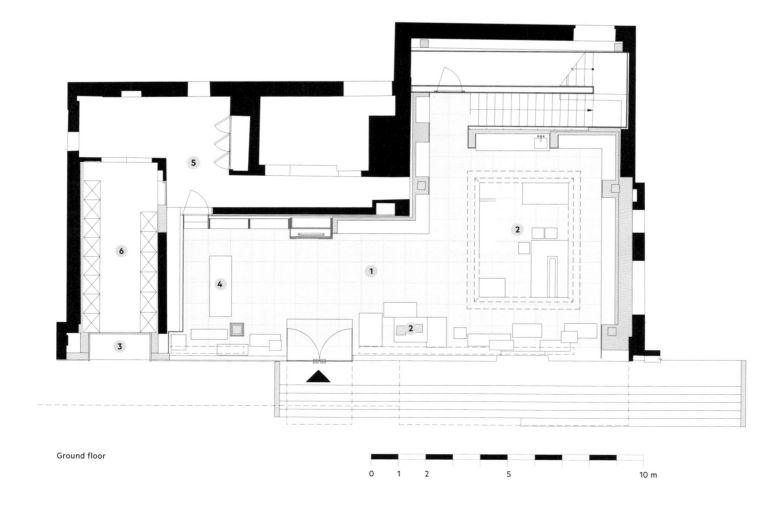

Ground floor

0 1 2   5   10 m

DESIGN REPUBLIC'S DESIGN COLLECTIVE
BY NERI&HU DESIGN AND RESEARCH OFFICE

WHERE Shanghai, China **WHEN** April 2012
CLIENT Design Republic **DESIGNER** Neri&Hu Design and Research Office (p.497)
TOTAL FLOOR AREA 7230 m² **SHOP CONSTRUCTOR** –
PHOTOS Shen Zhonghai

For avant-garde furniture retailer Design Republic, Neri&Hu explored the wraparound aesthetic both inside and out for its new Design Collective location on the outskirts of Shanghai. The design duo completely transformed the existing building that they inherited (and were not allowed to demolish) by wrapping it in opaque, carbon-fibre panels, printed with a graphic theme. Not only does this enigmatic new covering obliterate the previous identity of the structure; it also creates an introverted spatial platform for the furniture store inside. Both visually and experientially, all the visitor's attention is focused on the interior landscape. The main entrance is marked by what the designers call the 'steel funnel', a passage which serves as a transitional element from the urban context outside to the shop space within. Creating a sense of expectation, walking through this long entry tube also fosters a feeling of arrival when visitors find themselves in the three-storey exhibition hall where their introverted odyssey begins. The interior is

wrapped too, but in this case by a partly closed wooden staircase that runs around the main exhibition space, leading the visitor through all the multiple levels of the display. The staircase allows the furniture exhibits to be experienced from varying vantage points, in interesting voyeuristic snippets. As the visitor climbs higher through the gallery levels, the journey is given a new angle by the seven large openings in the roof which allow daylight to flood the exhibition space, relieving the rather claustrophobic atmosphere generated by the introverted displays.

1 An existing building is wrapped in a graphic carbon-fibre skin.
2 Inside, the corkscrew staircase provides a changing series of perspectives.

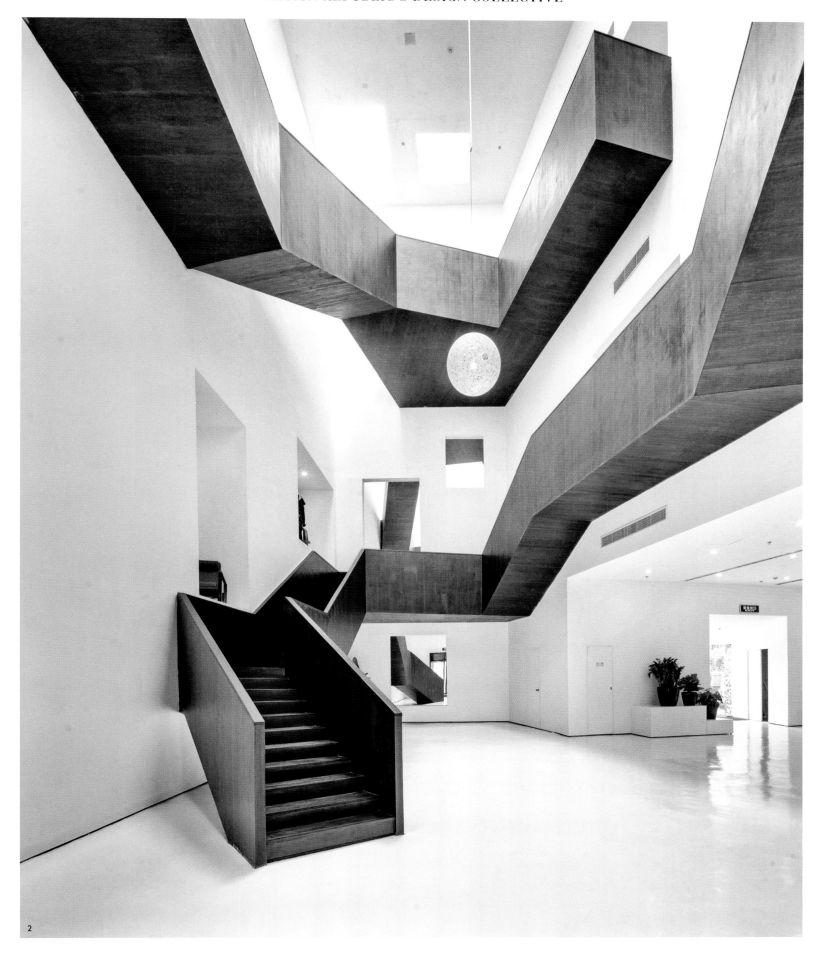

2

Variations on a wraparound theme

3 An intensely introverted interior throws
   all its emphasis on the items on display.
4 & 5 The use of white, particularly for the
   floor, dematerialises the space, so that
   the furniture almost seems to float.

A carbon-fibre wrapper covers the exterior and creates the interior experience

5

KOM
BY 2KUL INTERIOR DESIGN

WHERE Milicz, Poland **WHEN** July 2013
CLIENTS Edyta and Tomasz Defratyka **DESIGNER** 2kul Interior Design (p.490)
TOTAL FLOOR AREA 1710 m² **SHOP CONSTRUCTOR** Metalplast Consulting
PHOTOS Adam Marecik

A cultural centre that sells Christmas decorations? In the case of KOM, a multifunctional creative centre offering various facilities and workshops for individuals and groups, and both adults and children, that's not as strange as it sounds. Magdalena Urban and Agnieszka Koszutska of 2kul designed KOM based on the inspiration of the past: specifically, the history of the 1930s building as a factory producing seasonal baubles for the Christmas tree. The decorations made Milicz famous, and they have now become the key to making the new, multifunctional space attractive, while creating a link with the past by offering them for sale to a new generation. The complex consists of various facilities, including a café with space designed for children, workshop spaces and a conference room. But the star of the show is undoubtedly the so-called Chamber of Balls, a space which sells and exhibits the glittery Christmas decorations. Before buying your own, you can admire a unique collection of baubles made by the factory – some 6400 models, which were hand-crafted

here on the premises. The Chamber of Balls is lined with display cases in jewel-bright colours, each one with a quirky window framing the baubles collected inside. A sequence of freestanding display walls, each one a rich Christmassy red, occupies the centre of the space. They are studded with large balls made of dozens of smaller Christmas balls, and above them disco balls are suspended, increasing the festive effect. If this room fails to fill you with seasonal spirit, then you must have been *Scrooged*.

1 In the dark shell of the Chamber of Balls, bright display cases showcase the sparkling baubles and inspire customers to buy their own.
2 A sequence of red display walls is studded with balls made from dozens of small Christmas decorations.
3 Bright colours and rounded forms recur in other areas of the culture centre, like at the café.

Putting culture
into a Christmas bauble store

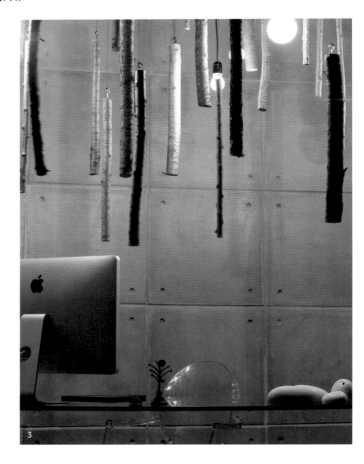

Raw nature riffs for art and craft objects

MDECOR
BY SERGEY MAKHNO

WHERE Kiev, Ukraine OPENING March 2012
CLIENT Sergey Makhno DESIGNER Sergey Makhno (p.498)
TOTAL FLOOR AREA 55 m² SHOP CONSTRUCTOR Sergey Makhno
PHOTOS Andrey Avdeenko

Selling design ceramics, sculptures, photographs and paintings old and new, MDecor is the manifestation of the long-cherished dream of architect Sergey Makhno and his wife Vladyslava to open a gallery space for stylish decorative objects and artworks by Ukrainian artisans, designers and artists. Naturally, Makhno designed the interior himself, basing it on a concept that he describes as 'neutral artistic minimalism with eastern notes'. The space is given a raw, natural look, thanks to concrete walls and floor and an abundance of untreated timber. Clusters of solid tree-trunk sections (they come from Zakarpattya silver fir trees), stripped of their bark, make impressive displays, and the sales desk is simply a sheet of glass atop four massive wooden blocks. Austere wooden storage cupboards with concrete tops line the walls, while above them on one side are rusty iron cubes used as a shelving system. Makhno designed all these, as he did the wire-cage ceiling lamps and the wooden branch installation that hovers over the table. Made

from cherry twigs, just one of the suspended elements is coloured celadon green, symbolising the uniqueness of the products for sale in the store. Behind the sales desk, decorative concrete panels conceal a storage space to the back of the store. Earthy and evocative, the materials used suggest authenticity, paralleling the honest handmade qualities of the works on show. Aside from the items on sale, there is little colour in the store, but the very restricted palette sets off the often subtle shades and finishes of the craft items on display.

1, 2 & 3 Concrete, untreated wood and rusty metal add up to a fitting display environment for the craft items on display.
4 Zakarpattya silver fir tree-trunks are used in clusters as displays, while an installation of cherry twigs hangs from the ceiling in this back-to-nature interior.
5 The austere wooden storage cupboards with concrete tops lining the walls create balance, while lighting brings materials and objects to life.

1

THE WOOD SPACE
BY HOUSEHOLD

WHERE London, United Kingdom **WHEN** January 2013
CLIENT Havwoods **DESIGNER** Household (p.495)
TOTAL FLOOR AREA 185 m² **SHOP CONSTRUCTOR** Unispace
PHOTOS Philip Vile and Steve White

Asked to create a showroom with the 'wow factor' for wooden-flooring brand Havwoods, Household came up with the idea of 'The Wood Space' – a showroom as destination, with pre-booked appointments designed to make a visit feel like an exciting event. A sense of arrival is conveyed by the scarlet 'timber ribbon' that guides visitors through the entrance and into an interesting, angular, wood-lined space. The interior design uses Havwoods' wood products almost exclusively, so that visitors encounter them as it were 'in action'. Customers see the products, touch them and stand on them. A major challenge was to feature the entire range of over 400 products, so Household designed a bespoke storage system that was hidden within the panelled walls. Each panel is made from a different wood, and once pushed it releases seamlessly to reveal the possibilities of that particular finish. This solution allowed the showroom to house 70 more samples than initially specified by the brief. The space is multifunctional, with showcase areas and intimate spaces for discussing orders that can be flexibly transformed to suit the audience. A series of interior stages and platforms with drop-in panels ensure that the space can be tailored to client specifications before they arrive, giving them a clearer idea of how the product looks in context. This kit also means that the space can be used to host design-related events, not only impressing potential clients but also ensuring that the space generates a buzz.

1 The Wood Space creates a sense of excitement thanks to a dynamic, angular design with pops of bright colour.
2 The interior design uses Havwoods' wood products almost exclusively.

3 The bespoke storage system, hidden within the wood-panelled walls, accommodates a huge range of samples.
4 The white Corian catwalk in centre of space acts as a tool for display of samples with clients, but also serves as additional storage and seating.
5, 6, 7 & 8 Showcase areas and intimate spaces for discussing orders alternate and can be easily transformed to suit individual visitors.

Putting the wow factor into wooden flooring

1 Entrance corridor
2 Timber stage
3 Catwalk
4 Product gallery storage
5 Sales desk
6 Meeting room
7 Kitchen
8 Elevator

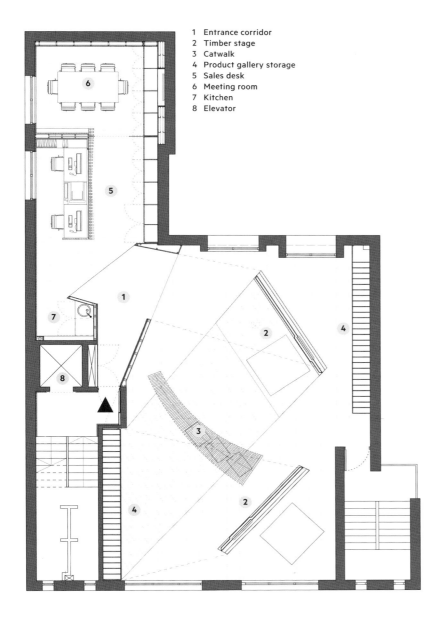

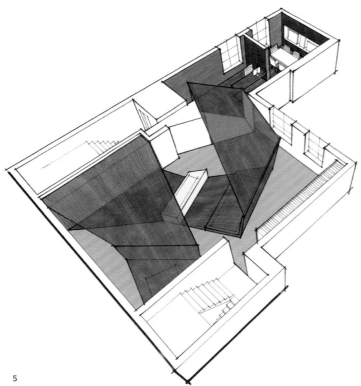

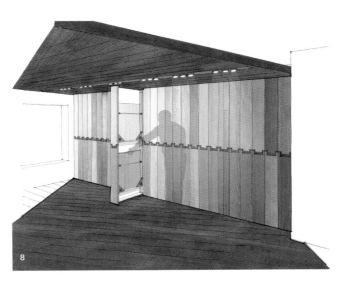

XYL
BY TONERICO

WHERE Tokyo, Japan **WHEN** August 2012
CLIENT XYL **DESIGNER** Tonerico (p.499)
TOTAL FLOOR AREA 120 m² **SHOP CONSTRUCTOR** –
PHOTOS Satoshi Asakawa

Families flock to children's furniture store XYL, not only for its furnishings, which are made from Japanese natural wood, but also for its collection of small school-related items, such as the iconic ransel (traditional school rucksack). Called in to design the store, Tonerico took its cue for the interior from the XYL product offering, which is unusually simple for children's goods and intended to be sustainable – one of the brand's aims is to promote forestry in Japan. Bearing this in mind, the designers decided that 'the space should not be for instant consumption but should be designed to express universality over time', says the Tonerico's Ken Kimizuka. The 'skeleton space' is white, with lace curtains and indirect lighting softening the effect. Within this, the designers created an organic egg-shaped space in Japanese natural (flooring) wood, with the areas in between this oval and the white box containing it used for display and to house the office area. 'The space has no edges and this provides a sense of security as if one were inside a nest', says Kimizuka.

A small house is placed in the centre and used as a drawing space. A series of branching tree silhouettes in wood form the display furniture for the small items and ransels. The tree forms heighten the contrast between the natural 'nest' and the inorganic white, rectilinear frame that surrounds it. 'The intent behind the open space structure was to express kindness, making something of a place for a new start for children', says Kimizuka.

1 An intriguing structure-within-a-structure lures kids and their families inside.
2 The design is based on the contrast between the white frame and the wooden oval it contains.
3 A small white house in the centre of the wooden space functions as a drawing station for visiting kids.

Fantasy without fuss for a kids' furniture store

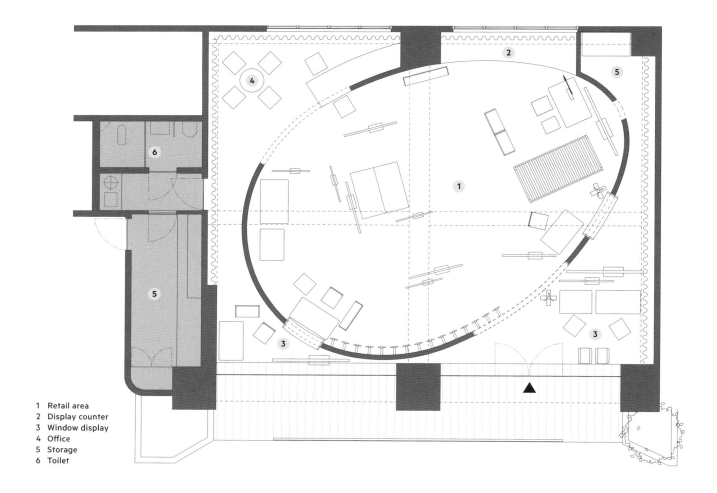

1 Retail area
2 Display counter
3 Window display
4 Office
5 Storage
6 Toilet

The intent of the space was to 'express kindness'

4 Materials and approach were both dictated by the principal product: natural wooden furniture for children, with school satchels an extra product line.
5 Tree-like structures create a playful, organic atmosphere.

MOBI

400

LITY

401

Making an art of automotive 'infotainment'

AMG PERFORMANCE CENTER
BY KAUFFMANN THEILIG & PARTNER
AND ATELIER MARKGRAPH

WHERE Beijing, China WHEN April 2012
CLIENT Mercedes-AMG DESIGNERS Kauffmann Theilig & Partner (p.496) and Atelier Markgraph (p.491)
TOTAL FLOOR AREA 380 m² SHOP CONSTRUCTOR Ambrosius Exhibition Design and Building
PHOTOS Andreas Keller Fotografie

With the inauguration of the AMG Performance Center in Beijing Sanlitun, Mercedes-AMG is breaking new ground. This is AMG's first stand-alone-store worldwide, as opposed to being integrated as a shop-in-shop system in a Mercedes-Benz dealership. The architectural design of the showroom was realised by Kauffmann Theilig & Partner, and the communication and media design by Atelier Markgraph. It occupies two levels and approximately 380 m² of floor space in a luxury mall. It aims to 'infotain' visitors about the world of AMG, its latest high-performance vehicles and their technological feats. In an exclusive lounge area on the upper floor, generous seating invites customers to relax and enjoy the exclusive brand atmosphere. The design concept of the AMG Performance Center focuses on the idea of a personal journey. On the way from the garage, where numerous AMG vehicles are available for a test drive, a trail of red downlights leads the way to the AMG exhibition on the entry level. A reduced but luxurious materials palette supports the concept of quality and elegance in the showroom: the ground-floor walls are clad in white high-gloss glass, with plenty of modern video and audio technology adding a multimedia buzz and reinforcing the brand message. Floors of shiny black granite create a strong contrast to the gleaming white of the back walls. From the street, the showroom makes use of a bold long-range effect through its high-visibility presentation window complete with rotating hub. During the day, passers-by can feast their eyes on star vehicles and themed events, while at night the rotating vehicle move in time with a choreography of light and sound.

1 The showroom exclusively respesents AMG products, highlighting the brand's pioneering role in design and technology.
2 Dynamic lighting was a key factor in the presentation of the high-performance brand (light planning: TLD Planungsgruppe).

3 The material palette features white high-gloss glass on the walls, plus floors and stairs of shiny black granite and dynamic LED light strips.
4 On the upper level of the space, a lounge area invites visitors to relax and absorb the atmosphere.
5 Modern video, audio technology and dramatic display spaces convey the brand message and adds multimedia excitement. The exhibition design and graphics were created by Totems Communication.
6 In the garage, top-spec AMG vehicles are available for a test drive.

A reduced but luxurious materials palette adds elegance in the showroom

Mobile fixtures for a feel-free brand

BUGABOO BRAND STORE
BY ...,STAAT CREATIVE AGENCY

WHERE Amsterdam, the Netherlands WHEN March 2013
CLIENT Bugaboo DESIGNER ...,staat creative agency (p.490)
TOTAL FLOOR AREA 150 m² SHOP CONSTRUCTOR J.G. Timmer
PHOTOS Ewout Huibers

'Not just a shop, but a workshop too' – that's the message behind mobility brand Bugaboo's first owned and operated brandstore on Amsterdam's Keizersgracht canal. The shop is part studio and part station – it's the place to try out and configurate the complete range of Bugaboo products. The space is divided over two floors, a main ground-floor shop area and an entresol above it. Entering the store, visitors immediately see the whole Bugaboo product and accessory range, displayed on a curved, 17-m-long wall cabinet. The product displays, like the simple counter, are made from white steel frames on chrome wheels, emphasising on Bugaboo's mobility brand values. As designer Jochem Leegstra says, 'By simply adding chrome wheels to all the freestanding displays, we not only emphasise Bugaboo's philosophy – freedom of movement – we also create a totally flexible store.' Behind the counter, a utility wall displays various stroller spare parts, so that any owner can get their 'vehicle' repaired on the

spot. And for Bugaboo newbies, the rear of the store contains a large 'product family' display which shows all the stroller models, which can be customised by the accessories in the long wall cabinet. A main focus in the store is the sleek and shiny mirror staircase with a Bugaboo-red interior, which leads up to the second floor. This has a more intimate look and feel, giving the space a creative, homey atmosphere. A large table here is the perfect place for meetings to discuss your very own stroller configuration.

1 Warhol flowers as wallpaper cheerfully welcome Bugaboo's visitors.
2 At the rear of the store, the entire Bugaboo collection of strollers is displayed.
3 Bugaboo's first brandstore occupies the ground floor and entresol of an Amsterdam canal house.
4 The mirror staircase is a feature of the space. Beside it is an array of Bugaboo spare parts.

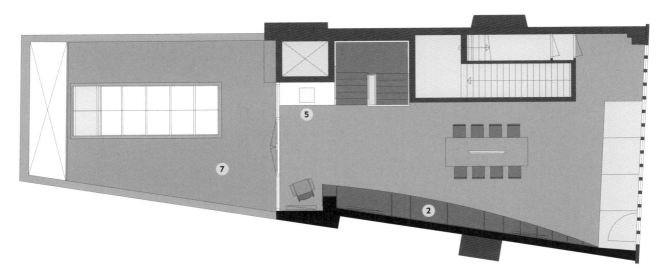

First floor

1 Stroller display
2 Product wall
3 Window display
4 Cash desk
5 Pantry
6 Toilet
7 Patio

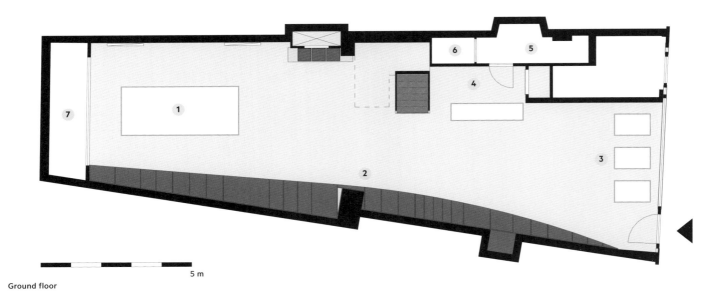

5 m

Ground floor

5 A showcase for parts allows customers to customise their stroller.
6 A meeting table in the space above means visitors can choose their options in comfort.
7 The upper floor is kept clear of the windows, creating a light, open effect.

CITROËN
EXPERIENCE CENTRE
BY CANDIDA TABET ARQUITETURA

1

WHERE São Paulo, Brazil **WHEN** April 2012
CLIENT PSA Peugeot Citroen do Brasil **DESIGNER** Candida Tabet Arquitetura (p.492)
TOTAL FLOOR AREA 140 m² **SHOP CONSTRUCTOR** Kross Engenharia
PHOTOS Guinter Parschalk and Eduardo Raimondi

For classic French car brand Citroën, studio Candida Tabet Arquitetura shaped a high-impact experience centre that appears anything but dated. The space plays with reflection, multiplying images through the abundant use of glass and mirrors to create a spectacular effect which, the designers say, could be achieved surprisingly quickly and easily due to the materials used. The centre is intended to embody the philosophy of the much-loved car brand, and visitors can savour the Citroën atmosphere over three floors devoted to Le Café Creative, La Boutique Citroën and La Galerie Creative, all linked by a dramatic staircase clad in coloured mirrors and translucent red glass inspired by car brake lights. Transparency is a key feature of the project, which is essentially contained within a seamless glass box that comes complete with solar and heat control. Outside, the space's video and LED screens can be seen from afar, their moving images creating a dynamic, mirage-like effect. The store appears like a shape-shifting, illuminated beacon from the outside, attracting people in and taking Citroën's brand message out onto the street. No less than three horizontal-axis tilting doors add to the inside-outside experience. Inside, the predominantly red and white interior achieves a cheerful graphic effect that showcases the cars on show. The façade frames the dramatic double-height entrance space, with its tall steel columns, and heightens the centre's lively impact on the neighbourhood's street scene: this is a space you don't even have to enter to enjoy.

1 The dramatic red and white staircase is a key element, drawing the three floors together.
2 The glass-skinned building is totally open to the street.

3

An inside space that's just as enjoyable on the outside

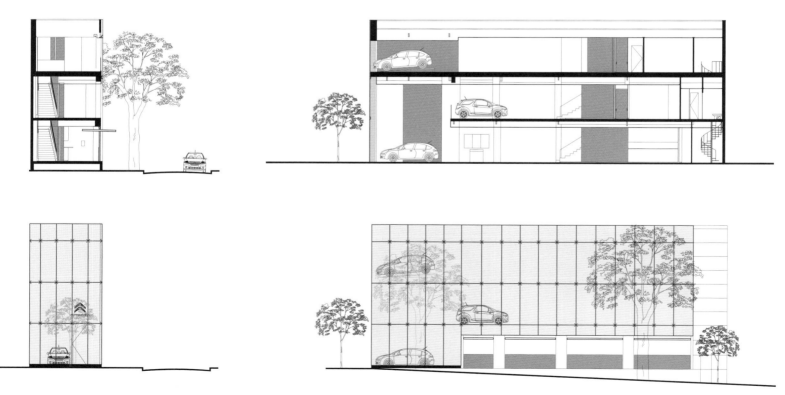

4

3 The lounge area, which, equipped with
  designer furniture, encourages visitors
  to stay.
4 Drawings show the importance of the colour
  red in articulating the design.
5 Citroën cars make unmissable focal points.
6 The high-impact bright red colour used
  throughout the interior has distinct
  motoring associations.

GIANT STORE
BY FABRIQUE

WHERE Amsterdam, the Netherlands **WHEN** July 2011
CLIENT Giant Benelux **DESIGNER** Fabrique [brands, design & interaction] (p.494)
TOTAL FLOOR AREA 500 m² **SHOP CONSTRUCTORS** Vanderoord Projects
PHOTOS Courtesy of Fabrique [brands, design & interaction]

Giant is the world's largest bicycle producer. The range of Giant is broad and deep: from racing bike to city bike, from bicycle pump to brake calliper. Design agency Fabrique developed a unique and scalable brand store for this Taiwanese manufacturer. The brand store, located in a historical building in the city of Amsterdam, is a real 'pampering shop' and not a full-to-overflowing glorified bicycle repair shop. The bikes are placed on well-lit catwalks, while clothing and accessories are displayed in showcases or display tables. The whole shop breathes space and structure. The shop is divided into two halves, one with city bikes for day-to-day use and the other with sports bikes. This division will be reflected in each Giant shop in the Netherlands. Fabrique used the colours blue, silver and grey throughout the shop. Silver painted brick walls and concrete flooring with huge signings on the wall in Giant's brand colour blue. The 'Repair & Go' area offers a rapid repair service, while the customer enjoys free coffee. If you are looking for a new bike, you are invited to walk around the bikes and view them at your leisure, or read a brochure at the picnic table and get an explanation from a salesperson. Buying a bike becomes a treat. The first flagship store on Van Woustraat in Amsterdam is a great success, and the concept is currently being rolled out in the Netherlands.

1　The store is divided into two sales areas, one for city bikes and one for sports bikes.
2　The bikes are presented on well-lit catwalks.
3　Customers can have their bikes repaired at the 'Repair & Go' area while they wait.

A unique and scalable brand store where the bikes are the heroes

RAPHA CYCLE CLUB
BY BRINKWORTH

1

WHERE London, United Kingdom **WHEN** July 2012
CLIENT Rapha **DESIGNER** Brinkworth (p.492)
TOTAL FLOOR AREA 130 m² **SHOP CONSTRUCTOR** Premier Shopfitting
PHOTOS Alex Franklin and James Purssell

The agony and the ecstasy of world road cycling – that was essentially what Brinkworth was asked to convey when commissioned to develop Rapha Cycle Club into an environment that would reflect the core cultural values of the Rapha brand heritage. The resulting space builds on Rapha's vision of a meeting place for the cycling community to eat, drink, watch bike racing and shop, totally immersing themselves in an environment dedicated to road cycling. The aesthetic reflects the Rapha approach of premium design and materials while referencing a workshop functionality. A flexible retail system displays not only apparel, but also unique products and Rapha's collection of cycling memorabilia. A double-height rear feature wall creates a backdrop for the iconic Rapha 'H' Van, a familiar element of the brand. Brinkworth has taken an unconventional approach to the layout, designing a space that places equal importance on social and retail aspects, delivering a blended experience. Bespoke cycle storage for visitors' bikes and tools for basic bike servicing and maintenance are available, making the club is a key destination for both city cyclists and racers alike. Integrated within the space is a custom-designed bar area with zinc-topped counter, reminiscent of timeless European café culture, underpinned by the Rapha branded cups and espresso machines. Visitors sit at laser-etched tabletops that feature famous alpine climbs, while watching races on large screens positioned within the space. Following the London flagship, the Brinkworth concept will roll out internationally, starting with Sidney, New York, Tokyo and Osaka.

1 Neutral solid concrete flooring is combined with the grey, white and pink Rapha colour scheme.
2 & 3 A double-height feature wall creates a backdrop for the iconic Rapha 'H' Van, a familiar element of the brand.
4 A flexible system displays not only merchandise, but also a collection of cycling memorabilia.

Retail gets social in a boldly blended space

SH

420

OES

421

1

Mobile store construction –
using a single hex key

2

ADIDAS ORIGINALS POP-UP STORE
BY D'ART DESIGN GRUPPE

WHERE Germany, Switzerland and Austria **WHEN** January 2011
CLIENT adidas **DESIGNER** D'art Design Gruppe (p.493)
TOTAL FLOOR AREA 40 m² **SHOP CONSTRUCTOR** Projektpilot
PHOTOS Daniel Schäfer

For a series of six pop-up stores for adidas Originals' Blue and Ransom collections, D'art Design Gruppe needed to produce a temporary and mobile solution that was thoroughly practical and quick to set up (the shops were intended to fulfil a guerrilla store function and would spring up unannounced overnight in various locations in Germany, Switzerland and Austria) while appearing hip and urban at the same time. Simplicity was the key to success here, and the designs utilised basic materials like steel tubes, exposed cables and simple light bulbs for lighting. Steel was combined with white mesh (a familiar sportswear material) for the stores' signature display with lighting elements. Everything was designed to be put together in a single day on site, using only one hex key. A further advantage of the steel construction was its flexibility when it came to display and to optimising whatever space the latest pop-up had to open in. Steel-pipe benches and floor lamps gave the spaces a welcoming, lounge-like feel. The iconic adidas trefoil was subtly visible on all the design elements. For example, the blue lampshades had little 'leaves' which daintily but discreetly presented the brand logo. On top of all this, the stores were a well-kept secret. Only invited guest knew the locations, which were communicated through social media channels – a strategy guaranteed to enhance the fast-moving and futuristic design.

1   The iconic adidas trefoil recurs on many elements throughout the store.
2   Basic materials like steel poles, white mesh and bare lightbulbs create a surprisingly sophisticated effect.
3   Benches were slightly sporty, while floor lamps added a homely touch.
4   Simplicity of design and construction was the key to success.

APPLE & PIE
BY STEFANO TORDIGLIONE DESIGN

WHERE Hong Kong, Hong Kong **WHEN** August 2012
CLIENT apple & pie **DESIGNER** Stefano Tordiglione Design (p.498)
TOTAL FLOOR AREA 85 m² **SHOP CONSTRUCTOR** Anzac
PHOTOS Courtesy of Stefano Tordiglione Design

Customers entering the apple & pie children's shoes store pass through a giant apple that surrounds the glass doorway – a clear signal that they are entering another world. Inside, they find an environment that's full of fantasy and fun, but still relaxed and laid-back. 'Our goal was to create a fun, welcoming, child-like environment, that was also practical for shopping', says designer Stefano Tordiglione. 'We made sure to have appealing design elements for both parents and kids, such as the child-sized Kartell seats that surround the play tables and the chalkboard wall filled with drawings to spark the imagination.' The space has lots of playful features, including apple-shaped seats (which very practically conceal storage) and diamond-shaped shelves, designed to resemble the lattice pattern often seen on pies. These make great niches for child-sized shoes. A sculptural tree design beautifies one wall, with apples hanging from its branches – it functions both as a lively display element and a visual feature in its own right. Around

the windows are semi-circular pie-like displays in white latticed wood. While such fantasy elements delight the kids, their parents will be impressed by more adult features – such as the Ethel lighting hanging from the ceiling, and the Giant Red Lamp from Anglepoise – which lend a 'design insider' feel to the store. Thanks to its combination of smooth curves and clean lines, a warm wooden floor and a colour palette that blends bold reds and bright greens with a calming mint and light beige, the store effectively inhabits the worlds of both youthful enthusiasm and mature sophistication.

1 A giant apple silhouette cheerfully greets shoppers and frames a playful but stylish interior.
2 Adults will enjoy the designer lighting – featuring Ethel ceiling lights and Anglepoise's Giant Red Lamps.
3 Kids are entranced by the large tree sculpture, lattice shelves and mini table Kartell chairs especially for them.

Youthful enthusiasm plus mature sophistication

BREUNINGER
SHOE DEPARTMENT
BY LIGANOVA

WHERE Stuttgart, Germany WHEN September 2012
CLIENT Breuninger DESIGNER Liganova (p.497)
TOTAL FLOOR AREA 2000 m² SHOP CONSTRUCTOR Liganova
PHOTOS Courtesy of Breuninger

With the ambition of establishing the 'best shoe destination in the fashion and premium segments', Liganova turned its attention to the 2000m² footwear space of Breuninger department store, located on the lower ground floor. A strong concept was clearly needed and the designers came up with one: a beautiful herringbone parquet floor is dotted with a wide variety of architectural display furniture, all under the combination of a light-coloured floating ceiling and a remarkable lighting installation featuring over 4000 LED-elements and able to create lighting effects from darkly mysterious to glowingly romantic. Within this impressive setting, the lighting helps to define visual axes and offers open views of the different style zones: Fashion, Designers, Pure Classic, Forever Young and Premium Shoes. Each one is an umbrella for a multi-brand offer – there are 250 brands and 40,000 shoes on display here, so the various theme areas help to create pockets of intimacy, assisting customer choice in a sea of footwear. The highly individual displays and furniture, all custom-produced by Liganova, greatly helps to break the space into manageable units. Displays vary from the rectilinear to the baroque, but a uniform palette of white and gold keeps the effect harmonious. Spectacle is a major aspect of a space like this, and on the stairs customers are met by a rainbow-coloured art installation designed by the Dutch artist John Breed, featuring 145 variously shod female legs – a surreal and fun touch. A bar (called Heels) and lounge seating area equipped with iPads help to promote first-class customer service.

1 A remarkable starry-night lighting installation features over 4000 glowing LED elements.
2 & 3 The designer areas make use of marble and onyx for a luxurious effect.
4 Seating adds colour, in red or blue velvet.

Variations on a theme for an epic shoe department

Architectural displays dot a herringbone floor

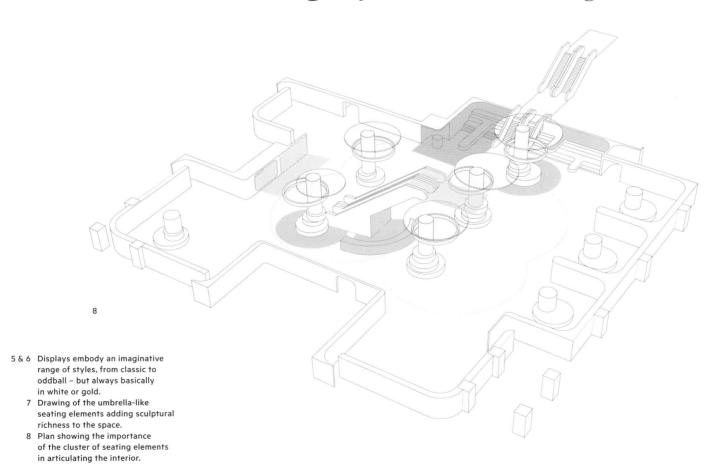

5 & 6 Displays embody an imaginative
        range of styles, from classic to
        oddball – but always basically
        in white or gold.
7 Drawing of the umbrella-like
   seating elements adding sculptural
   richness to the space.
8 Plan showing the importance
   of the cluster of seating elements
   in articulating the interior.

CAMPER TOGETHER
BY ATELIER MARKO BRAJOVIC

WHERE São Paulo, Brazil **WHEN** April 2013
CLIENT Camper **DESIGNER** Atelier Marko Brajovic (p.491)
TOTAL FLOOR AREA 90 m² **SHOP CONSTRUCTORS** Rodrigo Simões and Eduardo Rocha Franco
PHOTOS Fernando Laszlo

As part of its ongoing Camper Together series of projects, which involve offbeat collaborations with designers on store interiors and products, Spanish shoe brand Camper asked Marko Brajovic to design a shop in São Paulo. His response was to find inspiration in the local context, or as he says, 'in traditional folkloric Brazilian festivities, where involving environments are created by dense layers of coloured stripes.' Using only strips of cloth and shoelaces in the Camper brand's energising red, Brajovic created a fluid wave of scarlet that stretches from the shop front to the back of the store. Hanging like an arched canopy over the glass frontage and entrance, the crimson tide undulates in the interior, carving out a curved, cave-like space. Brajovic describes the installation as 'modelling different shapes that implement in the space a sensitive and scenographic experience, where the visitors are the everyday actors.' As well as adding vibrant colour, the cloth strips and shoelaces add an intriguing texture and a certain amount of movement.

Apart from the installation, which suggests an inverted field of red grass, the store is entirely white, although a soft, pinkish hue results from the colour reflected from above. The store layout is extremely simple: just three shelves on either side to display the products, and above them rows of uplighters that create interesting light and shadow effects on the rippling ruby ceiling. The rear of the store, however, is entirely red, with a scarlet counter (stamped with a subtle Camper logo) nestled among a curtain of red shreds.

1 The red strips hang like an arched canopy over the glass entranceway.
2 The undulating installation carves out a curving, cave-like space.
3 Cloth strips and shoelaces add an intriguing texture as well as colour to the store.

Red shreds create a vibrant, textured store

COCCODRILLO FOR VERSO
BY GLENN SESTIG ARCHITECTS

WHERE Antwerp, Belgium WHEN May 2012
CLIENT Coccodrillo for Verso DESIGNER Glenn Sestig Architects (p.495)
TOTAL FLOOR AREA 58 m² SHOP CONSTRUCTOR Fashion Club 70
PHOTOS Jean Pierre Gabriel

Antwerp's Coccodrillo is a well-known name in the shoe industry, much as the stylish city's Verso is a globally renowned temple of fashion. Putting the two together – as a Coccodrillo store within the third Verso boutique – clearly called for something special in terms of interior design. International architect Glenn Sestig has obliged with a space that is redolent of the era of *The Great Gatsby* (and so bang on trend) while remaining thoroughly contemporary in its stylish simplicity. Materials are the key to conjuring the atmosphere of understated luxury that is Glenn Sestig's hallmark. A herringbone wooden floor, with its period connotations, plus the rather Art Deco combination of green marble with warm, powdery tones, create a sumptuous but restful backdrop for the shoes on display. A focal point in the rather restrained yet glamorous space is the dramatic central column surrounded by an island bench seat. Like a piece of sculpture as much as an item of furniture, this ensemble is intended to evoke the salons and bars that were designed for the transatlantic cruise ships of the 1920s. Marble panels and shelves hug the periphery of the space, while dotted around the central area are custom-made elliptical tables perching on spindly legs. These have an elegant Art Deco presence, as do the glass and chrome wall lights. A matte black ceiling is a surprising and contemporary touch, which throws the rest of the interior into sharp relief. Spotlights here add sophistication to the lighting scheme.

1 & 2 Forms and materials hint an Art
Deco atmosphere.
3 Green marble, powder shades and
a herringbone floor evoke the 1920s.
A neutral palette allows the products
to really stand out.

436

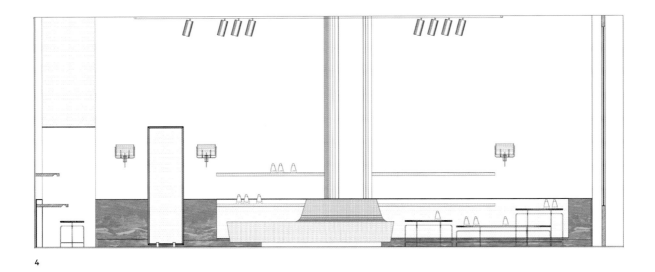

4

The Great Gatsby meets modern minimalism

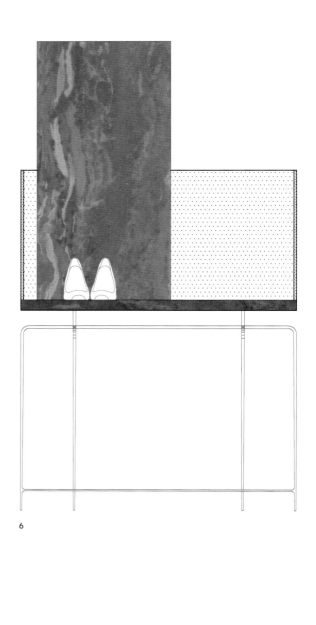

6

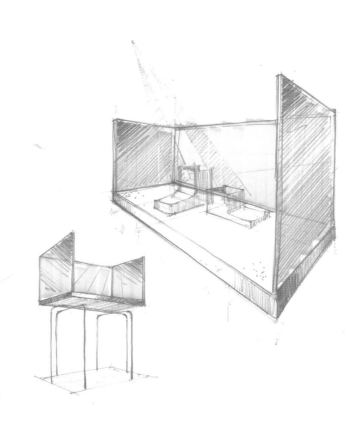

5

4 An elevation drawing of the shoe store.
5 & 6 An initial sketch of one of the custom-designed furniture pieces.
7 The elliptical display tables were custom-made.

DR. MARTENS
BY CHECKLAND KINDLEYSIDES

WHERE London, United Kingdom **WHEN** September 2011
CLIENT Dr. Martens **DESIGNER** Checkland Kindleysides (p.492)
TOTAL FLOOR AREA 20 m² **SHOP CONSTRUCTOR** Checkland Kindleysides
PHOTOS Paul Winch-Furness

It could have been an impossible challenge – Checkland Kindleysides had just two weeks and only 20m² in which to create an effective pop-up retail space for enduring British footwear brand Dr. Martens. But the resulting space, in Selfridges department store, benefited from a strong concept, thanks to the fact that it acted as the launch pad for the brand's 'First and Forever' campaign, which is based around people's memories of their first ever pair of Dr. Martens. While appealing to shoppers' memories, Checkland Kindleysides also channelled the history of the brand, in particular its industrial and artisanal heritage. The iconic boots are displayed in raw metal cages and on glass cabinets filled with iconic components of Dr. Martens, such as rubber compound beads (used to make their AirWair soles), reels of yellow thread and metal eyelets. The glass cabinets are left open, inviting shoppers to handle the materials and allowing the aromas of rubber and metal to permeate the air. For a further look behind the scenes, iPads tell the story of how the boots are made, and the sound of their manufacture is the pop-up space's background noise. Corresponding to the central arrangement of three display and seating units, three large mirrors visually extend the space, the central one stating, 'Everyone remembers their first pair of Dr. Martens', and inviting visitors to share their own recollections as part of an online campaign. As a finishing touch, the famous AirWair logo in yellow adorns wooden panels on either side of the space.

1 Three mirrors extend the space, the central one bearing stencils with the First and Forever campaign message.
2 Glass cases filled with yellow rubber compound beads make unusual displays.

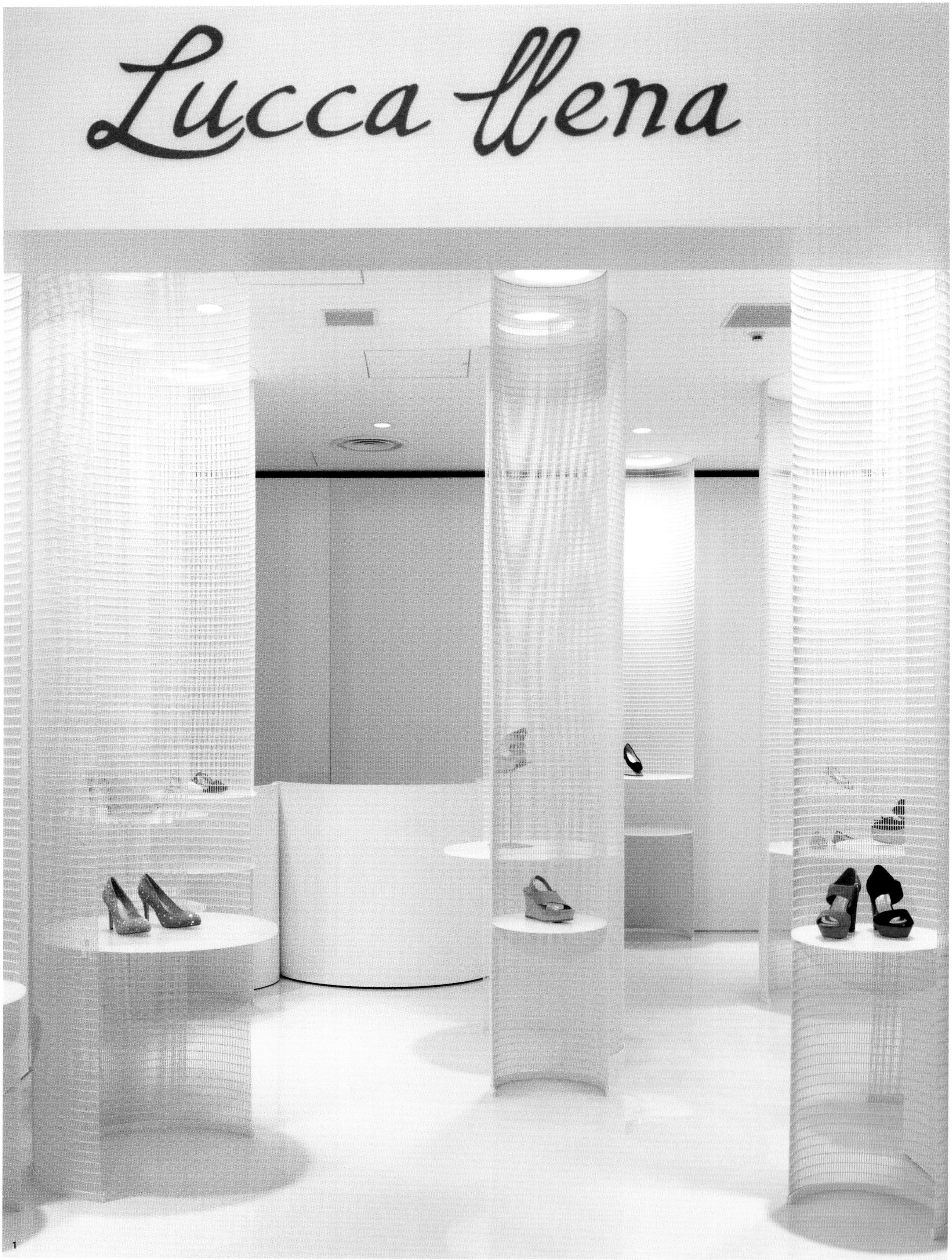

1

LUCCA LLENA
BY NOMURA / RYUTARO MATSUURA

WHERE Osaka, Japan **WHEN** April 2013
CLIENT J.B. **DESIGNER** Nomura / Ryutaro Matsuura (p.498)
TOTAL FLOOR AREA 54 m² **SHOP CONSTRUCTOR** Nomura
PHOTOS Nacása & Partners

A curvy and etherial landscape of wire-mesh columns greets visitors to the Lucca llena shoe store in Osaka, Japan. The colourful women's footwear sold in the shop is beautifully displayed in this all-white setting, in which the semi-circular wire mesh pillars alternately conceal and reveal the shoes in a tantalising way. The environment is refreshingly free of branding elements or other distractions from the main theme. The transparent metal displays, rounded forms and soft, neutral palette throw all the emphasis onto the shoes, allowing customers to consider them one by one as they navigate the restful but playful space. The wire-mesh fixtures have translucent loose shelves for the shoes that are made of honeycomb sandwich resin panels, adding to the light and airy effect. The columns vary in their circumference and angle, creating a sense of subtle variations on a theme. Ryutaro Matsuura, creative director of design studio Nomura, says he chose this approach in order to liberate shoppers from the set sales formula of wall shelves and display tables. 'The merchandise hovers like fruit on trees,' he says, describing the interior as 'a shoe forest' in which 'customers can enjoy meeting the merchandise and feeling a sense of exaltation. 'When the differences of the surrounding decorative environment are suppressed,' he continues, 'the items themselves begin to assert their presence.' He argues that this approach stimulates the imagination and curiosity of the customers, and that the cloud-like store allows them to choose the products that really fit their desires. 'At least, that's what we would expect,' he says.

1 Transparent wire-mesh semi-circular columns are fitted with translucent loose shelves made from honeycomb sandwich resin panels.
2 The subtle displays, rounded forms and pale palette allow the shoes to really stand out.

3 Soft downlighting, semi-transparent layers
and gentle shadows add to the effect.

1 Retail area
2 Cash desk
3 Storage

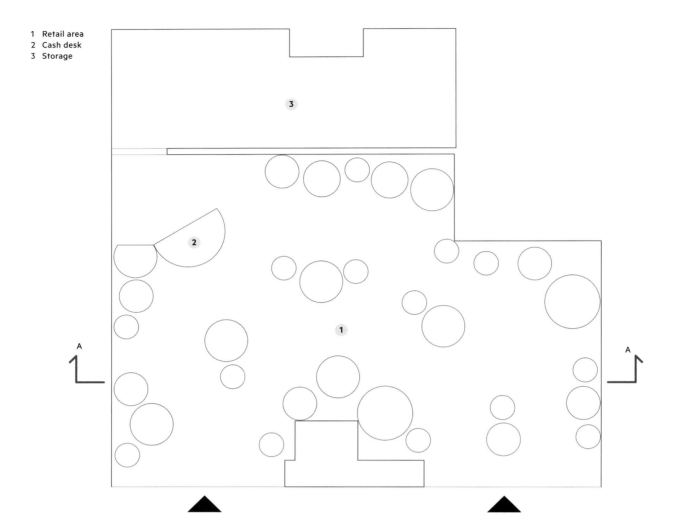

Transparent columns allow shoes to hover, like fruit on trees

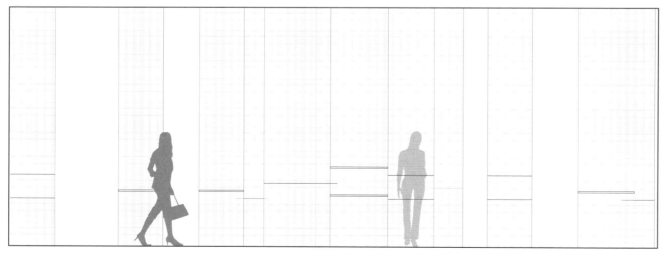

Section AA

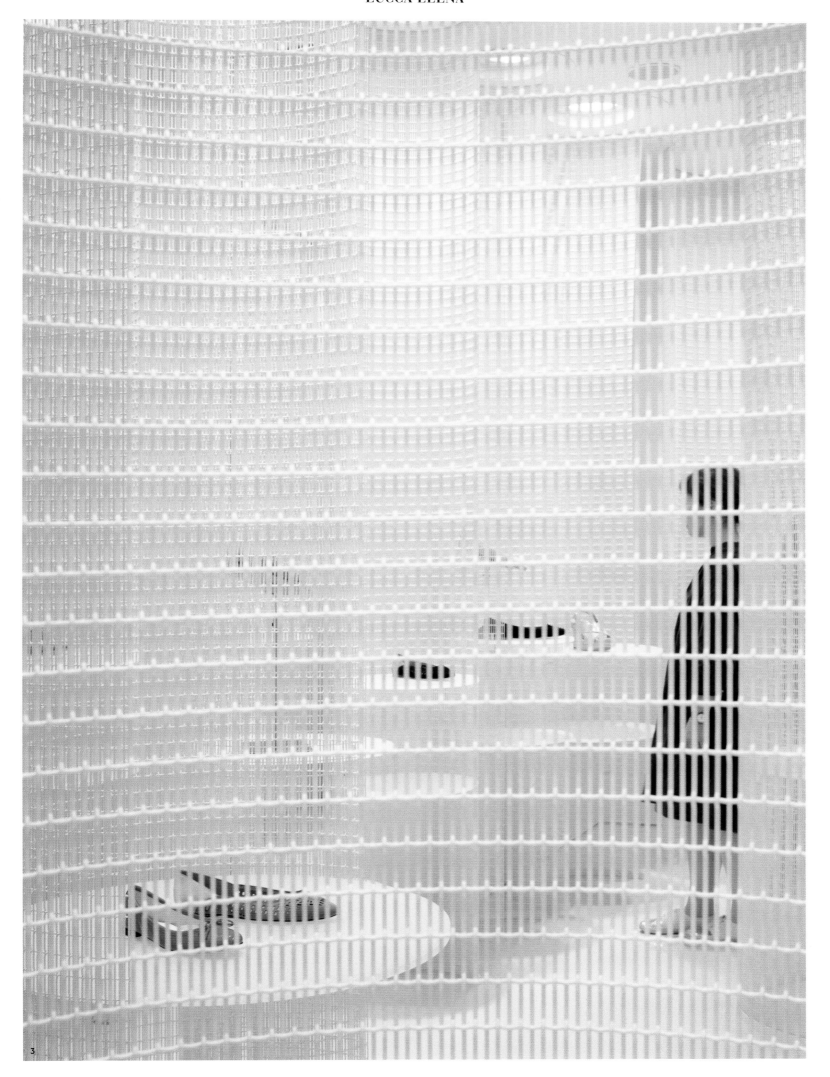

M DREAMS
BY BLU WATER STUDIO

WHERE Petaling Jaya, Malaysia WHEN November 2012
CLIENT Omniscent DESIGNER Blu Water Studio (p.491)
TOTAL FLOOR AREA 120 m² SHOP CONSTRUCTOR –
PHOTOS Lin Ho

Undulating shelves peel away from the walls in Melissa's M dreams store, creating dynamic display shelves for the Brazilian brand's quirky collection of shoes. Design company Blu Water Studio based the concept for the interior on paper, and the way it behaves when folded, bent or torn, hinting at the malleability of Melissa's plastic jelly shoes. An entirely white interior throws the brightly coloured shoes into sharp relief while furthering the paper concept. One arrestingly dark touch is the M dreams logo, finished in stainless steel and outlined in white lighting near the entrance. Signage is very subtle: the name Melissa also appears, but in white on white, on the scroll-like border – which the designers call the 'overhang' – that runs around the top of the walls. On the right-hand side of the store, shelves of various sizes curl out from the wall like ledges in a cave. Opposite them, on the left-hand side, the shelves branch out more elaborately, like fluttering ribbons captured in fluid silhouettes. Grey-tinted mirrors are placed between them, breaking up the effect and adding a touch of contrast, as well as allowing customers to see how the shoes look when they try them on, sitting on the soft, round moveable seating elements placed in the centre of the store. Here there are also clusters of display elements, resembling classical columns. Films of Melissa ad campaigns are projected onto the curtain-like overhang, adding an element of movement and theatre to the space.

1 On the left-hand side of the store, shelves unfurl like undulating ribbons.
2 A scroll-like border runs around the top of the space. Here the name Melissa appears, as do films of the brands ad campaigns.

Peeling paper inspires an intriguing interior

3 A cluster of freestanding displays resembles classical columns.
4 On the right-hand side of the store, shelves of various sizes curl out from the wall.
5 The M dreams logo in stainless steel is outlined in white lighting near the entrance.

1

M DREAMS
BY EDWARDS MOORE

WHERE Melbourne, Australia WHEN August 2012
CLIENT Melissa Shoes DESIGNER Edwards Moore (p.494)
TOTAL FLOOR AREA 60 m² SHOP CONSTRUCTOR Greg Scott
PHOTOS Peter Bennetts

How to capture the essence of the iconic Melissa plastic shoe in just 60 m²? That was the challenge facing the Edwards Moore designers, who were asked to provide space to display about 200 pairs of shoes together with seating for trying on and an easily accessible storage area. In an interesting take on the materiality of the plastic shoe, the designers reduced it to its most essential, molecular form, creating clusters of plastic particles reminiscent of balloons and bubbles. Into an otherwise stark and linear interior, they inserted nearly 300 environmentally friendly, 100% recyclable PTFE white plastic spheres, blurring the distinction between interior and exterior, ceiling and wall. The spheres, which are seamless and rotationally moulded, were sourced from local factories. The design was chosen as it is effective from both inside and outside: it allows natural light into the interior while balancing the need for an ever-changing shop window display. The cluster of particles creates a soft, organic welcoming space and product backdrop: the shoe display concept uses a series of visually unobtrusive, moveable holders that can be attached to any of the 300 PTFE bubbles using a suction cup. An oversized billboard acts as dividing wall between shop and storeroom, and can be easily changed to co-ordinate with the release of new shoe ranges by replacing the removable printed wallpaper graphic. The tables and sales counter were specially developed by the designers using the PTFE spheres to support a series of acrylic frosted surfaces for display and sales.

1 The bubbly interior, with its 300 spheres, is an ingenious way of evoking the essence of the Melissa plastic shoe.
2 The spheres, made of environmentally friendly, 100% recyclable PTFE, work as furniture, display and sculptural objects in the store.

RUNNERS POINT
BY DAN PEARLMAN

WHERE Dortmund, Germany WHEN March 2013
CLIENT Runners Point DESIGNER dan pearlman (p.493)
TOTAL FLOOR AREA 550 m² SHOP CONSTRUCTOR Serafini
PHOTOS Courtesy of Runners Point

Immersing customers in a world of running is no idle boast at Runners Point. The studio of dan pearlman designed the new flagship store which conveys the enthusiastic energy that every dedicated runner knows – and that has made the retailer Runners Point a winner since 1984. With an expansive 550 m² to play with, and Europe's largest collection of athletic shoes, among other products, to display, the designers set out to really make the space count with some dramatic running scenography. A centrally placed track, used to analyse customers' running style so as to select the most suitable shoe, seems even longer due to a mirrored wall, and a 15-m-long video wall provides an exciting and evocative backdrop of an idealised running scene. There's a distinct change of pace in the runners' lounge, where customers can read Runners Point's offering of articles online on iPads. The rest of the retail space, meanwhile, is divided into distinct brand sections that create separate zones and facilitate orientation, producing an eye-catchingly varied visual

impression. A poured concrete floor, sculptural wooden display elements and a turquoise and grey colour scheme all help to tie the separate areas together. At the store's entrance, which is extremely wide, three numbered lanes invite runners to sprint in off the street. A video screen offers a taster of what's inside on the video wall – a parkland scene that any runner would be happy to do laps in. In short, it's hard to imagine that any aspiring or experienced runner could pass this store without having to go in.

1 Sculptural elements, a poured concrete floor and a consistent colour scheme unify the various brand areas.
2 The technology-tinged runners' lounge has a video wall and iPads for customers to use.
3 The store is said to have Europe's biggest collection of athletic trainers.

4 A centrally placed track can be used to analyse customers' running styles.
5 The 15-m-long video wall adds drama and colour.

Three lanes invite runners to sprint in off the street

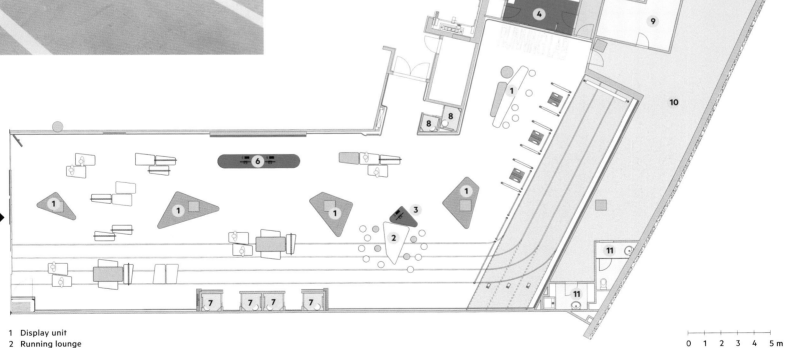

1 Display unit
2 Running lounge
3 Service desk
4 Running lab
5 Running academy
6 Cash desk
7 Fitting room men
8 Fitting room women
9 Staff-only area
10 Storage
11 Toilet

0 1 2 3 4 5 m

TELE

AN

SERV

456

COM

ND

ICES

457

Customer experience in the age of 'the cloud'

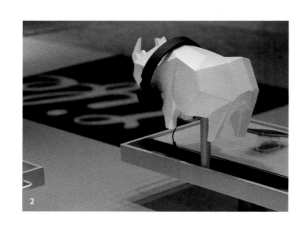

AER
BY COORDINATION ASIA

WHERE Shenzhen, China **WHEN** September 2012
CLIENT AISIDI **DESIGNER** Coordination Asia (p.492)
TOTAL FLOOR AREA 130 m² **SHOP CONSTRUCTOR** Shenzhen Ming Gao Decoration & Design
PHOTOS Courtesy of Coordination Asia

A black runway greets visitors to the AER digital lifestyle store with the message, 'App up your life' – a clear signal of what this brand is all about: keeping mobile-minded consumers connected, entertained and updated through a variety of online and offline apps. The AER space is a playground-like environment, complete with animal figures and giant Lego-like blocks, where customers are encouraged to discover, learn and have fun. Products are thematically presented in combination with related accessories, apps and carriers on custom-made presentation tables which literally 'serve up' the offerings on serving trays. Bold signage signals the various areas of the store, including the App Bar, where customers can try out the mobile apps on an interactive screen. Painted pegboard is used to cover the walls of the store, allowing for a flexible arrangement of the display shelves. Bright blue is combined with splashes of other vibrant colours, warm wood and black and white to create a bold effect. 'The hybrid form of the digital cloud can be traced in the

look and feel of the store', says Tilman Thürmer of Coordination Asia, the office which designed not only this store, but the whole AER brand. AER focuses not on selling products but on the whole mobile lifestyle, and the concept was based on in-depth research into China's mobile market. The name 'AER' was derived from the Greek word for air and loosely refers to the phenomenon of the 'cloud' which the store strives to embody – as Thürmer puts it, 'Celebrating the joy of sharing through wireless technology.'

1 Walls of bright-blue pegboard form a vibrant and versatile backdrop, while trays mounted on tables literally 'serve up' the store goods.
2 Playful touches like this yellow Rhino add to the flamboyant, fun atmosphere.
3 The App Bar, which encourages customers to try out the goods, is composed from giant, shiny Lego-like blocks.
4 A black runway forms the store entrance and sets the theme with its graphic message.

Light and contrast as branding elements

AND MARKET
BY ARCHICEPT CITY

2

WHERE Tokyo, Japan **WHEN** June 2011
CLIENT AND market **DESIGNER** Archicept city (p.490)
TOTAL FLOOR AREA 40 m² **SHOP CONSTRUCTOR** Hakusuisha
PHOTOS Atsushi Nakamichi

How to make a mobile retail outlet stand out in Japan's overcrowded market? That was the dilemma facing Archicept city's Atsushi Muroi when he was commissioned to design a new store for AND market – the country's first independent smartphone-focused retailer. 'Independent' was the key word here, with the retailer's freedom from major mobile carriers inspiring what Muroi calls the store's 'neutral' approach. 'Neutral means achromatic in terms of design', he says, explaining why he choose to rely on light, not colour, to create a distinctive environment. 'Our interior design symbolises the brand essence by depicting the balance of the brightness between black and white.' In order to create impact and attract shoppers to the space in the mall, Muroi designed a large circular ceiling light. Arranged in rows, these lights are 'not in the context of Japanese architecture and add a little bit of strangeness', he explains. 'They make the space quite unique and are attention-grabbing without strong colour.' Modular wall units on two of the interior walls display the items for sale in a very even manner, without privileging any one brand over the others. The units also create a rhythmic pattern corresponding to that of the ceiling lights, which is in turn echoed by the placement of the demo and display tables that occupy the central space. Rectangular shapes predominate in the displays and seating furniture, adding to the geometric effect. A white counter, boldly silhouetted against a black wall emblazoned with AND market's logo, adds a dramatic focal point to the store.

1 Rows of circular ceiling lights create a crowd-pulling effect.
2 Although the store lacks colour, its contrasting forms and modular design make for a high-impact graphic interior.

CHIANTIBANCA
BY CREA INTERNATIONAL

WHERE Poggibonsi, Italy **WHEN** May 2013
CLIENT ChiantiBanca **DESIGNER** CREA international (p.492)
TOTAL FLOOR AREA 300 m² **SHOP CONSTRUCTOR** Samarreda
PHOTOS Dario Garofalo

For a string of new branches in Tuscany, Italian bank ChiantiBanca was not afraid to do something different. It teamed up with Italian design studio's CREA international to devise a new concept that evokes Italy's fantastic food culture, by borrowing from traditional local eateries. The so-called 'restaurant experience banking' concept is designed to place ChiantiBanca's customer services within a friendly and familiar local context. There is not a traditional cash desk to be seen in the space. Instead, clusters of tables, surrounded by bar stools, chairs and cushioned seating cubes, project the welcoming ambience of a trattoria. Even the bank's brochures are arranged to look like restaurant condiments and accessories in the centre of the tables. But there are up-to-the-minute digital touches, including video teller machines (VTMs), replacing the standard ATMs, and a touch-screen wall displaying information and advertisements. Informal spaces at the front of the space functions as welcome zones, and there are also play areas for small children. The new concept store's material palette is earthy and warm and includes wood, Corten steel and soft shades of brown and green. A rustic touch is added by the installations of wooden roof 'beams' that add personality to the white ceiling and have a beneficial acoustic effect. With branches located in Florence's Piazza Duomo and in the towns of Poggibonsi, Fontebecci, Monteriggioni, it's appropriate that the materials and colours, as well as the concept, reflect local Tuscan traditions.

1 Installations of wooden 'roof beams' evoke the rustic local architecture.
2 On the restaurant-like tables, brochures are set out like restaurant accessories.

3

New bank concept channels local eateries

 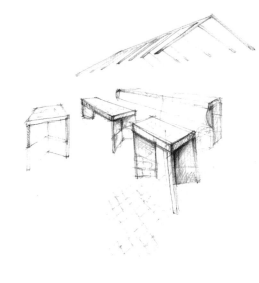  

3 Materials like wood, Corten steel and stone
   add to the earthy affect.
4 & 5 The colour palette is characterised by warm
   walnut and soft, olive green, with
   contrasting touches of viridian.

Blue cones enliven a bank interior

DEUTSCHE BANK
BY BEHF ARCHITECTS

3

WHERE Aalen, Germany **WHEN** May 2012
CLIENT Deutsche Bank **DESIGNER** BEHF Architects (p.491)
TOTAL FLOOR AREA 970 m² **SHOP CONSTRUCTOR** –
PHOTOS Bruno Klomfar

Dramatic blue conical structures characterise the branch interior concept that BEHF Architects created for Deutsche Bank. Called 'cones', these semi-closed spaces provide a discreet but not claustrophic environment for those more sensitive discussions between the bank and its customers. The lamellas surrounding these meeting rooms like dynamic blue blades were derived from the forward slash in the logo of Deutsche Bank. The conical spaces can be placed as desired in the space, depending on the needs of the particular branch. The blue lamellas add colour as well as corporate identity to an otherwise neutrally toned space. The interior as a whole is organised in an open fashion designed to be easy for customers to understand and navigate. The service and consultation zones are defined by different floor finishes (wood, linoleum and carpet), so that the functions of the areas can be deduced in an associative way. The central communications and marketing element of the space is known as 'the horizon'. This modular structure brings together formerly detached and isolated elements such as information brochures, tea and coffee making equipment, and promotional material. The flexibility of this system means that it can be applied to just about any branch, regardless of size or floor plan. The sales office meanwhile is deliberately separated from the customer area to ensure an undisturbed workplace for staff. The wooden furniture used in these areas was designed and produced exclusively for Deutsche Bank. In the client areas, plants, framed artworks and toys in the children's area humanise the space.

1   Blue conical meeting rooms are the
    signature of the space, but can be placed
    wherever a branch wants.
2   'The horizon' is a modular display
    structure that acts as the branch's main
    communication tool.
3   The blue lamellas are positioned with
    subtle cues like different floor treatments
    help customers to read the space.

KRUNGSRI EXCLUSIVE
BY CONCEPT I

WHERE Bangkok, Thailand **WHEN** October 2012
CLIENT Bank of Ayudha Public Company **DESIGNER** Concept i (p.492)
TOTAL FLOOR AREA 405 m² **SHOP CONSTRUCTOR** Pharapat Limited Partnership
PHOTOS Marc Schultz

When venerable Thai banking concern Krungsri (established 1945) decided to update its image, it turned to Interbrand for branding advice and Concept i for interior expertise. The makeover, for one of Thailand's largest commercial banks, would combine all aspects of brand identity, interior design and architecture. The aim was to create a simple, fresh and friendly customer experience, embracing the spirit of Krungsri's new motto, 'simplify your life'. The new interior concept was designed to refresh and consolidate the bank's brand identity, while creating an inspiring, retail-oriented environment. Part of the rethink involved clearly differentiating Krungsri's Exclusive Banking Centres from its standard branch environments. Using the basic profile of the newly redesigned standard branches, Concept i added more emphasis on service and luxury materials to the Exclusive Banking Centres. Tried-and-tested principles of retail design were also implemented to boost the centre's effectiveness, including open visibility, easy navigation, clear merchandise display and a focused graphic path leading to customer touch points. The resulting sleek, sinuous spaces are bathed in natural daylight. The furnishings are soft and homely, contemporary and welcoming, accented with textured fabrics and the brand's colour tones: a crisp, bright yellow balanced with warm neutral shades. The concierge counter is open and obvious for immediate personal contact – which is not always easy to come by in banks – and a luxurious reception area, dedicated touch-screen stations, high-tech VIP meeting rooms and personalised drinks and refreshments services continue the upmarket theme. Even Krungsri's heritage is not forgotten: specially commissioned large-format black-and-white photographs highlight the bank's Ayudhya origins.

1 The space invites customers into a centralised heart or comfortable hub, which feels more like a living room than a bank.
2 The concierge counter is open and obvious for immediate personal contact.

A retail-oriented approach for banking services

3 Rounded forms and comfortable furnishings
  create a friendly effect, while the brand's
  bright, crisp yellow contrasts with a warm,
  neutral palette.
4 The furniture and fixtures are inspired
  by the soft curves of the *prasart sang*,
  the traditional Thai roof form used on
  the bank's brand logo.

NOKIA
BY EVANSLUNDIN

WHERE Helsinki, Finland WHEN September 2012
CLIENT Nokia DESIGNER Evanslundin (p.494)
TOTAL FLOOR AREA 200 m² SHOP CONSTRUCTORS ISS Proko and Set Square Staging
PHOTOS Tuomas Uusheimo

Called in to redesign the Nokia Flagship Store in Helsinki, design office Evanslundin was asked to 'push the envelope' of normal technology stores regarding visual language and customer activities. At the same time, a white environment was requested in order to effectively showcase the jazzy colours of Nokia's product ranges. Evanslundin responded with a soft, white landscape of illuminated wall bays and floating ribbon tables. Although monochrome, the store is far from being minimal: the designers' strategy was to not hide the stock, but to put as much product on display as possible. The wall bays each contain 36 lit, oblong-shaped drawers, each capable of a range of display options. When closed, the edges of each draw are illuminated, but when pulled out, the whole drawer surface is lit, creating a futuristic vertical landscape of glowing displays, accentuating the product offering. The drawers can be pulled out in various configurations according to need, making for a flexible and versatile system. Additional display and demo space is provided by several linear tables which unfold and undulate at different heights. The product demos use imaging, navigation and music to encourage customer interaction with the products. The ribbon-like tables are destined and placed so that people can approach from any side and gather around the different demos. Contrast is added to the white-on-white store by bold blue graphics and by a home-like area composed of a brick wall backdrop and lounge-like furnishings – a chance for customers to imagine products in a domestic setting.

1   In an all-white store, bright blue wall
    graphics add contrast and interest.
2   Informal, ribbon-like tables invite customers
    to approach for a product demo.
3   Each wall bay has 36 illuminated drawers
    which can be pulled out to display products
    in virtually endless configurations.

472

RAIFFEISEN BANK KREUZPLATZ
BY DGJ AND NAU

1

WHERE Zurich, Switzerland WHEN July 2011
CLIENT Raiffeisenbank Zürich DESIGNERS DGJ (p.494) and NAU (p.497)
TOTAL FLOOR AREA 400 m² SHOP CONSTRUCTORS Glaeser Wogg, Salvini and Blaser Metallbau
PHOTOS Jan Bitter

Banks are the kind of institutions that are all too often seen as faceless corporations. Perhaps that's why so many faces adorn new-look Swiss bank Raiffeisen in Zurich, a collaboration by design offices DGJ and NAU, which features curving walls perforated with abstracted portraits of historical residents from the local area. With the kind of personality more usually associated with high-end retail projects, Raiffeisen's 'open lounge' is a response to changing conditions in banking, which dissolve the traditional barriers between customers and employees. Advanced technologies make the banking infrastructure largely invisible; employees access terminals concealed in furniture elements, while a robotic retrieval system grants 24-hour access to safety deposit boxes. This shifts the bank's role, allowing it be become a light-filled, inviting environment – an open lounge where customers can learn about new products and services. Conversations can start spontaneously around a touch-screen equipped info-table, while meeting rooms allow for more private discussions. Elegantly flowing walls blend the different areas of the bank into one smooth continuum, from the customer reception at the front to the employee workstations towards the back. The walls are also placed to allow different grades of privacy and to maximise daylight throughout, while also acting as a membrane mediating between the open public spaces and more intimately scaled conference rooms. Portraits of the quarter's most prominent past residents like Böklin, Semper and Spyri adorn the walls, their abstracted images the result of advanced digital production techniques. While intricately decorative, the design grounds the bank in the area's cultural past, while creating a distinctly futuristic look.

1 The portraits on the walls have a historical theme but were executed using advanced technology (a collaboration with ROK – Rippmann Oesterle Knauss).
2 Muted meeting rooms shift the palette from white to beige.

An inviting open space, free of visible banking infrastructure

1 Entrance lobby
2 ATM
3 Reception
4 Cash desk
5 Lounge
6 Meeting room
7 Offices
8 Main office
9 Kitchen
10 Toilets

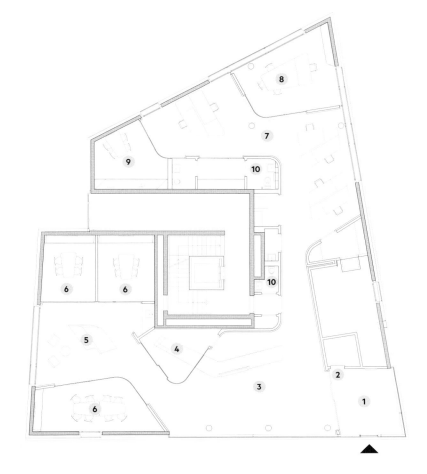

3 The meeting rooms offer privacy and
   pockets of intimacy.
4 The bank is designed as a lounge with the
   banking terminals concealed inside pieces
   of furniture.
5 The abstract images on the walls are made
   up of 12-mm CNC-perforated Hi-macs Panels.

5

RAIFFEISEN BANK SCHAFFHAUSEN
BY DGJ AND NAU

WHERE Schaffhausen, Switzerland **WHEN** May 2013
CLIENT Raiffeisenbank Schaffhausen **DESIGNERS** DGJ (p.494) and NAU (p.497)
TOTAL FLOOR AREA 200 m² **SHOP CONSTRUCTORS** Wickli Metallbau, Glaeser Wogg, Waldvogel Schreinerei
PHOTOS Roger Frei

Adding colour and richness to the interior of Swiss bank of Raiffeisen's new Schaffhausen branch are dramatic walls of glass shingles in warm, gold-toned colours, backlit by LED lights so that they glow. The walls, a modern take on the local tradition of stained glass, give a strong identity to an otherwise calm, neutral interior, the result of a collaboration between design offices DGJ and NAU. The whole ground floor of the bank is conceived as a spacious, open meeting place which flows over the entire elongated (originally medieval) floorplan, from the entrance on the Bahnhofstrasse through to the inner courtyard. The open organisation allows for good natural lighting, straightforward wayfinding for the customer and transparency regarding the bank's internal processes. Built-in furniture helps to define various zones in the space, and touches of colour (rich, warm yellows and reds) on these elements echo the palette of the patterned walls. Meanwhile the background palette, in cool white and grey, sets off the jewel-like brilliance of the glass. For the glass mural walls, the designers drew on the tradition of painted façades in the historic centre of Schaffhausen. Collaborating with ROK – Rippmann Oesterle Knauss, the designers digitally processed these murals to create an abstract pattern composed of overlapping rhomboid glass shingles. The end result references the Raiffeisen brand's original honeycomb logo and anchors the interior to local history. It also works to attract the interest of passers-by through its combination of colour, radiance and pattern.

1 Feature walls were inspired by colourful murals in the historic centre of Schaffhausen which were reinterpreted using contemporary computer-based technologies.
2 The diamond motif recurs in the glass used for walls and windows.
3 Black diamonds partly screen the façade, creating an intriguing effect.

4 The coloured glass walls are backlit using
  LEDs to create a bright, warm atmosphere.
5 The feature murals were made from glass
  shingles, arranged in overlapping patterns.
6 The 8-mm glass panels were hung on
  stainless steel brackets afixed to the walls.

Sensuous glass tiles create a warm, vibrant atmosphere

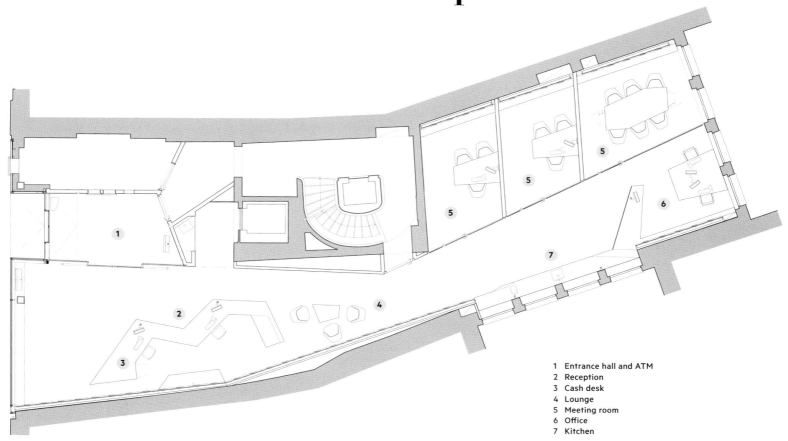

1 Entrance hall and ATM
2 Reception
3 Cash desk
4 Lounge
5 Meeting room
6 Office
7 Kitchen

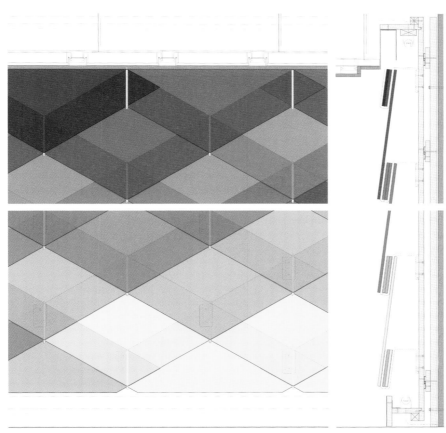

6

SUGAMO SHINKIN BANK
BY EMMANUELLE MOUREAUX
ARCHITECTURE + DESIGN

WHERE Tokyo, Japan **WHEN** December 2012
CLIENT Sugamo Shinkin Bank **DESIGNER** emmanuelle moureaux architecture + design (p.494)
TOTAL FLOOR AREA 714 m² **SHOP CONSTRUCTOR** Shiraishi Construction
PHOTOS Nacása & Partners (Daisuke Shima)

For the Ekoda branch of the Sugamo Shinkin Bank, Emmanuelle Moureaux, who always bases her work on colour and its ability to shape spatial effects, created the concept of 'a rainbow shower'. By surrounding the space with a forest-like façade of brightly coloured sticks, placed rather randomly outside the actual physical space of the branch, she has tied together the interior of the store and the street beyond. While 29 sticks are dotted outside the glass façade, there are also 19 inside it. By encroaching onto the street, the coloured sticks add to the public space and entice visitors into the bank: 'This rainbow shower returns colours and some room for playfulness back to the town,' explains Moureaux. She adds that the client brief called for a space that 'customers feel happy to visit.' When visitors enter the bank – the fourth branch Moureaux has designed for Sugamo Shinkin – they find themselves in an informal open space: an indoor terrace filled with a variety of colourful chairs, resembling a café more

than the average bank. Two further glazed courtyards separate this informal meeting area from the rest of the space. Each one appears as a glass vitrine and contains bamboo trees, a kind of real forest reflecting the metaphorical one created by the coloured sticks. Each of the layers in the interior is filled with daylight and with shadows and reflections, adding an outdoor feel to the interior experience.

1 The 9-m-high coloured sticks occupy the 2-m zone outside the glass façade.
2 The lounge-like interior has the forest of coloured sticks on one side, with real trees growing in the glass vitrines on the other.

A rainbow forest of sticks adds a playful aspect to the town

3 Chairs in rainbow hues are used throughout the bank's interior.
4 The various glazed layers fill the interior with daylight and complex shadows and zreflections.

VZ FINANZPORTAL
BY DGJ AND NAU

2

WHERE Zurich, Switzerland **WHEN** January 2013
CLIENT VZ VermögensZentrum **DESIGNERS** DGJ (p.494) and NAU (p.497)
TOTAL FLOOR AREA 150 m² **SHOP CONSTRUCTOR** Glaeser Wogg
PHOTOS Roger Frei

Having created a successful online financial services platform, VZ VermögensZentrum asked DGJ and NAU to design an interface for its VZ Finanzportal web brand. The challenge was to create a multifunctional space, while conveying a tangible real-world identity for the Finanzportal's digital presence. The designers responded with a concept that reinterprets VermögensZentrum's logo in a spatial way, as a sculptural, multifunctional desk defining three separate zones (for informing, advising and training clients). The result is not so much a piece of furniture as an architectural element, snaking and twisting through the space in a manner reminiscent of a Moebius strip. It morphs from counter to table to shelf to screen support, with lighting emphasising its several changes of character, although the material – white, glossy Hi-Macs – is the same throughout. A contrasting warm hardwood floor sets off the sleek white floating desk, while suspended white ceiling elements set with LED bands in parallel lines add to the high-tech aesthetic.

They also reflect and balance the angular movement of the desk below. At the back of the space, a hardwood wall contains a long strip of screens – evoking the brand's online roots and screening the warmer, more intimate meeting areas that lie behind the front office. These spaces are furnished rather more conventionally, with custom design tables and Arper Catifa chairs. In the evening, the sculpted space comes to life thanks to an animated multimedia projection, designed to lend a tangible face to the immaterial universe of finance.

1 The contemporary display units and lighting give the space a somewhat futuristic feel.
2 The suspended ceiling elements balance the angular movement of furniture and fittings below.

DESI
PROD

488

GNER
TILES

489

…,STAAT CREATIVE AGENCY
De Ruyterkade 143
1011 AC Amsterdam
the Netherlands
+31 20 5721 388
contact@staatamsterdam.nl
staatamsterdam.nl

(p.318, p.406)

An international creative agency based in Amsterdam, the Netherlands, …,staat was established in 2000. The agency states that it consists of 'original thinkers, who know no limits and deliver fully integrated branding concepts. From strategy to concept to design, with passion, turning the everyday into the iconic.'

2KUL INTERIOR DESIGN
Ul. Moniuszki 7/1
51-610 Wrocław
Poland
+48 600 281 323
biuro@2kul.pl
2kul.pl

(p.386)

2kul Interior Design was founded by Magdalena Urban, Agnieszka Koszutska and Ewa Lewicka as a group of freelance designers. The group works on projects for business clients, public institutions and private clients, and on commissions including architecture, interior design, furniture and graphics.

42 ARCHITECTS
Unit 2.3, 1-5 Vyner Street
London E2 9DG
United Kingdom
+44 790 6621 482
info@42architects.com
42architects.com

(p.112)

42 Architects is an architectural studio based in London, established in 2009 by Johan Berglund. The practice works internationally on cultural, residential and commercial projects, providing full architectural, landscape and interior design, event and exhibition design services for both public and private sectors.

A L M PROJECT
5544 Hollywood Blvd.
Los Angeles, CA 90028
United States
+1 323 5700 571
studio@almproject.com
almproject.com

(p.324, p.356)

A l m project is a multidisciplinary Hollywood-based design studio founded in 2007 by Austrian Andrea Lenardin Madden. Its focus is on architecture, identity and packaging design. 'Growing up in Vienna, where culture and the arts are a prominent part of the daily discourse, has greatly influenced my approach to architecture and design', says Andrea Lenardin Madden. 'Sensitive to the relevance of place and time, a l m strives to design distinctive environments capable of retaining past, present and future memories.'

AEKAE
Talwiesenstrasse 17
8045 Zurich
Switzerland
+41 43 960 2061
mail@aekae.com
aekae.com

(p.044, p.222)

Aekae is an ideas-driven design studio founded by Fabrice Aeberhard and Christian Kaegi in 2006. With a holistic approach to design, the studio works with international clients across multiple disciplines on a diverse range of projects, including interiors, furniture, products, luxury goods, transportation and branding. It has a special interest in the reuse of materials and the lifecycle of objects.

AIGNER ARCHITECTURE
Redwitzstrasse 4
81925 Munich
Germany
+49 89 9089 9628
info@aigner-architecture.com
aigner-architecture.com

(p.036)

Aigner architecture was founded in 2000 by Marie Aigner, who completed her architectural studies in Germany and France as well as gaining a degree in engineering and architecture at Technischen Universität in Munich. She subsequently collaborated with the architecture studios S.O.M and Richard Meier in New York and Atelier 11 in Paris. Since its foundation, the office has completed projects in Germany, Switzerland, the UK, the USA and Oman, and has won a number of awards.

ANAGRAMA
Guillermo Prieto #400,
Colonia San Pedro
San Pedro Garza Garcia,
NL 66236
Mexico
+52 818 336 6666
hello@anagrama.com
anagrama.com

(p.322)

International branding firm Anagrama was founded by Gustavo Muñoz, Sebastián Padilla and Mike Herrera in 2008. It has offices in Monterrey and Mexico City and a global client list representing various industries. As well as brand development, Anagrama works on the design and development of objects, spaces, software and multimedia projects. Its aim has always been to 'break the traditional creative agency scheme, integrating multidisciplinary teams of creative and business experts.'

ARCHICEPT CITY
5-4-35-1104 Minamiaoyama,
Minato-Ku
107-0062 Tokyo
Japan
+81 3 6427 6409
muroi@archicept-city.com
archicept-city.com

(p.078, p.460)

Archicept city, founded in April 2013 by Atsushi Muroi, works mainly on experience branding and spatial design. With a degree in architecture, Muroi formerly worked for Hakuhodo, a major advertising agency in Japan. His novel experience-branding methodology is a hybrid approach based on strategic spatial design and advertising-oriented communication activities. Awards include the Red Dot Best of the Best (2011), Good Design Awards (2009 and 2011), and Cannes Lions Design (finalist 2009).

ART BUREAU 1/1
Ul. Myasnitskaya 24/7,
Building 1
101000 Moscow
Russia
+7 495 621 5669
studio@1over1.ru
oneoverone.ru

(p.062, p.142, p.262)

The name of Art Bureau 1/1 reflects the office motto: 'all we do is unique, each design is the only one of its kind'. The bureau's aim is to reflect its own and its clients ideas about art, aesthetics and taste, whether in commercial or private designs. The team of eight specialises in interior design, architecture and decoration.

AS DESIGN SERVICE
Room A, 8/F, New Timely
Factory Building
497 Castle Peak Road
Lai Chi Kok, Kowloon
Hong Kong
+852 2191 6433
info@as-hk.com
as-hk.com

(p.296, p.300, p.304)

AS Design founders Four Lau and Sam Sum believe that the ideal design contains 'sense and sensibility': practicality and aesthetics. Thanks to their imagination, market sense and determination, AS Design has grown into a thriving firm. The agency has worked on the identity of brands in Hong Kong, Mainland China and the South Pacific region, as well as interiors for retail, hospitality, commercial and residential projects.

ATELIER DU PONT
89 rue de Reuilly
75012 Paris
France
+33 1 5333 2410
adp@atelierdupont.fr
atelierdupont.fr

(p.014, p.278)

Founded in 1997 by Anne-Cécile Comar, Philippe Croisier and Stéphane Pertusier, Atelier du Pont is a multi-polar agency that oscillates between public and private projects, architecture and urban planning, exterior and interior work. Although architecture (in particular public housing and facilities) is an essential part of the agency's work, the office finds interiors 'a breath of fresh air, giving free rein to our imaginations and allowing us to experiment with extravagant materials and to create places that are both outside time and of their time.'

ATELIER MARKGRAPH
Ludwig-Landmann-
Strasse 349
60487 Frankfurt am Main
Germany
+49 69 979 930
contact@markgraph.de
markgraph.de

(p.402)

A leading agency for spatial communication, Atelier Markgraph is based in Frankfurt am Main. This interdisciplinary design and planning provider creates tangible spatial experiences for companies, brands and themes for clients all over the world. Using leading edge technologies, Markgraph produces surprising spatial productions at the interface of business, culture and science – from exhibitions through media productions to corporate architecture.

ATELIER MARKO BRAJOVIC
Rua Apinajés 440
05017-000 São Paulo
Brazil
+55 11 2371 9206
atelier@markobrajovic.com
markobrajovic.com

(p.432)

The idea of the hybrid obsesses the multidisciplinary Atelier Marko Brajovic, with offices in São Paulo, Brazil, and Barcelona, Spain. Founded in 2009, the atelier works on projects in Miami, Dubai, Aixi, Shanghai, Barcelona, Rio de Janeiro and São Paulo, in the areas of architecture, scenography, interior and product design. The office believes in 'creating spaces that communicate brands through a narrative, multi-sensorial and immersive experience.'

BEHF ARCHITECTS
Kaiserstrasse 41
1070 Vienna
Austria
+43 1 524 1750
contact@behf.at
behf.at

(p.338, p.466)

BEHF Architects, a Vienna-based international architectural practice, was established by the principals Armin Ebner, Susi Hasenauer and Stephan Ferenczy in 1995. Since then, BEHF has executed a wide range of award-winning projects in Europe and Asia, based on its understanding that good architecture is the result of good communication, and that architecture should be an intricate part of the corporate culture and message of the client.

BETWIN SPACE DESIGN
3F, 685-383 Seongsu1-
ga2-dong, Seongdong-gu
133-112 Seoul
Korea
+88 2 6402 9665
betwinspace@gmail.com
betwin.kr

(p.006, p.156)

Betwin Space Design states that it obtains results through 'the sharing of ideas on the characteristics of our business, and sharing the value of our ideas through cooperative work, creating more value through enjoying pleasant collaborations with a lot of people.'

BLOCHER BLOCHER PARTNERS
Herdweg 19
70174 Stuttgart
Germany
+49 711 224 820
info@blocherblocher.com
blocherblocher.com

(p.010, p.308)

With offices in Stuttgart, Mannheim and New Delhi, Blocher Blocher Partners was founded in 1989 by architect Dieter Blocher and interior designer Jutta Blocher. The firm's core activities are architecture and interior architecture with a focus on event-oriented retail concepts. In cooperation with its subsidiaries Blocher Blocher Shops and Blocher Blocher View, the company works in brand development, mono brand concepts, corporate, retail and graphic design, as well as in communication, public relations, decoration concepts and visual merchandising.

BLOCK722ARCHITECTS+
Patision 57
10433 Athens
Greece
+30 21 0361 7081
info@block722.com
block722.com

(p.192)

BLOCK722architects+ is an Athens-based architectural practice, named after the urban block in Athens where it was founded. Established in 2009 by Sotiris Tsergas and Katja Margaritoglou, the office undertakes complete project management in the residential, retail and business fields. The design process begins with a thorough conceptual approach and by integrating the interior design into this phase, the desired unified architectural result is achieved regarding the project as a whole.

BLU WATER STUDIO
B-1-1, Block B, 1F
Megan Avenue 1, 189, Jalan
Tun Razak
50400 Kuala Lumpur
Malaysia
+603 2163 4689
bluw@bluwaterstudio.com
bluwaterstudio.com

(p.446)

Established by Lai Siew Hong in 2010, BluWater Studio is an award-winning design studio providing interior design consultancy services and specialising in hotels, resorts and restaurants. The studio's goal is 'to create unique and distinctive designs, bringing the client instant recognition while maximising the consumer's experience.'

BRINKWORTH
4-6 Ellsworth Street
London E2 0AX
United Kingdom
+44 20 7613 5341
info@brinkworth.co.uk
brinkworth.co.uk

(p.184, p.284, p.418)

Adam Brinkworth established Brinkworth, one of the UK's leading creative design agencies, in 1990. The office specialises in interior, architectural, graphics and brand design. Based in London, Brinkworth's clients include Nike, Ben Sherman, Selfridges, Carhartt, Dabbous, Diesel LBi, Supreme, Dinos Chapman, Hugo Boss, Converse, Karen Millen, Heineken, Tinello, Foot Patrol, All Saints and Casio.

CANDIDA TABET ARQUITETURA
Rua Fidalga 505
05432-070 São Paulo
Brazil
+55 11 3034 6441
info@candidatabet.com
candidatabet.com

(p.412)

Founded in 2000, Candida Tabet Arquitetura realises residential, commercial and institutional projects, creatively combining architecture and interior design. The office's projects are developed on the basis of research into materials and on elaborate construction, always taking into consideration the environments in which they are to come to life.

CHECKLAND KINDLEYSIDES
Charnwood Edge,
Cossington
Leicester LE7 4UZ
United Kingdom
+44 116 2644 700
heidi@checklandkindleysides.com
checklandkindleysides.com

(p.440)

The UK-based creative firm Checkland Kindleysides was established by Jeff Kindleysides in 1979. The multidisciplinary studio specialises in defining strategy, brand identity, retail environments, workplace, events, in-store merchandising, furniture design, digital and graphic communications. It brings together a collaborative mix of talents and skills to create compelling, category leading brand experiences in a wide range of global and local markets.

COMO PARK STUDIO
Artemisstraat 90
1076 DW Amsterdam
the Netherlands
+31 6 1228 6454
info@comoparkstudio.com
comoparkstudio.com

(p.186, p.216)

Como Park Studio specialises in interior architecture, concept development, branding, identity, design and execution in the areas of retail, hotel, hospitality and other. Based in Amsterdam, the office works internationally on large and small-scale projects.

CONCEPT I
Q House Convent, 4F
38 Convent Road, Silom,
Bangrak
10500 Bangkok
Thailand
+66 2632 0876
admin@concept-i-design.com
concept-i-design.com

(p.468)

Founded in 1996 by CEO Geoff Morrison, Concept i is an award-winning, international design studio dedicated to creative and commercially sustainable design solutions. With a strong focus on retail and leisure sectors, the firm prides itself on adding exceptional value to design and providing high-calibre client services. With offices in Bangkok, Shanghai and Istanbul, Concept i works across the Far East and Middle East regions.

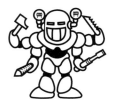

CONFETTI
Sevillaweg 132
3038 TW Rotterdam
the Netherlands
+31 10 4762 627
info@confettireclame.nl
confettireclame.nl

(p.106)

Confetti is a company uniting different disciplines under one roof. A one-stop shop, Confetti prides itself on understanding what clients want to say, and translating that into a 3D design. Projects include interiors for schools and stores, shop display windows and booths for events.

COORDINATION ASIA
4F, 244 Liaoning Road,
Hongkou District
200080 Shanghai
China
+86 21 6276 0206
hello@coordination-asia.com
coordination-asia.com

(p.458)

Coordination Asia was founded by German architect Tilman Thürmer (who also set up Coordination Berlin with Jochen Gringmuth and Flip Sellin). The award-winning design and architecture agency specialises in creating high-impact environments for museums, exhibitions, retail and hospitality clients. Driven by the quest for fresh ideas and extraordinary design solutions, Coordination Asia has collaborated with the Shanghai Museum of Glass and the Shanghai Film Museum, among others.

CORNEILLE UEDINGSLOHMANN ARCHITEKTEN
Konrad-Adenauer-Ufer 83
50668 Cologne
Germany
+49 221 335 5370
info@cue-architekten.de
cue-architekten.de

(p.210, p.256)

Founded by Yves Corneille and Peter Uedingslohmann in 2002, Corneille Uedingslohmann Architekten is dedicated to finding comprehensive solutions in the fields of architecture and shop design. With its long-term clients, the company shares a history of successful projects that have featured in national and international publications and won various awards and prizes.

CREA INTERNATIONAL
Via Olmetto 9
20123 Milan
Italy
+39 02 3656 3870
info@creainternational.com
creainternational.com

(p.462)

CREA international is an integrated multidisciplinary design company based in Milan. According to its original Physical Brand Design working methodology, it aims to create competitive values for clients by harnessing service design innovation and delivering effective brand design experiences within physical space. Founded in 2002 by Alberto Pasquini and co-managed by Marco Bini and Stefano Carone, the company specialises in naming and branding, retail design, architecture, hospitality and real estate and product design.

CRENEAU INTERNATIONAL
Hellebeemden 13
3500 Hasselt
Belgium
+32 11 24 79 20
info@creneau.com
creneau.com

(p.030)

Creneau International is a global agency that connects brands, spaces and consumers through design concepts. Established in 1989, the Hasselt-based office provides a full service, from concepts and consultancy to graphics, interiors, and F&B support for projects including hospitality, retail and branding.

D'ART DESIGN GRUPPE
Am Zollhafen 5
41460 Neuss
Germany
+49 21 3140 307
hello@d-art-design.de
d-art-design.de

(p.422)

D'art Design Gruppe is one of the leading agencies for spatial communication in Germany, in which creative design skills are merged with interdisciplinary expertise. A recipient of numerous international design awards, D'art Design Gruppe designs brand experience and adventure spaces for clients such as adidas, arte, Bogner, Electrolux, Grundig, Panasonic and Philips since more than 20 years. D'art Design Gruppe is guided by the Managing Directors Jochen Höffler, Guido Mamczur, Freddy Justen and Dieter Wolff.

DALZIEL AND POW
5-8 Hardwick Street
London EC1R 4RG
United Kingdom
+44 20 7837 7117
info@ dalziel-pow.com
dalziel-pow.com

(p.136)

Dalziel and Pow is an integrated design consultancy which was cofounded in 1983 by David Dalziel. The company offers a full range of design services, from brand positioning, identity design and retail design, through to graphic design, photographic art direction and digital design. The approach is holistic, which results in successful brand environments and communications. The ambition is 'to create great customer experiences.'

DAN PEARLMAN
Kiefholzstrasse 1
12435 Berlin
Germany
+49 30 5300 0560
office@danpearlman.com
danpearlman.com

(p.226, p.312, p.452)

dan pearlman is a strategic creative agency with a '360° approach' covering everything from strategic positioning and brand development to implementation in brand and leisure environments. The agency says it is 'passionate about creating holistic, sustainable and creative concepts and experiences using strategic processes, innovative methods and a creative, interdisciplinary and intercultural team.'

DASTRO RETAILCONCEPTS
Zwaanshals 510
3035 KS Rotterdam
the Netherlands
+31 6 5021 2538
dastro@dastro.nl
dastro.nl

(p.108)

In 2007 Rob Hoogendijk founded Dastro Retailconcepts, a Rotterdam design agency whose name highlights the firm's core business: retail design. Dastro has gathered experience in various branches of the industry thanks to projects for fashion, shoe, perfumery and jewellery stores, as well as pharmacies, opticians, and spaces belonging to the automotive and telecoms sectors. One of Dastro's clients is supermarket Spar.

DENIS KOŠUTIĆ
Florianigasse 7/8
1080 Vienna
Austria
+43 699 1947 9990
contact@deniskosutic.com
deniskosutic.com

(p.154, p.166)

Denis Košutić aims at a new, anti-traditional perception of the role of architecture in the modern world, translating trends from fashion and design into the language of everyday life and seeing architecture as a matter of consumption and not a monument to eternity. His office works on projects from restaurants, clubs, shops, houses, apartments and hotel apartments to furniture, and also cooperates with graphic designers, PR advisors and furniture producers.

DESIGNLSM
The Bath House
58 Livingstone Road
Hove BN3 3WL
United Kingdom
+44 12 7382 0033
info@designlsm.com
designlsm.com

(p.214)

Steve La Bouchardiere and Simon McCarthy founded designLSM in June 1988. Since then, the award-winning practice has worked on interior design, architecture and graphic design services for hotels, restaurants, bars, retail and residential properties. Clients range from independents to iconic brands in hospitality and retail, and while most projects are UK based, the office is also active in Europe, the Middle East, the USA, India and China.

DFROST
Hauptstaetterstrasse 59 A
70178 Stuttgart
Germany
+49 711 664 817
info@dfrost.com
dfrost.com

(p.024)

Founded in Stuttgart, Germany, in 2008 by Nadine Frommer, Christoph Stelzer and Fabian Stelzer, dfrost is a visual marketing and retail design agency. From POS consulting to retail architecture to communications and window design, the agency is interdisciplinary, comprising experienced retail marketing experts, project, event and communications executives, architects and graphic and design professionals. It prides itself on offering 'innovative solutions for the successful presentation of products and brands at the point of sale.'

DISTILLERY
315 Outram Road
#13-01 Tan Boon Liat
Building
169074 Singapore
Singapore
+65 6224 3221
info@distillerystudio.net
distillerystudio.net

(p.052)

Distillery is a Singapore-based interior design studio led by Australian interior designers Paul Semple and Matthew Shang and driven by 'all that influences, stimulates, and provokes us'. The office specialises in hotel and resort design, luxury residential projects, restaurants and hospitality, retail design including branded environments, prototype development and flagship stores as well as unique standalone boutiques and retail entities, and specialist custom-designed furniture and detailed joinery design.

DGJ
Riedtlistrasse 27
8006 Zurich
Switzerland
+41 44 382 1062
zurich@dgj.ch
dgj.ch

(p.474, p.478, p.486)

Founded in 1999, Drexler Guinand Jauslin Architekten (DGJ) is an international architectural office based in Zurich, Frankfurt and Rotterdam. In parallel to planning and realisation, the firm researches in the field of design methodology and sustainability. The integration of new technologies, associated with a sustainable approach, is also part of its approach. Office projects range from urban planning to interior design.

DITTEL ARCHITEKTEN
Rotenwaldstrasse 100/1
70197 Stuttgart
Germany
+49 711 4690 6550
info@d-arch.de
d-arch.de

(p.096)

Founded in 2005 by Frank Dittel, Dittel Architekten develops distinctive spaces with passion. The interdisciplinary office's 23 architects, interior designers and communication designers aspire to create an intriguing, characteristic and exclusive look for every brand or company.

DOEPEL STRIJKERS
Heer Bokelweg 155
3032 AD Rotterdam
the Netherlands
+31 10 2733 158
office@doepelstrijkers.com
doepelstrijkers.com

(p.282)

After working together at MVRDV architects in the early 1990s, architect Duzan Doepel and interior architect Eline Strijkers both started their own practices. In 2007 they joined forces. Today, Doepel Strijkers produces innovative interiors, architecture and urban strategies based on what it calls 'co-creative and participatory design trajectories related both to the fields of art and theory.' Recent projects have included homes, restaurants, schools, shops and offices.

DUCCIO GRASSI ARCHITECTS
Via San Marco 48
20121 Milan
Italy
+39 02 2906 3196
info@ducciograssiarchitects.com
ducciograssiarchitects.com

(p.232, p.236)

Duccio Grassi Architects (DGA) develops concepts for buildings, boutiques and showrooms. Clients include Max Mara, Zara, Canali, Guru, Guess by Marciano, Penny Black, Max&Co, Ceramiche Refin, Iris Ceramica, and many others. DGA has also designed furniture for Emmebi, Minotti Cucine and Viabizzuno. The studio has won awards in Paris, New York and Los Angeles and has offices in Milan and Reggio Emilia.

EDWARDS MOORE
90 Moor Street, Fitzroy
Melbourne 3065
Australia
+61 3 8060 1840
hi@edwardsmoore.com
edwardsmoore.com

(p.240, p.450)

Edwards Moore was founded in 2009 by Ben Edwards and Juliet Moore – both qualified architects who are 'passionate about design and the human experience, believe that architectural and artistic thinking can apply to varying types of projects, and have an ambition to bring ideas to life, to inspire and delight.' It has established itself as a design studio based on innovation and conceptual thinking, with an international perspective. The office works on a range of projects from small-scale objects to large-scale buildings and infrastructure.

EMMANUELLE MOUREAUX ARCHITECTURE + DESIGN
Tounkyo Bldg 3F
1-14-14 Uchikanda,
Chiyoda-ku
101-0047 Tokyo
Japan
+81 3 3293 0323
contact@emmanuelle.jp
emmanuelle.jp

(p.074, p.482)

French architect Emmanuelle Moureaux has lived in Tokyo since 1996, establishing her own office, emmanuelle moureaux architecture + design, in 2003. Inspired by the Japanese tradition of sliding screens, she has created the concept of shikiri, which literally means 'dividing space with colours'. She uses colour as a 3D layering element to build up her interiors, working on a wide range of architecture, interior, furniture and product-design projects. Moureaux is also an Associate Professor at Tohoku University of Art and Design.

EVANSLUNDIN
16 Southam Street
London W1 05PH
United Kingdom
+44 20 3582 7290
info@evanslundin.com
evanslundin.com

(p.472)

Evanslundin is a London design agency with extensive experience in delivering unique and high-quality built solutions to a variety of clients ranging from private individuals to multinational corporations. Earlier clients include Hilton, Waldorf Astoria, Cutler & Gross and Nokia. The office states that its approach is 'focused on inventing bespoke spatial solutions that truly embody a brand and fully reflect its ideology whilst creating engaging experiences for consumers.'

FABIO NOVEMBRE
Via Perugino 26
20135 Milan
Italy
+39 02 504 104
info@novembre.it
novembre.it

(p.194)

Since 1966, I've responded to those who call me Fabio; since 1992, I've responded to those who also call me "architect". I cut out spaces in the vacuum by blowing air bubbles, I make gifts of sharpened pins so as to ensure I never put on airs. My lungs are imbued with the scent of places that I've breathed, when I hyperventilate it's only so I can remain in apnea for a while. As though I were pollen, I let myself go with the wind, convinced I'm able to seduce all that surrounds me.' – Fabio Novembre

FABRIQUE [BRANDS, DESIGN & INTERACTION]
Jollemanhof 13
1019 GW Amsterdam
the Netherlands
+31 15 2195 600
info@fabrique.nl
fabrique.nl

(p.416)

In 1992, Jeroen van Erp, Theo Wolters and René Bubberman started Fabrique, which has since grown into an agency with more than 85 enthusiastic artists, engineers and storytellers. The multidisciplinary agency now has offices in Amsterdam, Rotterdam and Delft and works on various assignments for consumer brands, service companies, government, education, the entertainment industry and cultural institutions.

FAK3
Universal Building, 2F
5-13 New Street
Sheung Wan, Hong Kong
Hong Kong
+852 2964 9950
design@fak3.com
fak3.com

(p.088)

Johnny Wong and Miho Hirabayashi founded the award-winning boutique design studio FAK3 in Hong Kong in 2004. They say: 'Our philosophy is to create memorable experiences, stimulating the senses through the poetic blending of space, light and meticulous detailing.' The office specialises in hotels, restaurants and retail design.

FOURFOURSIXSIX
48 Oxford Street
London W1D 1BF
United Kingdom
+44 20 7323 2060
info@fourfoursixsix.com
fourfoursixsix.com

(p.326)

Founded in 2006 by Daniel Welham and Tim Ridd, Fourfoursixsix is an international architecture practice with offices in London and Bangkok. The office's research-based design process features 'an ability to work within highly varied typologies which, coupled with our international positioning, has allowed the company to undertake a diverse range of worldwide commissions within a number of project disciplines.'

FRANK AGTERBERG / BCA
Acacialaan 11
1560 Hoeilaart
Belgium
+32 2 673 0633
contact@frankagterberg.com
frankagterberg.com

(p.178)

Frank Agterberg / BCA is a full-service marketing agency headed by founder and creative director Frank Agterberg. Spread over Europe, this organic team of creative individuals and pragmatic fixers share their international experience and expertise from a broad variety of marketing disciplines. Projects include brand building, graphic design, fashion shows, product presentations, store design, retail- and window displays, tradeshows and showrooms.

FREITAG
Binzmühlestrasse 170b
8050 Zurich
Switzerland
+41 43 210 33 33
drivein@freitag.ch
freitag.ch

(p.034)

In 1993, two graphic designers, brothers Markus and Daniel Freitag, were looking for a functional, water-repellent and robust bag to hold their drawings. Inspired by the colourful heavy traffic that rumbled through the Zurich transit intersection in front of their flat, they designed a messenger bag made of old truck tarpaulins, used bicycle inner tubes and car seatbelts. The rest, as they say, is history. Freitag bags are still designed, cut and crafted in Zurich.

GLENN SESTIG ARCHITECTS
Fortlaan 1
9000 Ghent
Belgium
+32 9 240 1190
contact@
glennsestigarchitects.com
glennsestigarchitects.com

(p.070, p.434)

Glenn Sestig studied architecture at the Henry Van de Velde Institute in Antwerp. He went to found his own architectural firm in 1999. The focus of the firm is to realise contemporary, chic projects. Glenn Sestig 'aims to evolve cities into better places' by applying his signature cosmopolitan and luxurious style to stores, bars, nightclubs, residential buildings, renovations, temporary projects and products.

HEIKAUS CONCEPT
Hessigheimerstrasse 63
74395 Mundelsheim
Germany
+49 71 4396 9290
mail@heikaus.de
heikaus.de

(p.196, p.272)

Heikaus Concept designs and implements architectural concepts for domestic and international customers from many different industries. The company was founded in 1977 as Heikaus Lichttechnik (lighting technology) in Ingersheim, Germany. Projects include 'anything from an attractive optician to appealing shoe and fashion stores', with distinctive fashion environments being a particular speciality.

HOUSEHOLD
135 Curtain Road
London EC2A 3BX
United Kingdom
+44 20 7739 6537
sian@household-design.com
household-design.com

(p.392)

Household is a London-based customer experience design consultancy. Founded in 2004, the company partners global brands to transform retail and leisure environments – from format design, to pop-ups, spas and online. Household combines idea innovation with creative execution across interiors, communications and digital to enhance the customer's shopping and leisure journey. It has extensive expertise in food, luxury, home, beauty and technology.

i29 INTERIOR ARCHITECTS
Industrieweg 29
1115 AD Duivendrecht
the Netherlands
+31 20 6956 120
info@i29.nl
i29.nl

(p.372)

Founded by Jaspar Jansen and Jeroen Dellensen, award-winning i29 interior architects describes itself as a creative and versatile interior design studio. Their aim is to create intelligent designs and striking images. 'Space is the leitmotiv, the result always clear, with a keen eye for detail. Our approach is practical yet based on strong ideas articulated in clear concepts. We try to get to the core of things but keep it looking simple. Our clients are open minded and involved', says Jansen.

IPPOLITO FLEITZ GROUP
Augustenstrasse 87
70197 Stuttgart
Germany
+49 711 993 392 330
info@ifgroup.org
ifgroup.org

(p.364, p.378)

Ippolito Fleitz Group is a multidisciplinary, internationally operating design studio based in Stuttgart. Currently, Ippolito Fleitz Group is a creative unit comprising 37 designers and covering a wide range of design territory, including strategy, architecture, interiors, products, graphics and landscape architecture. Its projects have won over 170 international and national awards.

ITO MASARU DESIGN PROJECT / SEI
101 Daikanyama Tower
1-35-11 Ebisunishi,
Shibuya-ku
150-0021 Tokyo
Japan
+81 3 5784 3201
sei@itomasaru.com
itomasaru.com

(p.148, p.160)

Masaru Ito was born in Osaka, Japan in 1961 and graduated from Tokyo Zokei University in 1987. He established his own studio, SEI, after working in Kawasaki Takao's office. Since then, he has built a reputation as an interior maverick due to his quest for novel ideas and awareness of fashion. His motto is, 'always have the consumer's point of view.'

JAKLITSCH/GARDNER ARCHITECTS
115 W 27th Street,
9th Floor
New York, NY 10001
United States
+1 212 6209 166
info@jaklitschgardner.com
jaklitschgardner.com

(p.242)

Jaklitsch/Gardner Architects (J/GA) is an award-winning, New York City-based studio with expertise in designing commercial and residential buildings and interiors, furnishing and objects. Over the firm's 15 year history, J/GA has built several-hundred projects throughout North and South America, Europe, Asia and the Middle East – giving the firm an international perspective on design. The firm's principals, Stephan Jaklitsch and Mark Gardner, are actively involved in all stages of every project.

JAYME LAGO MESTIERI ARCHITECTURE
Alameda Casa Branca 851
Jardins
01408-001 São Paulo
Brazil
+55 11 3062 2885
contato@jlm.arq.br
jlm.arq.br

(p.118)

Jayme Lago Mestieri Architecture was founded in 1999, in São Paulo, Brazil. Since then, the office has produced over 700 projects, mostly involving commercial and public spaces as well as restaurants. The studio has designed several flagships and chain stores along with branding and retail concepts and today represents over 30 brands in Brazil. It also has a shopping centre division which specialises in malls.

JC ARCHITECTURE
144 Chaozhou Street
10649 Taipei
Taiwan
+886 2 2351 2998
info@johnnyisborn.com
johnnyisborn.com

(p.330)

JC Architecture (JCA) is a multidisciplinary design firm founded in 2010 by Johnny Chiu and Nora Wang. Its projects include architecture, interiors, industrial design and jewellery design. JCA says that it operates 'like a studio think-tank, always pushing imagination into every corner of its work, and breaking the boundaries between architecture and design.'

JOSÉ CARLOS CRUZ ARQUITECTO
Rua Fernão Lopes, 157 1º
Dto. B
4150-318 Porto
Portugal
+35 12 2616 3408
arch@josecarloscruz.com
josecarloscruz.com

(p.092)

After several years in partnership with other architects, José Carlos Cruz launched his own company in 2004. His work is inspired by frequent visits to major world cities and focuses on engaging with the practical realities and lifestyles of each client, seeking to give each project an individual character tailored to its site.

KAUFFMANN THEILIG & PARTNER
Zeppelinstrasse 10
73760 Ostfildern
Germany
+49 711 451 22 0
info@ktp-architekten.de
ktp-architekten.de

(p.402)

The office Kauffmann Theilig was established in 1988, changing its name in 1995 to Kauffmann Theilig & Partner. The award-winning office, run by Andreas Theilig, Dieter Ben Kauffmann and Rainer Lenz and located near Stuttgart in Germany, specialises in planning and realising projects in all fields of building construction, as well as corporate architecture and exhibition design for companies such as adidas, Mercedes-Benz, Liebherr, Boehringer Ingelheim, Seele and ADVA.

KOIS ASSOCIATED ARCHITECTS
33 Vasileos Konstantinou Avenue
10674 Athens
Greece
+30 21 0724 4433
info@koisarchitecture.com
koisarchitecture.com

(p.048, p.358)

Kois Associated Architects (KAA) is based in Athens and was founded by architect Stelios Kois in 2007. KAA works in all fields of design, ranging from urban projects to private buildings, interiors, furniture and products. The design ethos of the multidisciplinary studio is the synchronized engagement in practice and research that leads to the evaluation and generation of new solutions.

KONCEPT STOCKHOLM
Grev Turegatan 29
11438 Stockholm
Sweden
+46 85 4587 900
info@koncept.se
koncept.se

(p.290)

Koncept Stockholm is a company with clients and commissions throughout the world. With a base in Stockholm, the office's 55 employees work within the fields of design, architecture and concept development, on projects in the hotel, retail and office sectors. Koncept aims to design unique environments that create increased value and give clients a competitive advantage.

LANDINI ASSOCIATES
43 Rainford Street, Surry Hills
Sydney 2010
Australia
+61 2 9360 3899
studio@landiniassociates.com
landiniassociates.com

(p.334, p.362)

Landini Associates was established in 1993 by Mark and Rikki Landini. Mark was previously creative director of the Conran Design Group and Fitch RS and Rikki worked in corporate planning and PR. Based in Sydney, the office practices architecture, interior, graphic, product, furniture and digital design and is currently active in Australia, the USA, the UK, Korea, the UAE and Singapore.

LAUTREFABRIQUE ARCHITECTS
Anciennes Fabrique Crozel,
La Galicière
38160 Chatte
France
+33 476 648 577
info@lautrefabrique.com
lautrefabrique.com

(p.350)

Founded in 2001 by Jean-Pascal Crouzet, Lautrefabrique works internationally, offering the full range of architectural services, on all scales. The office favours a pragmatic approach focusing on promoting straightforward, common sense solutions in both public and private markets.

LIGANOVA
Herdweg 59
70174 Stuttgart
Germany
+49 711 652 200
info@liganova.com
liganova.comh

(p.428)

A specialist in integrated brand retail, marketing and production Liganova claims to 'blur the boundaries between classic brand communication and POS marketing, designing cutting-edge brand experiences while preserving the brand's own identity.' Its clients include Tommy Hilfiger, Calvin Klein, adidas, Cartier, Nespresso and Mercedes. The office was founded by Bodo Vincent Andrin and Michael Haiser, in 1995 and today employs over 200 people.

LINE-INC.
Kazami Bldg 2F+3F
1-1-6 Higashiyama,
Meguro-ku
153-0043 Tokyo
Japan
+81 3 5773 3536
line@line-inc.co.jp
line-inc.co.jp

(p.018, p.198, p.258)

Takao Katsuta founded Line-Inc. in 2002. Since then, the office has completed over 600 projects (including retail, bars, offices, restaurants, beauty salons and exhibition stands) and now works worldwide, in Shanghai, Hong Kong, Hawaii, London, and New York as well as in Japan. Katsuta states that the office's strength is 'our experience and our ability to manipulate flexible ideas and inspirations.'

MINISTRY OF DESIGN
20 Cross Street #03-01
048422 Singapore
Singapore
+65 6222 5780
studio@modonline.com
modonline.com

(p.084)

Ministry of Design was founded by Colin Seah in 2004. Since then, it has established an international reputation for its lifestyle-inspired design work. Projects range from boutique hotels to master plans and malls. Seah was recently dubbed a 'Rising Star in Architecture' by Monocle. He has been invited by the Singapore Tourism Board to redefine Singapore as a destination for 2020 and beyond.

MOVEDESIGN
2-5-20-203 Kusagae,
Chuoku
810-0045 Fukuoka
Japan
+81 92 986 4095
info@movedesign.jp
movedesign.jp

(p.082)

Founded in 2003 by Mikio Sakamoto, MOVEDESIGN has a solid track record in both architecture and interiors. The office's portfolio includes a number of salons, as well as retail spaces, private houses, bars and restaurants. The studio's design philosophy is: 'we can "MOVE" people's heart with design.'

MYKITA
Brunnenstrasse 153
10115 Berlin
Germany
+49 30 2045 6645
mail@mykita.com
mykita.com

(p.058)

A supplier of handcrafted eyewear since 2003, Mykita combines precise craftsmanship, high-end technologies a self-contained network. A constant search for intelligent technical solutions, the creative use of materials and a wealth of experience in eyewear design are behind the brand's collections, which are now available in 70 countries. A key factor in the company's success is its holistic business philosophy, which unites all departments and the in-house workshop under a single roof: The Mykita Haus in the heart of Berlin.

NAU
Riedtlistrasse 27
8006 Zurich
Switzerland
+41 44 382 1062
info@nau.coop
nau.coop

(p.474, p.478, p.486)

NAU is an international, multidisciplinary design firm, spanning the spectrum from architecture and interior design to exhibitions and interactive interfaces. As a futurist office creating both visual design and constructed projects, NAU melds the precision of experienced builders with the imagination and attention to detail required to create innovative exhibits, public events and architecture.

NERI&HU DESIGN AND RESEARCH OFFICE
88 Yuqing Road
200030 Shanghai
China
+86 21 6082 3777
info@nhdro.com
neriandhu.com

(p.382)

Lyndon Neri and Rossana Hu are the founding partners of Neri&Hu Design and Research Office, an inter-disciplinary, international architectural design practice based in Shanghai, China. The office won an AR Award for Emerging Architecture in 2010 from Architectural Review (UK), was selected as one of the AD 100 top talents in architecture and interior design in 2013 by Architectural Digest China, was named one of the Design Vanguards in 2009 by Architectural Record (USA), and was Overall Winner at the 2011 INSIDE Festival.

NOËL DOMINGUEZ ARCHITECTE
8 rue Sorbier
75020 Paris
France
+33 1 4797 1810
studio@noeldominguez.com
noeldominguez.com

(p.328)

Noël Dominguez Architecte is an architectural firm established in Paris in 2007 by Noël Dominguez-Truchot. He says: 'The practice is interested in the emotional potential and physical qualities of "a place" regardless of styles or fashion, envisioning architecture as something you are embedded in more that something you look at.'

NOMURA / RYUTARO
MATSUURA
1-11-26 Higashikagaya,
Suminoe-ku
559-0012 Osaka
Japan
ryutarou_matsuura@
nomurakougei.co.jp
nomuradesign.cn/nomura_
design/en/professional/
matsuura

(p.442)

Ryutaro Matsuura, one of the creative directors of Nomura, is in demand for his high-profile retail stores, restaurants, hotels and shopping centres. Nomura has a long history – about 120 years, to be exact. It was founded in 1892 by Taisuke Nomura who specialised in displaying chrysanthemum dolls, which were popular in Japan during that era.

OHLAB
Jose Abascal 27 7-Iz
28003 Madrid
Spain
+34 915 227 555
info@ohlab.net
ohlab.net

(p.064)

Paloma Hernaiz and Jaime Oliver direct OHLAB, an office devoted to urban analysis and cultural research through design, architectural practise and urban strategy. Prior to establishing the office in Madrid in 2007, the designers gained nine years of professional experience in New York, Shanghai and Beijing collaborating with offices such as OMA.

OPENAIR STUDIO
7 Narathiwas soi 10, Sathorn
10120 Bangkok
Thailand
+66 2676 0707
wit@openairstudio.com
openairstudio.com

(p.168, p.202, p.286)

OpenAir Studio, founded by Wit Chongwattananukul in 2008, is an interior design firm based in Bangkok which aims to create 'timeless and elegant architectural environments employing high quality materials and fine craftsmanship' and demonstrating 'an optimal relationship between objects and space, approaching each project considering its own spatial needs, and constructing a sculptural experience through it.'

PLAJER & FRANZ STUDIO
Erkelenzdamm 59/61
10999 Berlin
Germany
+49 30 616 5580
studio@plajer-franz.de
plajer-franz.de

(p.124, p.206, p.266)

Plajer & franz studio is an international and interdisciplinary team consisting of 50 architects, interior architects and graphic designers based in Berlin. All its activities are carried out in house. Clients include Karl Lagerfeld, Galeries Lafayette, BMW, Mini, Puma, Timberland and Pierre Cardin. The studio has also established itself in the premium sector of luxury residential projects and hotels, both in Europe and Asia.

PROPELLER DESIGN
5-9 Takezono-cho
659-0055 Ashiya
Japan
+81 797 255 144
info@propeller-design.com
propeller-design.com

(p.274)

Yoshihiro Kawasaki established Propeller Design in 2006. The office is active in various fields, including boutiques, beauty salons, showrooms, exhibition spaces, restaurants, displays and products. Major projects have included ASK Academy Schwarzkopf in Tokyo and the Daab VIP room for Toyota Motor Corporation. Propeller Design has won several prizes for its work inside and outside Japan.

RAFAEL DE CÁRDENAS /
ARCHITECTURE AT LARGE
611 Broadway, Suite 627
New York, NY 10012
United States
+1 212 965 8755
enquiry@
architectureatlarge.com
architectureatlarge.com

(p.374)

Rafael de Cárdenas / Architecture at Large was founded in 2006 as a small office in Chinatown, NYC and has now expanded to include a London studio. The practice has a wide-reaching portfolio with projects in architecture, interiors, temporary spaces, and object design. Recently, the studio has completed work for Baccarat, Nike and Nordstrom. The practice states: 'We favor the strategic over the thematic, the cosmopolitan over the typological, and the atmospheric over the static. Ever-focused on the contemporary, we take diligent note of the past while day-dreaming the future.'

SERGEY MAKHNO
Mejigorskaya Street 17,
apartment 6
04071 Kiev
Ukraine
+38 067 555 5515
mahnodesign@gmail.com
mahno.com.ua

(p.388)

Sergey Makhno is a Kiev-based architect and designer whose workshop creates both residential and commercial interiors in an eclectic combination of styles. With ten years of experience, the office focuses not only on overall structure, but also on decorative details, furniture and accessories. Over 100 completed projects include apartments, cottages, offices and restaurants all over the country.

SPECIALNORMAL
9-21-306 Hachiyama-cho,
Shibuya-ku
150-0035 Tokyo
Japan
+81 3 6416 0948
info@special-normal.com
special-normal.com

(p.252)

Specialnormal is a multidisciplinary design office based in the heart of Tokyo. It was founded by Shin Takahashi in June 2011 and since then has built a notable retail portfolio. Projects also include graphic design, package design and creative direction. Takahashi studied interior design at Kuwasawa Design Institute, Tokyo, and later worked on retail projects at Klein Dytham before founding Specialnormal.

STEFANO TORDIGLIONE
DESIGN
3F, 37 Staunton Street
SOHO, Central,
Hong Kong
Hong Kong
+852 2840 1100
info@tordiglione.com
stdesign.it

(p.426)

Stefano Tordiglione Design offers a range of architectural and design services covering retail, hospitality, commercial and residential as well as product development, project management, graphic design and creative consultancy. Collectively, the team has professional experience from Europe and the USA. Stefano Tordiglione, the Italian creative director and founder, is a designer and artist with extensive industry experience acquired in Italy, New York and London.

STUDIO ARTHUR CASAS
Rua Itápolis 818
0124-5000 São Paulo
Brazil
+55 11 2182 7500
casas@arthurcasas.com
arthurcasas.com

(p.340)

Arthur Casas' team of designers, architects and urbanists work from São Paulo and New York, building globally to great acclaim in cities such as Tokyo, Paris, and Rio de Janeiro. The office states: 'From the object to the landscape, inside and out, the creative process of Studio Arthur Casas is intimately connected to a horizontal scale, where the main concern is dialogue in the conception of programmes that can be as diverse as a chair or an entire neighbourhood, influenced by a spirit both modernist and contemporary that is Brazilian but also cosmopolitan.'

STUDIOMFD
Tussen de Bogen 60
1013 JB Amsterdam
the Netherlands
+31 6 2858 2916
info@studiomfd.com
studiomfd.com

(p.344)

Studiomfd was founded in 2006 by Martijn Frank Dirks, who says: 'I don't design offices, shops, houses, logos, websites or furniture; I design ways of working, selling, living, appearing, presenting or sitting: made exclusively for you… I reach my results by using your content. This is the starting point of every project.'

SUPERMACHINE STUDIO
57/7 Soi Chokchairuammit
16/13 Jompol, Jatujuk
10900 Bangkok
Thailand
+66 2276 6279
pitupong@gmail.com
supermachine.wordpress.com

(p.288)

Supermachine Studio is a multidisciplinary design studio, founded in Bangkok in 2009 by architect Pitupong Chaowakul. With a team of six designers, the studio's portfolio is diverse and includes architecture, interior, product and exhibition design, as well as art installations.

TONERICO
#902, 6-18-2 Jingumae,
Shibuya-ku
150-0001 Tokyo
Japan
+81 3 5468 0608
tonerico.inc@nifty.com
tonerico-inc.com

(p.100, p.130, p.396)

Founded in 2002 by Hiroshi Yoneya, Ken Kimizuka and Yumi Masuko. Tonerico focuses on architecture, interiors, furniture and industrial design. The office exhibits conceptual work around the world and has received several awards including the first prize in the 2005 Salone Satellite Design Report Award. Tonerico collaborates with manufactures such as Arflex Japan, Cassina, Muji and Panasonic.

UP
37 Greenpoint Avenue
Brooklyn, NY 11222
United States
+1 646 8203 529
whatsup@theupstudio.com
theupstudio.com

(p.042)

UP studio is an architecture and design firm that believes all disciplines can live together within a given project. The studio prides itself on its ability to solve problems through a multifaceted, collaborative design process to reach an integrated solution.

UPSTAIRS_
323B Beach Road
199558 Singapore
Singapore
+65 6299 0650
studio@upstairs.sg
upstairs.sg

(p.174, p.246)

Founded in 2011 by Dennis Cheok, who describes himself as 'a trained architect and chronic design busybody', UPSTAIRS_' avowed aim is 'to conceptualise and cultivate and collaborate as a design network across diverging disciplines, practices, and geographic boundaries, working with creative minds, brands and personalities to conjure and create spaces, products, graphics, installations, and then some.'

WILSON BROTHERS
21 Chippendale Street
London E5 0BB
United Kingdom
+44 7973 667 654
info@wilsonbrothers.co.uk
wilsonbrothers.co.uk

(p.184, p.284)

The Wilson Brothers joined forces in 2004. Oscar specialises in 2D-image creation and handcrafted typography, and Ben is a 3D industrial designer. Together, they work on creative projects with an international client list, which includes Nike, Supreme, Puma, Stussy, Brooks England, Sony, Honda, MTV, Virgin Atlantic and Twentieth Century Fox.

SH

ADDR

500

OP
ESSES

501

16AOUT COMPLEX (p.148)
by Ito Masaru Design Project / SEI
5-5-4-A1F Minamiaoyama, Minato-ku
107-0062 Tokyo
Japan
16aout-complex.com

ADIDAS ORIGINALS POP-UP STORE (p.422)
(temporary store)
by D'art Design Gruppe
Germany, Switzerland and Austria
adidas.com

AER (p.458)
by Coordination Asia
L4S-031-032, Coco Park
666 South Road, Longgang District
518000 Shenzhen
China

AMG PERFORMANCE CENTER (p.402)
by Kauffmann Theilig & Partner and
Atelier Markgraph
N3-12, 11 Sanlitun Road, Chaoyang District
100027 Beijing
China
mercedes-amg.com

AMICIS WOMEN (p.154)
by Denis Košutić
Tuchlauben 14
1010 Vienna
Austria
amicis.at

AND MARKET (p.460)
by Archicept city
3-2-5 Kasumigaseki, Chiyoda-ku
160-6090 Tokyo
Japan

ANGELICO (p.082)
by MOVEDESIGN
543-101 Fujiki, Oaza, Hyogomachi
8490915 Saga
Japan

AOYAMA MIHONCHO (p.100)
by Tonerico
4-2-5 Shibuya, Shibuya-ku
150-0002 Tokyo
Japan
takeo.co.jp

APPLE & PIE (p.426)
by Stefano Tordiglione Design
Shop# 206, 2/F One Island South
2 Heung Yip Road
Wong Chuk Hang, Hong Kong
Hong Kong
appleandpie.com

AS GOOD AS NEW (p.372)
(temporary store)
by i29 interior architects
Rozengracht 191
1016 LZ Amsterdam
the Netherlands
thisisasgoodasnew.com

AT HOME 103 (p.156)
by Betwin Space Design
79 Hwa-dong, Jongno-gu
110-210 Seoul
Korea
vve.co.kr

BACCARAT (p.374)
by Rafael de Cárdenas / Architecture at Large
635 Madison Avenue
New York, NY 10022
United States
baccarat.com

BACK TO SCHOOL (p.106)
(temporary store)
by Confetti
Bijenkorf
the Netherlands

BACKLASH (p.160)
by Ito Masaru Design Project / SEI
8-7 Uguisudani-cho, Shibuya-ku
150-0032 Tokyo
Japan
backlash.jp

BAMBINI (p.166)
by Denis Košutić
Tuchlauben 7
1010 Vienna
Austria
bambini-fashion.com

BAX-SHOP (p.108)
by Dastro Retailconcepts
Olympiastraat 2
4462 GG Goes
the Netherlands
bax-shop.nl

BEAN POLE (p.006)
by Betwin Space Design
B1, D-CUBE CITY
360-51 Shindorim, Guro-gu
152-706 Seoul
Korea
beanpole.com

BILDER & DE CLERCQ (p.318)
by ...,staat creative agency
De Clercqstraat 44
1052 NG Amsterdam
the Netherlands
bilderdeclercq.com

BORK (p.378)
by Ippolito Fleitz Group
Ul. Sadovaya-Spasskaya 3
Moscow
Russia
bork.ru

BREUNINGER SHOE DEPARTMENT (p.428)
by Liganova
Marktstrasse 1-3
70173 Stuttgart
Germany
e-breuninger.de

BUCHERER (p.010)
by Blocher Blocher Partners
Residenzstrasse 2, Palais an der Oper
80333 Munich
Germany
bucherer.ch

BUGABOO BRAND STORE (p.406)
by ...,staat creative agency
Keizersgracht 500
1017 EH Amsterdam
the Netherlands
bugaboo.com/bugaboostore

BURMA (p.014)
by Atelier du Pont
16 rue de la Paix
75002 Paris
France
bijouxburma.com

CA4LA (p.018)
by Line-Inc.
1F-2F Piazza Building
4-26-18 Jinguumae, Shibuya-ku
150-0001 Tokyo
Japan
ca4la.com

CADENZZA (p.024)
by dfrost
Rathaus Galerien Innsbruck
Maria Theresien Strasse 18
6020 Innsbruck
Austria
cadenzza.com

CAMPER TOGETHER (p.432)
by Atelier Marko Brajovic
JK Iguatemi Mall
Av. President Juscelino Kubitschek 20
04543-011 São Paulo
Brazil
camper.com

CAPITAL ZEN (p.168)
by OpenAir Studio
Zen Department Store, Central World
494 Rajdamri Road
10330 Bangkok
Thailand

CATALINA FERNÃNDEZ (p.322)
by Anagrama
Ave. San Pedro #202, Local 4 Centro Comercial
XO, Colonia del Valle
San Pedro Garza García, NL 66240
Mexico

CHIANTIBANCA (p.462)
by CREA international
Via Fermi Angolo via Mameli
53036 Poggibonsi
Italy
chiantibanca.it

CHOBANI SOHO (p.324)
by a l m project
150 Prince Street
New York, NY 10012
United States
chobanisoho.com

CITROËN EXPERIENCE CENTRE (p.412)
by Candida Tabet Arquitetura
Rua Oscar Feire 1009
01426-001 São Paulo
Brazil
blog.citroen.com.br

COCCODRILLO FOR VERSO (p.434)
by Glenn Sestig Architects
Schuttershofstraat 9 A/B
2000 Antwerp
Belgium
coccodrillo.be

CROCODILE CONCEPT BOUTIQUE (p.174)
by UPSTAIRS_
#02-237/278 VivoCity
1 Harbourfront Walk
098585 Singapore
Singapore
crocodileinternational.com

CTC COLOURTOCOLOUR (p.178)
by Frank Agterberg / BCA
Raadstede 24
3431 HA Nieuwegein
the Netherlands
ctc-store.nl

DESIGN REPUBLIC'S DESIGN COLLECTIVE (p.382)
by Neri&Hu Design and Research Office
A7 Design Collective, JSWB
5369 Jiasong Road, Qingpu District
201704 Shanghai
China
thedesignrepublic.com

DEUTSCHE BANK (p.466)
by BEHF Architects
Schubarstrasse 13
73430 Aalen
Germany
deutsche-bank.de

DIAGEO CONCEPT STORE (p.326)
by Fourfoursixsix
Rama IV Road
10110 Bangkok
Thailand

DIESEL VILLAGE (p.184)
(temporary store)
by Brinkworth and the Wilson Brothers
Regent Street
London
United Kingdom
diesel.com

DR. MARTENS (p.440)
(temporary store)
by Checkland Kindleysides
Selfridges
400 Oxford Street
London W1A 1AB
United Kingdom
drmartens.com

DURASAFE (p.084)
by Ministry of Design
Westech Building
237 Pandan Loop #01-06
128424 Singapore
Singapore
durasafe.com.sg

ERNO LASZLO (p.088)
by FAK3
Time Square
1 Matheson Street
Causeway Bay, Hong Kong
Hong Kong
ernolaszlo-hk.com

EVEN MEGASTORE (p.118)
by Jayme Lago Mestieri Architecture
Av. Santo Amaro 1411
04505-001 São Paulo
Brazil
evenmegastore.com.br

EYE CANDY (p.030)
by Creneau International
Turnhoutsebaan 5/400
2110 Wijnegem
Belgium
eyecandy.be

FARMÁCIA LORDELO (p.092)
by José Carlos Cruz Arquitecto
Urbanização de São Lourenço, Lote 16, Lordelo
5000-179 Vila Real
Portugal
farmacialordelo.com

FILSON (p.186)
by Como Park Studio
9 Newburgh Street
London W1F 7RL
United Kingdom
filson.com

FREITAG STORE LAUSANNE (p.034)
by Freitag
Rue Neuve 6
1003 Lausanne
Switzerland
freitag.ch

FREUDENHAUS (p.036)
by Aigner Architecture
Hohenzollernstrasse 4
80801 Munich
Germany
freudenhaus.com

GALERIES LAFAYETTE (p.124)
by plajer & franz studio
Pacific Place Shopping Mall
Jalan Sudirman Kav. 52–53, Level B1
12190 Jakarta
Indonesia
galerieslafayette.co.id

GIANT STORE (p.416)
by Fabrique [brands, design & interaction]
Van Woustraat 59-63
1074 AC Amsterdam
the Netherlands
giantstore-amsterdam.nl

GRIGIO (p.192)
by BLOCK722architects+ /
Katja Margaritoglou and Sotiris Tsergas
Proxenou Koromila Street 51
54622 Thessaloniki
Greece

HAT CLUB (p.042)
by UP
103 Mercer Street
New York, NY 10012
United States
hatclub.com

HIT GALLERY (p.194)
by Fabio Novembre
Times Square
1 Matheson Street
Causeway Bay, Hong Kong
Hong Kong
hitgallery.com

HOCHSTETTER (p.196)
by Heikaus Concept
Simeonstrasse 13
54290 Trier
Germany
hochstetter.de

J.I (p.198)
by Line-Inc.
3F Maison Mode, Skyone Plaza, 56 Section
2 Renmin South Road
610016 Chengdu
China
lessin.cn

JUST CAVALLI (p.202)
by OpenAir Studio
Zen Department Store, Central World
494 Rajdamri Road
10330 Bangkok
Thailand
justcavalli.com

KARL LAGERFELD (p.206)
by plajer & franz studio
194 boulevard St. Germain
75007 Paris
France
karl.com

KOM (p.386)
by 2kul Interior Design
Ul. Dąbrowskiego 3
56-300 Milicz
Poland

KOMPLEMENTAIR MEN (p.044)
by Aekae
Im Viadukt 21
8005 Zurich
Switzerland
komplementair.ch

KRUNGSRI EXCLUSIVE (p.468)
by Concept i
Capital Tower, G/F All Seasons Place
87/1 Wireless Road, Lumpini, Pathumwan
10330 Bangkok
Thailand
krungsri.com

KULT (p.210)
by Corneille Uedingslohmann Architekten
Neumarkt 18a
50667 Cologne
Germany
guna.de

LA CHAMBRE AUX CONFITURES (p.328)
by Noël Dominguez Architecte
60 rue Vieille du Temple
75003 Paris
France
lachambreauxconfitures.com

LACOSTE (p.214)
by designLSM
52 Brompton Road
London SW31BW
United Kingdom
lacoste.com

LES BÉBÉS CUPCAKERY (p.330)
by JC Architecture
149-4 Chaozhou Street
10649 Taipei
Taiwan
lesbebescupcakery.com

LEVI'S (p.216)
by Como Park Studio
Kalverstraat 167
1012 XB Amsterdam
the Netherlands
levistrauss.com

LINEA PIU (p.048)
by Kois Associated Architects
N.Kalogera Street 24
84600 Mykonos
Greece
lineapiu.gr

LOBLAWS (p.334)
by Landini Associates
60 Carlton Street
Toronto, ON M5B 1J2
Canada
loblaws.ca

LOFT (p.130)
by Tonerico
3-8-3 Marunouchi, Chiyoda-ku
100-0005 Tokyo
Japan
loft.co.jp

LUCCA LLENA (p.442)
by Nomura / Ryutaro Matsuura
3F Grand Front Osaka
3-1 Ofukacho, Kita-ku
530-0011 Osaka
Japan
luccallena.jp

M DREAMS MALAYSIA (p.446)
by Blu Water Studio
Lot G341, 1 Utama Shopping Centre
1 Lebuh Bandar Utama
47800 Petaling Jaya, Selangor
Malaysia
mdreams.com

M DREAMS AUSTRALIA (p.450)
by Edwards Moore
QV Melbourne
Corner Swanston and Lonsdale Streets
3000 Melbourne
Australia
melissaaustralia.com.au

MAKING THINGS (p.222)
by Aekae
Geroldstrasse 23
8005 Zurich
Switzerland
makingthings.ch

MALMAISON (p.052)
by Distillery
270 Orchard Road, Unit 01-01
238857 Singapore
Singapore
thehourglass.com

MARC O'POLO (p.226)
by dan pearlman
Theatinerstrasse 1
80333 Munich
Germany
marc-o-polo.com

MAX MARA CHENGDU (p.232)
by Duccio Grassi Architects
1/F-2/F Yanlord Shopping Mall, 1 Section
2 Renmin South Road
610016 Chengdu
China
maxmara.com

MAX MARA HONG KONG CENTRAL (p.236)
by Duccio Grassi Architects
Shop G1 & M12-16, G/F Prince's Building
10 Chater Road
Central, Hong Kong
Hong Kong
maxmara.com

MDECOR (p.388)
by Sergey Makhno
Stolichne Hwy 101
Kiev
Ukraine

MERKUR HOHER MARKT (p.338)
by BEHF Architects
Hoher Markt 12
1010 Vienna
Austria
merkurhohermarkt.at

MINI PACEMAN CONCEPT STORE (p.240)
by Edwards Moore
250 Chapel Street
3181 Prahran
Australia
minipaceman.com.au

MISTRAL (p.340)
by Studio Arthur Casas
JK Iguatemi Mall
Av. President Juscelino Kubitschek 20
04543-011 São Paulo
Brazil

MUSSLER BEAUTY (p.096)
by Dittel Architekten
Am Höhenpark 4
70192 Stuttgart
Germany
mussler-beauty.de

MY BOON (p.242)
by Jaklitsch/Gardner Architects
4-1 Cheongdam-dong, Gangnam-gu
135-900 Seoul
Korea
boontheshop.com

MYKITA (p.058)
by Mykita
109 Crosby Street
New York, NY 10012
United States
mykita.com

N.TYLER (p.246)
by UPSTAIRS_
#B2-118 The Shoppes at Marina Bay Sands
2 Bayfront Avenue
018972 Singapore
Singapore
n-tyler.com

NOKIA (p.472)
by Evanslundin
Aleksanterinkatu 46
00100 Helsinki
Finland
nokia.com

NOTE ET SILENCE. (p.252)
by Specialnormal
3F MINT Kobe
7-1-1 Kumoidori, Chuo-ku, Hyogo-ken
651-0096 Kobe
Japan
ambidex.co.jp/note_et_silence

OLD AMSTERDAM CHEESE STORE (p.344)
by studiomfd
Dam 21
1012 JS Amsterdam
the Netherlands
oldamsterdam.nl

OLYMP & HADES (p.256)
by Corneille Uedingslohmann Architekten
Paunsdorfer Allee 1
04329 Leipzig
Germany
guna.de

ONITSUKA TIGER (p.258)
by Line-Inc.
4-24-14 Jinguumae, Shibuya-ku
150-0001 Tokyo
Japan
asics.co.jp/onitsukatiger

PARIS (p.136)
by Dalziel and Pow
Quilín Shopping Centre
Mar Tirreno 3349, Local 1127,
Comuna de Peñalolen
Santiago
Chile
paris.cl

PATCHI TAKHASSUSSI (p.350)
by Lautrefabrique Architects
Takhassussi Road, Bldg #309
2150 Riyadh
Kindom of Saudi Arabia
patchi.com

PODIUM JEWELLERY (p.062)
by Art Bureau 1/1
Malaya Nikitskaya 2/1
Moscow
Russia
podiumfashion.com

PODIUM MARKET (p.142)
by Art Bureau 1/1
Trade House Gallery Moscow
Okhotny Ryad 2
Moscow
Russia
podium-market.com

PODIUM SPORT (p.262)
by Art Bureau 1/1
Trade House Gallery Moscow
Okhotny Ryad 2
Moscow
Russia
podiumfashion.com

PUMA (p.266)
by plajer & franz studio
1-5-4 Nishi-Shinsaibashi, Cyuo-ku
542-0086 Osaka
Japan
puma.com

RAIFFEISEN BANK KREUZPLATZ (p.474)
by DGJ and NAU
Zeltweg 93
8032 Zurich
Switzerland
raiffeisen.ch

RAIFFEISEN BANK SCHAFFHAUSEN (p.478)
by DGJ and NAU
Bahnhofstrasse 30
8200 Schaffhausen
Switzerland
raiffeisen.ch

RAPHA CYCLE CLUB (p.418)
by Brinkworth
85 Brewer Street
London W1F 9ZN
United Kingdom
rapha.cc

RELOJERIA ALEMANA (p.064)
by OHLAB
Port Adriano
07180 Port Adriano, Calvia, Mallorca
Spain
relojeriaalemana.com

RIO (p.070)
by Glenn Sestig Architects
Lange Kruisstraat 29
9000 Ghent
Belgium
riostore.be

RUNNERS POINT (p.452)
by dan pearlman
Thier Galerie Dortmund
Westenhellweg 102
44137 Dortmund
Germany
runnerspoint.com

SOHO (p.272)
by Heikaus Concept
Fleischstrasse 52
54290 Trier
Germany
soho-moden.de

SOV DOUBLE STANDARD CLOTHING (p.274)
by Propeller Design
2F JP Towers
2-7-2 Marunouchi, Chiyoda-ku
100-0005 Tokyo
Japan
doublestandard.jp

SPRINKLES ICE CREAM (p.356)
by a l m project
9631 South Santa Monica Blvd.
Beverly Hills, CA 90210
United States
sprinklesicecream.com

STELLA CADENTE (p.278)
by Atelier du Pont
102 boulevard Beaumarchais
75011 Paris
France
stella-cadente.com

STILLS (p.282)
by Doepel Strijkers
Cornelis Schuytstraat 16
1071 JH Amsterdam
the Netherlands
stills.eu

SUGAMO SHINKIN BANK (p.482)
by emmanuelle moureaux architecture + design
1-55-1 Asahigaoka, Nerima-ku
176-0005 Tokyo
Japan

SUPREME (p.284)
by Brinkworth and the Wilson Brothers
2-3 Peter Street
London W1F 0AA
United Kingdom
supremenewyork.com

SWEET ALCHEMY (p.358)
by Kois Associated Architects
Kolokotroni 9
11521 Athens
Greece
parliaros.gr

T2B (p.362)
by Landini Associates
Shop 15G, Westfield Sydney
450 George Street
2000 Sydney
Australia
t2btea.com

TADASHI SHOJI (p.286)
by OpenAir Studio
Centra Chidlom, Central World
494 Rajdamri Road
10330 Bangkok
Thailand
tadashishoji.com

TANK STORE (p.288)
by Supermachine Studio
2F Mega Bangna
39 Moo 6 Bangna-Trad Road
10540 Bangkok
Thailand
e-tankstore.com

THE WOOD SPACE (p.392)
by Household
6-12 Tabard Street
London SE1 4JU
United Kingdom
havwoods.co.uk

TIGER OF SWEDEN STORE CONCEPT (p290)
by Koncept Stockholm
St James
210 Piccadilly
London W1J 9HL
United Kingdom
tigerofsweden.com

UM (p.296)
by AS Design Service
Shop L214, KK Mall
5016 Shennan East Avenue, Shenzhen, PRC
Shenzhen
China

UM COLLEZIONI (p.300)
by AS Design Service
Shop 9, Winman Mall
Macau
Macau

UMIX (p.304)
by AS Design Service
Shop 2027, Sands Cotai Central
Macau
Macau

URBANEARS BOXPARK (p.112)
by 42 Architects
2-4 Bethnal Green Road
London E1 6GY
United Kingdom
urbanears.com

VZ FINANZPORTAL (p.486)
by DGJ and NAU
Beethovenstrasse 24
8002 Zurich
Switzerland
finanzportal.vermoegenszentrum.ch

WEIN & WAHRHEIT (p.364)
by Ippolito Fleitz Group
Main-Taunus-Zentrum
65843 Sulzbach am Taunus
Germany
wein-wahrheit.de

WORMLAND (p.308)
by Blocher Blocher Partners
Centroallee 128
46047 Oberhausen
Germany
wormland.de

XYL (p.396)
by Tonerico
1-18-15 Tomioka, Koutou-ku,
135-0047 Tokyo
Japan
xyl.jp

YOUTOPIA (p.312)
by dan pearlman
Bachstrasse 2-4
88214 Ravensburg
Germany
bredl.com

ZOFF (p.074)
by emmanuelle moureaux architecture + design
Mitsui Outlet Park Iruma
1369-1 Miyadera, Iruma-shi
358-8515 Saitama
Japan
zoff.co.jp

ZOFF PARK HARAJUKU (p.078)
by Archicept city
6-35-3 Jingumae, Shibuya-ku
150-0001 Tokyo
Japan
zoff.co.jp

CREDITS

POWERSHOP 4
New Retail Design

PUBLISHER
Frame Publishers

PRODUCTION
Marlous van Rossum-Willems

AUTHOR
Jane Szita

GRAPHIC DESIGN CONCEPT
Cathelijn Kruunenberg

GRAPHIC DESIGN
Matte.nl

PREPRESS
Beeldproductie

COVER PHOTOGRAPHY
Dennis Lo

PAPER
115 gsm Arctic Volume White
Wibalin Buckram

TRADE DISTRIBUTION USA AND CANADA
Consortium Book Sales & Distribution, LLC.
34 Thirteenth Avenue NE, Suite 101
Minneapolis, MN 55413-1007
T +1 612 746 2600
T +1 800 283 3572 (orders)
F +1 612 746 2606

DISTRIBUTION REST OF WORLD
Frame Publishers
Laan der Hesperiden 68
1076 DX Amsterdam
the Netherlands
frameweb.com
distribution@frameweb.com
ISBN: 978-4-91727-15-3

© 2014 Frame Publishers, Amsterdam, 2014

All rights reserved. No part of this publication may be reproduced or transmitted in any form or by any means, electronic or mechanical, including photocopy or any storage and retrieval system, without permission in writing from the publisher.

Whilst every effort has been made to ensure accuracy, Frame Publishers does not under any circumstances accept responsibility for errors or omissions. Any mistakes or inaccuracies will be corrected in case of subsequent editions upon notification to the publisher.

The Koninklijke Bibliotheek lists this publication in the Nederlandse Bibliografie: detailed bibliographic information is available on the internet at http://picarta.pica.nl

Printed on acid-free paper produced from chlorine-free pulp.
TCF ∞ Printed in Poland. 987654321

RECEIVED

JAN 2   2015

HUMBER LIBRARIES
NORTH CAMPUS

RECEIVED

JAN 2   2015

HUMBER LIBRARIES
NORTH CAMPUS